D0016753

LIVING IN A
MATERIAL
WORLD

LIVING IN A MATERIAL WORLD

★ ★ ★ ★ ★

THE COMMODITY CONNECTION

KEVIN MORRISON

John Wiley & Sons, Ltd

Copyright © 2008   Kevin Morrison

Published by   John Wiley & Sons Ltd, The Atrium, Southern Gate, Chichester,
                     West Sussex PO19 8SQ, England

                     Telephone   +44 1243 779777

Email (for orders and customer service enquiries): cs-books@wiley.co.uk
Visit our Home Page on www.wiley.com

Other Wiley Editorial Offices

John Wiley & Sons Inc., 111 River Street, Hoboken, NJ 07030, USA

Jossey-Bass, 989 Market Street, San Francisco, CA 94103-1741, USA

Wiley-VCH Verlag GmbH, Boschstr. 12, D-69469 Weinheim, Germany

John Wiley & Sons Australia Ltd, 42 McDougall Street, Milton, Queensland 4064, Australia

John Wiley & Sons (Asia) Pte Ltd, 2 Clementi Loop #02-01, Jin Xing Distripark, Singapore 129809

John Wiley & Sons Canada Ltd, 6045 Freemont Blvd, Mississauga, ONT, L5R 4J3, Canada

Wiley also publishes its books in a variety of electronic formats. Some content that appears in print
may not be available in electronic books.

Library of Congress Cataloging-in-Publication Data:

Morrison, Kevin, 1964–
   Living in a material world : the commodity connection / Kevin Morrison.
      p. cm.
   Includes bibliographical references and index.
   ISBN 978-0-470-51891-5 (cloth : alk. paper)
   1. Commodity futures.   2. Commodity exchanges.   I. Title.
   HG6046.M67 2008
   332.64′4–dc22

                                        2008019028

British Library Cataloguing in Publication Data

A catalogue record for this book is available from the British Library

ISBN 978-0-470-51891-5 (HB)

Typeset in 10.5/15pt Sabon by Aptara Inc., New Delhi, India
Printed and bound in Great Britain by TJ International Ltd, Padstow, Cornwell, UK

To Melina and Carly for all your help and support during writing this book, which I could not have done without you both. A very big thanks to my sisters Annette and Caroline, and their families, for their help, support and encouragement. To Mum and Dad for their constant support and guidance. To Michael G for wading through the early drafts and the synopsis for this work. And to my in-laws for their patience. I also owe a debt of gratitude to all the people that took time from their busy lives to talk to me about the subjects in this book. It is their knowledge and vast experience that I have tried to convey in this work.

Contents

Introduction

The record oil and food prices seen in 2008 has triggered debates about an impending energy and food crisis that has not been experienced for decades. At the same time that the people are becoming more concerned about global warming. This book attempts to examine some of the factors behind the rise in energy and food, otherwise known as commodities, prices and explain how they are interlinked together with the battle against climate change.

Some people think commodities are a subject of interest only for farmers, miners, oil companies, traders or business journalists like myself. But the link between what I write about every day – energy, metals and agriculture – and the discussions I have had at home with family and friends about the cost of filling up the car, the power bill or whether I should offset the carbon from my next plane journey, sent me off in a different direction.

I wanted to write a book about the connection between the consumer and the raw materials we use every day and to link the chain from the businesses that extract the materials, the governments that set the laws and the commodity markets where raw material prices are determined. In the simplest of acts we take raw materials for granted; like switching on a light or turning up the heating. I wanted to show

how commodities are relevant to every body, every day – and how they are more relevant now than they have been at any time since the last oil shock nearly three decades ago (my memories of which include going to bed by candlelight during the energy rationing and three-day weeks of the 1970s).

Everything we consume – whether through buying something, eating or even our physical actions – involves, at some level, the use of metals, fossil fuels or agricultural produce, which we take from planet Earth and use to make our lives more comfortable, more productive or more manageable. Our high-tech 'lifestyles' depend on the secure supply of these raw materials. They are transformed into mobile phones, laptops, iPods, t-shirts and cars with brand names that help shape our identity; both inwardly (how we feel about or reward ourselves) and outwardly (how we project ourselves through our material possessions to friends, neighbours and colleagues). The focus of this book is on the materials that lie behind these lifestyle acquisitions: 'pre-logo', you might say.

The effect of increasing global demand for commodities has pushed up prices of materials from oil and copper to corn and wheat, forcing consumers to pay more for the many 'necessities' of life, from a loaf of bread to their quarterly electricity bill. This era of high oil and food prices is no passing phase: the supply of many key natural resources is stretched to the limit. This is not only driven by extravagant consumption in the West, but by the emergence of hundreds of millions of new consumers in China and India, and other developing countries in Asia, the Middle East and Latin America.

Higher winter heating bills and more expensive trips to the petrol station have gone some of the way to alerting us all to the importance of commodities, but the consumer is still largely detached from the raw materials that they use each day. When we listen to music on our iPods or drive to the shop, we don't really have to think about the materials that have enabled us to do it. There's a long journey for many commodities from source to consumer. Minerals start with their extraction from the ground, pass through the phases of refinement, fabrication, manufacture, logistics, retail and finally enter the home as finished consumer goods. It's no wonder most people have little idea where exactly their stainless steel teapot or copper-bottomed saucepan comes from. 'Made in China' doesn't tell the full story. This book attempts to shed some light on the commodity connection and explain why it matters.[1]

I have written this book for the informed consumer, as well as those more closely involved in the world of commodities: investors, producers, industrial consumers and the go-betweens. Rather than trying to cover all commodities in depth (I would need to write an encyclopaedia to do that) I have focused on some of the most important raw materials that show the connection between personal consumption, the politics of supply and how these commodities are traded. I have included a chapter on the environmental effects of our use of the Earth's resources and how increasingly we will pay for the 'services' that the environment has so far provided for free: clean air, water, fertile soil and the biodiversity of animal and plant life. The environment is increasingly entwined with business and government policy. The advent of carbon markets has put a price on something we have taken for granted – clean air. For the first time we will all (producers and consumers) have to pay for our polluting ways.

Paying for a cleaner environment through a market mechanism is still a relatively new development. Fine-tuning is taking place and there is a greater will by regulators, politicians and companies to see that carbon markets work. Carbon pricing is becoming an integral part of the commodities market and will eventually determine what fuels are used and how the land is allocated for crop growing and grazing livestock.

From 2003 to 2007 I was the Financial Times's Commodities Correspondent. It was a unique position in many ways, as few newspapers around the world have a dedicated commodities writer. They might have an oil reporter or an environment writer, but not someone solely focused on the raw materials world. At the FT, I was reporting on the front line of this 'once in a generation' boom, witnessing the wide-range repercussions for consumers, investors and geopolitics.

The opaque world of commodities has gone from the back page of the newspaper to the front. Headlines about record oil prices, dire climate change warnings, higher food prices, energy security and

China's demand for more raw materials are now commonplace. This book is an attempt to thread all these events together and to bring a historical perspective to the trends we are witnessing.

Researching this book has taken me from Tamil Nadu in southern India, where the farmers might have little more than a field the size of a basketball court, to the US Midwest, where cornfields stretch for hundreds and thousands of acres. I have stood on the trading floors of commodity exchanges in New York, Chicago and London where billions of dollars are traded each day, and lunched with the investors whose fortunes are made or undone by these markets. I've also had meetings with miners in South Africa, biofuels producers in Iowa, climate change pact negotiators in Bali and policymakers in Washington. These diverse sets of people are all connected in some way to the commodities world.

While sitting in my own kitchen with my laptop I have kept in mind the average consumer sitting in their kitchen sipping coffee and reading the paper or cooking a meal. The kitchen, in particular, is as much the epicentre of the commodities world as the trading floors or the closed-door meetings of the world's largest commodity cartel, the Organization of the Petroleum Exporting Countries (Opec), and here's why . . .

At breakfast time, most people use an electric kettle to boil water for their morning cup of tea or coffee. Most of the world's electricity is generated from coal-fired power stations (Energy Information Administration, 2007a) and coal is the biggest source of carbon dioxide emissions, which the overwhelming majority of scientists conclude is a key contributor to global warming. Making tea and coffee, I hasten to add, is not the biggest factor in global warming. Nevertheless there is a direct connection between those dirty chimneys at the power station and you wandering bleary-eyed into the kitchen on a grey Monday morning to make an early morning cuppa.

The electricity travels from the power station to your kitchen through a convoluted network of wires which are largely made from copper, the best conductor for electrons. The economic development of China and its great rival India have triggered one of the biggest expansions of power generation networks in history and this is consuming vast quantities of copper. As a consequence the price of the red metal has quadrupled over the past five years, triggering a global crime wave in copper theft.

Lots of people like milk with their morning cuppa and most of this comes from cows, although goat and sheep milk as well as soya milk are popular too. The keeping of livestock to meet the world's growing appetite for dairy products and meat, means most of the world's grains and oilseeds go to animal feed. A greater share of grains and oilseeds is also being used for making biofuels. The combination of the growing demand for dairy and meat products together with government-imposed mandatory renewable fuel targets has caused an escalation in agriculture prices, leading to the steepest climb in global food prices for a generation.

The demand for raw materials has not only increased because of higher living standards in the world's two most populous countries, China and India. The Middle East and Russia have also boosted economic growth on the back of the high oil price, while Brazil's improving economy is primarily due to its emergence as a global agricultural-export superpower. The rise in living standards has come at a time of unparalleled population growth, technological and scientific breakthroughs, political upheaval and economic and trade liberalization.

Economic growth in developing countries has accelerated global growth at a faster pace than at any time since the 1960s. In the 1950s and 1960s, the world economy rose by 5 % due to the reconstruction of Europe and Japan, as well as the economic competition between the US and the Soviet Union. The two oil shocks in the 1970s slowed growth to about 4 %, and then to 3 %, which became the average economic growth rate of the 1980s and 1990s.

Higher oil and food prices together with the credit crisis in the US have prompted economists to cut global economic growth rates to around 3 % for 2008. Some experts cite this as the start of a prolonged downturn in the global economy. Others take the view that the build up in sovereign funds in China along with Middle Eastern and other Asian countries, accumulated on the back of higher energy prices, will see more reliance on the developing world as the engine of global growth. This will maintain strong demand for energy, agriculture and metals as well as the emission of greenhouse gases at a higher level (a worrying trend).

The effect of economic growth in developing countries translates into rising income for the average worker beyond their basic needs for food and shelter, creating hundreds of millions of new consumers who aspire to the affluent lifestyles of developed nations. They are competing for the very thing that Americans, Europeans and Japanese have taken for granted in recent decades: a cheap, abundant supply of energy, food and consumer goods.

Two decades after Madonna's mid-80s hit song *Material Girl*, which endorsed materialism, was released, the cult of consumption is stronger than ever. Our appetite for material goods is like an ever-expanding waistline; our hunger for energy grows unabated and we allow precious resources like water to literally run away down the drain.

China has already had a profound effect on the supply and demand of raw materials, but there is a long way to go before its citizens have income parity with more affluent countries. The average Chinese consumer has a living standard that is a fifth of those who live in its island territory of Hong Kong and about a quarter that of the average consumer on the island of Taiwan, of which China claims ownership.[2] The Chinese government wants to bridge the gap in living standards between the mainland and its near neighbours.

The creation of hundreds of millions more 'material girls' (and boys) has prompted a scramble for the natural resources to build the 'material world' that Madonna sang about. China has become one of the biggest investors in Africa to secure supplies of raw materials. It is shaping its foreign policy around its resource needs and forming special relationships with resource-rich countries, such as Argentina, Australia, Brazil, Canada and South Africa, as well as nations that are mostly off-limits to Western countries, such as Sudan and Iran.

The world's most populous nation has emerged after a long slumber to reassert its position among the largest economies. China's rapid growth has led to one of the biggest movements of people in history. Hundreds of millions of Chinese are moving from rural areas to urban dwellings connected to the electricity network, and spending more disposable income on protein-rich food, electronic consumer goods and motorbikes or cars.

This movement in China is reflective of a global trend. More of the world's population are born into the developing world and more are living in cities than on the land. The year 2007 marked the first time in history that a greater number of people lived in cities and towns than in rural areas globally. This development is changing the dynamics of the supply and demand of raw materials; urban dwellers on average consume more material goods, energy and food than their rural brethren.

As the world endures its strongest period of economic growth in more than 40 years, raw materials are becoming more and more sought after. This demand has led to rapid commodity price increases over the past five years, posing the threat of inflation as consumers react to higher food and power bills and more expensive car fuel.

The credit crisis in the sub-prime home lending market in the US in 2007 is the second financial bubble in the last decade, following the bursting of the dot com bubble in April 2000. It is not the first financial meltdown we have seen towards the end of a decade in recent times: the Asian currency crisis and the Russian default came in the late 1990s and the stock market crash in the late 1980s, when companies who had over-borrowed were hit by rising interest rates. The credit crisis of 2007 followed a prolonged period of loose money supply where interest rates were kept below their long-term average.

The combination of easy credit and high oil prices is eerily similar to the economic conditions in the early and late 1970s at the time of the world's first two oil shocks, both of which were followed by recessions.[3] The 1970s was the last time the world was seriously concerned about the supply and price of raw materials, and I refer to this period throughout the book.[4]

In December 1976, the US government issued a report on resource availability by the National Commission on Supplies and Shortages,[5] which looked at the issue of whether the US was running out of resources and whether the country was dependent on importing raw materials from foreign countries (Eckes, 1978). The report concluded that resource exhaustion was not a serious threat to economic growth for the next quarter of a century; which was pretty much true, as the concern about resource availability only became apparent again after 2001. This report mirrored one that was done almost a quarter of a century earlier by the Paley Commission, which was set up by the government of President Harry Truman in 1952. The Paley Commission was also asked to look into the same issue of resource availability. It recommended a 'materials policy' for the US to secure an adequate and dependable flow of materials (US Geological Survey, 2001). The recommendation was never enacted because of the complex nature of having a centralized body for buying materials.

All this underlines a cyclical pattern of commodity demand, supply and prices, albeit a very long cycle that unfolds over decades. Each time it has been broken by an economic slowdown, the uptake of new technology and changes in consumption habits. This time consumer behaviour has largely been resilient to higher commodity prices.

One of the most striking events of this decade is that oil prices have jumped to more than $100 a barrel. Conventional thought, up until the last few years, was that if the oil price rose above $40 a barrel the global economy would slow down. It would seem it takes a lot more than $100 a barrel to change people's consumption habits.

One reason the world has been able to live with a higher oil price is the decline in the US dollar. Commodities are priced in US dollars, so if the dollar weakens, the probability of commodity prices rising is greater. A lower dollar has increased the value of Euros, British sterling and Japanese yen, which means those currencies can purchase more dollar-denominated assets such as commodities. Devaluation of the dollar prompted many British and Europeans to fly to New York for their Christmas shopping in late 2007. This example of consumer spending, where people are prepared to travel long distances in search of a bargain, sums up the consumer age – the 'Material Girl' is alive and kicking.

The developing world, where oil demand has been greatest, has largely been insulated from high oil prices. The Asian Development Bank estimated that more than half the governments it surveyed in the Asia Pacific region still controlled fuel at low price levels in order to cushion the effect of higher prices on consumers (Asian Development Bank, 2007). But the subsidy comes at an increasing cost. The oil-producing countries, Saudi Arabia, Qatar, Venezuela and United Arab Emirates (UAE) all provide large subsidies for fuel consumption, stimulating a domestic demand that threatens to grow at a faster rate than new supplies. If the trend continues, it could lead to less oil for exports to China, the US, Japan and Europe. Egypt and Iran are also big subsidizers, inspiring an oil-smuggling market between Iran and its neighbours, as well as Egypt and Palestine.

The major beneficiaries of high oil prices are Middle Eastern oil exporters, who have reaped record receipts from every barrel they ship. This has seen a dramatic rise in the region's economy, which has outpaced global economic growth rates for the past eight years (International Monetary Fund, 2007). The Middle East is spending on new infrastructure and oil and gas projects, as well as topping up public coffers (International Monetary Fund, 2007).[6] According to the Asian Development Bank's World Outlook 2007, the sovereign wealth fund of Abu Dhabi – the biggest oil-producing emirate of the UAE – had $875 bn at the end of June 2007. The large amounts of expenditure and saving by Middle Eastern governments is dependent on higher oil prices, which is something that these governments can help influence through Opec. With bulging pockets, Arab oil sheiks and sultans are broadening their economic influence by acquiring established businesses such as ports in the West, as well as taking large stakes in the world's biggest investment banks.

The higher oil price has revived Russia's fortunes, and a decade after it was begging the world for money, the bear is back with an assured bite. Under President Putin, the Russian government has resumed control of oil and gas production. This resource nationalism has spread to other countries including Venezuela and Bolivia. Governments play a key role in the supply of raw materials, with a majority of the world's oil production coming from state-owned companies. The world's largest copper producer is Codelco, owned by the Chilean government.

Many more countries have been opened up to private foreign investment, including the oil-rich nation of Libya in northern Africa. As a consequence of the commodities boom and the subsequent economic expansion of resource-based industries, developing nations from Azerbaijan to Zambia have taken steps to look more like market economies with a privatized banking sector, floating and partial exchange rates. This has led to an explosion in foreign exchange trading in currencies of developing nations. Trade between developing and transition countries is greater than that between developed nations, another reason why the prices of these raw materials have largely been immune from recent economic hiccups in the developed world.

This book takes a look at the evolution of the modern commodity industry from local and regional trading exchanges to global operators. In Chapter 1 I discuss energy, the largest member of the commodity family. Energy's economic value and political importance outweighs all else; its use and its policies affect all parts of the commodity chain.

The chapter explains why energy prices are high and likely to remain so for years to come. Unlike the 1970s when the oil price skyrocketed on supply disruptions following the Arab oil embargo in 1973 and Iran's Islamic revolution in 1979, this time around prices are high because of demand.

Growth in demand comes at a time when supplies of oil and gas have fallen in developed countries, leaving more of the world's oil supplies in the hands of Opec; and gas with Russia and a handful of Middle Eastern producers. The rise in oil price has also triggered the biggest search in history for alternative sources of energy; giving the venture capitalists on the west coast of the US a new industry on which to focus.

Energy demand has revived the coal industry at a time when the world is becoming more and more concerned about the need to cut carbon emissions to prevent global warming. Coal, the dirty polluter, is conversely now more popular than ever.

Chapter 2 examines how the energy and agricultural sectors are becoming increasingly connected through the use of grains and oilseeds for making biofuels for transportation. Government policies are having the unintended consequences of pushing up food prices; the biggest proponent is the US ethanol policy, which has boosted the demand for corn. It is not just the US that has embraced biofuels though: Indonesia has emerged as a large producer of palm oil, used for making biodiesel which is exported to Europe. This has come at a cost, with vast areas of tropical forests cleared for palm oil plantations, making the archipelago nation the world's third largest emitter of greenhouse gases. All this puts a question mark over the greenness of biofuels and industry expansion, at a time when many countries are confronting water scarcity and more extreme weather conditions that could be related to climate change.

The chapter also looks at the impact of increasing meat consumption on the supply of grains and oilseeds. The influence of government subsidies on the agricultural sector is examined. Reducing agricultural subsidies is the subject of the Doha round of the World Trade Organization talks in order to make the balance fairer between farmers in the developing world and the developed world, which currently receives all of the farm subsidies.

Chapter 3 looks at the emergence of the environment as a commodity and how it is now an integral part of the energy and agricultural markets. Both sectors are big contributors to greenhouse gas emissions. Carbon pricing is a market mechanism that will force agriculture and energy producers to pay more attention to the environmental costs of industry. In addition to clean air, the chapter looks at how market mechanisms have created a price for biodiversity and water based on their scarcity value.

Chapter 4 takes as its focus one metal without which our electronic age would not exist. Copper is a vital component of the energy sector, where it is a conductor and transformer of electricity; and in transportation, where it is used in the wiring of planes and cars.

Increasingly it is also used for clean energy solutions such as wind farms and hybrid cars.

China has awakened the commodity markets and none more so than metals. In base metals, copper, aluminium, nickel and zinc, China accounts for between 20 and 25 % of global demand. China's role in spiking demand for metals, especially copper, is examined. Lack of investment in new production capacity in metals, energy and agriculture from the early 1980s and throughout the 1990s, until the beginning of this decade, has meant that the world is scrambling to respond to the wave of China and India's industrialization.

The final chapter looks at the trading of commodities. Following the collapse of the former Soviet Union and the transformation of the Chinese economy, most of the world participates in a market-based economy. This is also true of commodity markets, which have gone global. Chapter 5 looks at the evolution of commodity markets from bit player in the financial world to the main stage.

By the end of 2007 oil was hovering at more than $90 a barrel, wheat had gone through $10 a bushel and soya beans were at 34-year highs, capping a year when gold, nickel, zinc, lead, tin, silver, platinum, corn and oil all hit record highs. Many of these high prices have been described as a sign of speculative activity and the US government is launching an inquiry into the role of speculators in commodity futures markets. Commodities have attracted hedge funds, but there are few specialized funds that only look at commodities; many more have brought in commodity specialists from banks and research houses to trade commodities.

The role of hot money, synonymous with hedge funds and its influence on commodity prices, will certainly find some excesses and wrongdoings, but it is not the reason for one of the most prolonged commodity price booms in the modern era; rather, it is money that is following strong supply and demand trends for natural resources.

Commodity markets have also attracted pension funds, university endowment funds and foundations, which previously were cautious about this market's reputation for volatility. In addition, private investors are increasing their exposure to commodity markets, previously off limits to many individual investors because of the perceived risk. Investment banks have devised new vehicles to attract private investors to commodity markets such as exchange-traded funds (ETFs). Investment banks have beefed up their commodity trading businesses, having ditched these departments at the end of the 1990s when commodities trading was out of fashion. Oil traders are the 'pin-up boys' of Wall Street; commanding some of the biggest bonuses too.

The burgeoning commodity exchanges in China[7] and India are extending the global reach of commodity trading. As is the electronic age, which has helped create commodity trading arcades in Gibraltar, suburban London, Chicago and New York. And commodity markets are emerging in the form of deregulated power markets and the newly created emissions markets (Domanski and Health, 2007).[8] A further sign that investment fashion has changed is that ExxonMobil is the world's biggest company by market value, a mantle held by Microsoft during the dot com years.

Commodities are also the backbone of one of the largest corporate takeover bids ever made when BHP Billiton made a $150 billion offer to its mining rival Rio Tinto. This conjures up parallels with the takeover by AOL, the US internet service provider, which bought TimeWarner, the media conglomerate, using AOL's inflated share market price during the height of the dot com bubble. The BHP Billiton–Rio Tinto merger could be another metaphor for the resource boom.

Commodity markets are cyclical: higher prices attract substitution and destroy demand, and guessing prices, as in the futures market, falls into two camps – bulls and bears. There is another dimension to the supply of natural resources, which straddles academic theory and economics; one side believing in peak supply and the other side adhering to the cornucopia club where the prevalent thought is of resource abundance.

This is nowhere better illustrated than the bet made between Julian Simon and Paul Ehrlich in 1980 over how the prices of five metals – copper, chromium, nickel, tin and tungsten – would move during the ten years leading up to September 1990. Ehrlich, an environmental scientist at Stanford University, argued in his book *The Population Bomb* that the rate of population growth was outstripping growth in the supply of food and resources (Ehrlich, 1968).[9] But Simon, who was professor of business administration at the University of Maryland, did not agree with this view and challenged Ehrlich to a bet. The price of each metal fell over the period of the bet and Simon won. Simon, a known doom-slayer, wrote in his book *The Ultimate Resource 2* that the fall in prices was, 'not surprising; the odds were all against them because the prices of metals have been falling throughout human history. From my point of view, the bet was like shooting fish in a barrel. Of course I offered to make the same bet again, at increased stakes, but the Ehrlich group has not taken up the offer.' (Simon, 1996).

Simon died in 1998, but had he lived and made the same bet in 2000 for another ten-year period, he would be losing the bet so far. The price of copper has risen by 260 %, nickel rose by 210 %, tin has gained 165 % and chromium and tungsten have risen by double-digit figures.[10] This demonstrates, like any investment, that it is all to do with timing. If either Simon or Ehrlich had selected any metal or commodity this decade, so far it would show that prices are higher in 2008 than in 2000. In its April bulletin for 2007, the Reserve Bank of Australia, which oversees an economy that is among the world's largest mineral exporters, said that the recent increase in real metals prices is by far the largest of the last century for these commodities, and that the level of real metals prices is now above its century average. In contrast the recent upturns in food and non-food agricultural prices have been comparatively small, and these prices are still well below their century average levels.

The trough for commodities was in 1999 when gold and other metals sunk to long-term lows. It was at the time when the dot com economy was climbing to its peak and oil was recovering from below $10 a barrel. Yet, as we have already explained, prices in early 2008 were still breaking long-term highs, which meant the commodity price boom had completed eight years. The year 2008 represents its ninth, making this cycle the longest price rise since the post-war trough to

INTRODUCTION | 15

peak boom between 1943 and 1951. The early 1970s boom lasted for three years, followed by two years of decline, and a four-year increase between 1975 and 1979 (Cashin and McDermott, 2002).

It is easy to get caught up making bets in the midst of an exceptional period, thinking this is the new norm. I heard about paradigm shifts when I was writing about the dot com phenomenon in the late 1990s and at the turn of the millennium, and I have heard it again in relation to commodities. However, I do think commodity prices will remain relatively high for the foreseeable future. The cost of climate change, pollution mitigation and cleaner energy technologies will underpin higher energy prices. The demand for food to feed the world's growing population will impact food prices in the same way.[11] Eventually prices will fall, with substitution and the adoption of new technologies. With more people in the world, the threat of global warming and higher commodity prices, the impetus for technological and government policy solutions has never been greater.

Notes

1. According to the Mineral Commodities summaries for 2007, published by the US Geological Survey, the value added to GDP by major industries that consume processed mineral materials is $2130 billion, or 16 % of the total US economy.
2. This is based on the per capita income estimates from the Central Intelligence Agency – The World Factbook.
3. Barsky and Kilian (2000) wrote that the stagflation of the 1970s was caused more by loose monetary conditions than the high oil prices that were prompted by the Arab oil embargo in 1973 and the deposing of the Shah in 1979.
4. Another comparison with the 1970s is the number of disaster-themed films that have been made. *The Day After Tomorrow*, the two-hour long 2004 film, shows accelerated global warming where the North Atlantic current is shut down and the northern hemisphere descends into a deep freeze. In the 1970s Charlton Heston starred in *Soylent Green*, which was based on global-warming science and was set in an overcrowded New York City in 2022 where there is a heatwave all year

long and, with food scarcity, people turn to a concoction of soya and lentils, which is where the film gets its name 'soylent'. There are also several serious films that have been made about climate change, such as Al Gore's *Inconvenient Truth*, for which he won a Hollywood Oscar in 2007.

5. The National Commission on Supplies and Shortages was set up in September 1974 to look into resource exhaustion, the consequences of the nation's growing dependence on imported materials, the ability of the free market to deal with shortages and the adequacy of government for handling materials problems (US Office & Technology Assessment, 1985).

6. The oil exporters of the Arabian Gulf are spending at least $800bn over the next five years, and they are also managing to save more than 40 % of their oil income. The IMF estimates that the region's oil and gas receipts will have topped $650bn last year and will rise to $750bn this year, a four fold increase on levels at the start of the decade.

7. The BIS said in its December 2007 quarterly report that the surge in activity on the Chinese commodity exchange was the main factor behind the rapid expansion in trade of agricultural commodities in the second half of 2007.

8. Over-the-counter (OTC) trading of commodity derivatives has also grown rapidly. According to BIS statistics, the notional value of OTC commodity derivatives contracts outstanding reached $6.4 trillion in mid-2006, about 14 times the value in 1998. At the same time, the share of commodities in overall OTC derivatives trading grew from 0.5 % to 1.7 % (Domanski and Heath, 2007).

9. Ehrlich states on the first page that 'Overpopulation is now the dominant problem in all our personal, national, and international planning.'

10. Prices were taken from the London Metal Exchange website from January 1, 2000 to December 30, 2007.

11. Population and population growth are major determinants of the demand for food. The United Nations estimates that the world population is about 6.5 billion and growing at a rate of 76 million annually as at 2005. The UN projects the world population to reach 9.1 billion by 2050, peaking at 9.5 billion by the year 2070.

1

Energy

'Time is the only capital that any human being has, and the one thing that he can't afford to lose.'

Thomas Edison

The Return of King Coal Adds a Warm Glow

A visit to the Forbidden City in the centre of Beijing provides a fascinating insight into China's rich historic past. For almost five centuries the imperial palace was home to 24 emperors, and the city – a vast array of ancient preserved wooden buildings – was the political centre of the Chinese government throughout the Ming and the Qing dynasties. But it is outside the Gate of Heavenly Peace, looking across the stretch of tarmac separating the old imperial palace from Tiananmen Square under the watchful gaze of Mao, where you get a real picture of the China of today, and of tomorrow. The 12-lane road is clogged with cars, four-wheel drives, trucks and buses. One or two cyclists are glimpsed in the traffic, but pedal power is a fringe mode of transport on the first proper ring road in Beijing, millions of Chinese having ditched their bicycles in favour of cars.

The Forbidden City was once China's most important symbol of power. Today the Volkswagen Santana and Jetta, the Geely or Xiali mark individual power and wealth of the Chinese consumer. The icon of Mao just a few hundred metres away is a stark contrast to the symbols of capitalism on the road ahead, marking the dualism of a China still strongly connected to its past while intent on progression. The main goal of the Chinese Communist leadership today has moved beyond equality between its citizens to economic equality between Chinese people and those in the developed world. And, in the process, for China to regain its mantle as the world's most powerful economy, a position it last held during the fifteenth century (Kynge, 2006).[1] China is now pursuing the same trappings of the modern lifestyle long enjoyed in the US, Europe and Japan. It is a trend that you'd think would be applauded by proponents of the US car industry, where the car is viewed as a symbol of freedom and wealth. But the growing demand for motor vehicles among the increasingly affluent Chinese is creating a huge dilemma for the global energy sector.

In 2007 China overtook Japan as the world's second largest car market. It is predicted to become the biggest in the next decade, overtaking the United States by 2015. It's a dramatic turnaround for China, especially when you consider that in 1990 it had in total around a quarter of the number of cars on British roads. In the space of 25 years it will have become the largest car market in the world (International Energy Agency, 2007; Department of Transport, 2007). The fact that more Chinese citizens are able to afford cars is thanks to China's nearly unbroken 30-year economic expansion. China has become the 'workshop for the world', as factory owners in the West relocate their manufacturing facilities to China to take advantage of the lower wages and industrious work ethic of the Chinese. But the 37 million cars and 60 million motorcyclists on China's roads[2] need fuel, and, increasingly, imported fuel: China was last self-reliant for its oil in the mid-1990s. Its thirst for oil is growing fast, which has prompted the Chinese government and many of its state-owned companies to scour the world for other sources. What is striking is that they're going to places the US dares not, such as Sudan and Iran;

completely changing the world geopolitical landscape. The number of cars, trucks, SUVs and vans on Chinese roads is expected to increase to a staggering 270 million by 2030 according to the International Energy Agency, so barring a major technological breakthrough in automobile engines or alternative fuel supply (neither of which is expected to be commercially available within the next ten years) China will need even more fuel. China is expected to become as 'addicted' to oil as the US within the next 20 years.

The transferral of much of the world's manufacturing industry to China has also stimulated one of the largest movements of humans in history. Its cities have doubled in size in the past 20 years and hundreds of millions of Chinese citizens have moved from the countryside to apartments equipped with electricity – a stark contrast to their rural dwellings, which were largely without power. About 200 of China's cities have a population of more than one million, and about 40 % of its total population of 1.3 billion live in cities, with another 130 million expected to move from rural to urban areas over the next ten years (International Energy Agency, 2007).

Power for the People

Electricity in the vast majority of Chinese homes is generated by coal-fired power stations. Until 2007 China was self-sufficient in coal (as home to the largest coal reserves in the world, it should be!). But China has been building more power stations to provide electricity for expanding demand; its power network expansion in 2006 alone was bigger than the electricity generation of the entire UK. It would be inconceivable to think of Britain, or indeed any other country, installing as much electricity generation capacity in one year. It has plans on the drawing board to expand its power network even further, which would equate to the construction of new infrastructure as large as the entire power grid built across Europe since the Second World War – that's all the homes, buildings, restaurants, factories and sports venues stretching from the Baltic countries to the west of Ireland, and from the tip of Norway to the Greek Islands in the Mediterranean.[3]

This planned expansion will light up millions of new homes, for even greater numbers of consumers (many of whom will become car owners for the first time). The country's demand for energy is so great that it is projected to overtake the United States as the world's largest consumer of energy, coal, oil and nuclear power at the end of the decade. Considering that as recently as 2005, the US consumed over a third more energy than China, it represents growth of astronomical proportions. The scale and the speed of the increase meant that in the three years prior to 2005, China's increase in energy demand was the equivalent of all of Japan's annual energy needs,[4] and at this pace China's need for more energy supplies has become critical, pushing oil prices above $100 a barrel in 2008.

The increase in electricity consumption is primarily due to more homes connecting to the power network, which in turn stimulates the demand for consumer electronic goods. Rapid income growth and declining prices mean that almost every home in Chinese cities now has at least one television, a washing machine and refrigerator. Air-conditioning systems are now found in four of every five homes. These appliances account for more than a fifth of total residential energy (International Energy Agency, 2007). Electrical gadgets may well have improved the quality of daily life for Chinese consumers, but these appliances in fact suck much more electrical power than their equivalents in developed countries and emit much more carbon pollution. This is one of the reasons why China's energy demand has risen so rapidly.[5]

The Comeback King

Coal's re-emergence as a major fuel source is a significant factor in the rise of CO_2 emissions. Coal overtook wood during the 1800s[6] as the world's major fuel source and fuelled the Industrial Revolution in Britain and the United States of America. It was during this era that the phrase 'King Coal' was coined by 19th century economist William Stanley Jevons who said: '(Coal) stands not beside but entirely above all other commodities.' King coal held onto its crown in the US until just after the Second World War when oil from the Middle East and Venezuela changed things,[7] by which stage the US was the largest coal consumer in the world. Usage declined further in the 1930s when coal was banned from US homes, and a decade later in trains. By the 1950s and 1960s, nuclear and gas were set to replace coal altogether – that is until the Three Mile accident halted the expansion of nuclear power. Gas was ready to step in, and between 1975 and 2002 every power station built in America was gas-fired (Goodell, 2006). But gas, too, had its shortcomings.

China's industrial revolution has followed the pattern of Britain's industrialization, which started about 250 years ago, in that it is fuelled by coal and has stimulated the renaissance in global demand for the black rock. In China's case coal is burned in power stations, not the home or factory; it is out of sight and out of mind for most consumers, who rarely make the connection between switching on a light or watching the television and the emission of greenhouse gases. An inconvenient truth much less acknowledged is the role of the always-on internet-connected world in boosting electricity demand from coal-fired stations.

Coal's re-emergence confounds predictions in the second half of the 20th century that coal had a dim future. Coal was used to heat the Victorian-built home in London that I lived in as a child. It wasn't very effective; while it heated the room where the fire was located, the rest of the house was freezing. It was my job to fill a bucket with coal from the cellar (which today is probably used for the wine collection of an Islington family). Our coal was delivered each autumn by the coalman, who would empty sacks of coal down the coalhole (a feature of Victorian houses) in front of the doorstep. But the coalman's days were numbered when hundreds of thousands of UK households switched to natural gas in the 1960s and 1970s, piped from the new gas fields in the North Sea straight to people's houses. The gas central heating system that replaced our antiquated coal fires heated the whole house with the flick of a switch. It was great – I no longer needed to sleep under five blankets or to huddle around the small electric fire in the lounge. Nor was it necessary to do those cold trips down to the cellar each night. That was it – coal was history, and gas was the future.

Coal's perceived decline in the 1980s and 1990s and the popularity of gas was due to the efficiency of gas-fired generating plants. They convert more primary energy into electricity than coal-fired plants and they are cheaper to build than coal or nuclear plants and gas is a cleaner fuel than coal and oil. This view was endorsed in the 1980s when coal mines across Britain were closed. The price of coal had plummeted and the government-owned mines were now uneconomic: they had no place in the Conservative government of Margaret Thatcher. The decision led to bitter battles between police and British coal miners. The closure of the British coalmines was another sign that the world had moved beyond coal.

The gas coming from the North Sea territory was not enough to heat, light and power Britain; now gas is piped from Norway, Belgium and shipped from Algeria and Qatar. The decline in gas supplies from politically secure areas such as the North Sea and the Gulf of Mexico has left consumers more reliant on Russia, the Middle East and Indonesia for gas supplies. The political risks long associated with oil imports now apply to gas; in particular, Russia, which has used its market position as the world's largest exporter to threaten cuts in supply to some consumers if they do not pay. Gas exporters have also become friendlier with each other, raising fears about the creation of a gas Opec (Organization of the Petroleum Exporting Countries).[8]

Coal has resurfaced, and Britain is now importing record volumes. The port of Immingham in Lincolnshire on the east coast of England is the largest import point for coal in Britain; the mountains of coal around the port turn the snow black in winter and the coal dust which rises into the air in the summer has to be hosed down with water. Much of the coal feeds the nearby Drax power station, the largest of its kind in the UK. Coal still accounts for less than half of Britain's electricity power supply (Energy Information Administration, no date).

Coal's key role in the British Industrial Revolution was firing the first steam engine that started the railway revolution. This, in turn, helped move vast quantities of commodities – from grains to minerals – from producer to industrial consumer. Steam turbines were used for electricity generation: the efficiency of steam turbines has improved vastly since the 19th century. The size of the coal-fired power station has increased too, by 1500 times from the start of the 20th century, which means more coal can be burned to produce more power (Jaccard, 2006).[9]

Coal can easily be transported via railways and boats, so it can be moved from pit to power station without the political connotations associated with gas or oil pipelines. Coal also has the largest of all fossil fuel reserves in the world. Global coal reserves are concentrated in North America, the former Soviet Union, China, India, Australia and South Africa. These reserves of fossil fuels are finite; something which demand for electricity shows no sign of being. Its abundance and perceived low political risk has also made coal cheaper than the fossil fuel alternatives, gas and oil. Gas prices have risen because they are linked to oil prices: most gas is exported on a sales contract between the buyer and seller whereby the price is indexed to oil prices, in order to ensure that gas remains competitive. Coal prices rose by more than 50 % last year, but they remain competitively cheap compared with oil and gas.

Coal Play

The increase in energy demand globally is largely due to the simple fact that there are more people living on the planet. The world's population is projected to reach 8.2 billion by 2030, from 6.4 billion in 2005. The population rise in the second half of the 20th century corresponded to a huge increase in energy demand. A trend that looks set to continue in the first third of the 21st century.[10]

The world's demand for energy is projected to rise by 55 % by 2030 from 2005 levels (International Energy Agency, 2007). This means more power stations, and more copper and aluminium electricity lines to transmit the electrons from power stations to homes, factories, offices and street lights. Less than a fifth of the world's energy supply is projected to come from less polluting sources, such as nuclear, hydro, biomass, wind and solar. The majority of the increased demand will be met by power generated from fossil fuels.

Most of the rise in the world's population is occurring in the developing world. China and India are expected to remain the world's two most populous countries over this period, but both countries have hundreds of millions of citizens living without electricity, and those who are connected are subject to frequent power shortages. The respective Beijing and New Delhi governments have plans to connect most of their citizens to power networks in the next 25 years. Hundreds of new power stations will be built. Many will be fuelled by coal. So vast is the planned increase in coal demand that the two countries are expected to account for about 80 % of the world's coal growth by 2030, and 40 % of the world's increase in oil demand over the same period.

China relies on coal because it has its own vast reserves, in addition to imports from relatively safe producers such as Australia and South Africa. Coal is also far cheaper than nuclear and natural gas, and since China is not bound by the Kyoto Protocol or any other international pact limiting emissions, it is basically unhindered. The new power stations China is building will undoubtedly breach the emissions levels that the Kyoto signatories are attempting to abide by. All this has earned China the unenviable title of the world's largest polluter; a position it has won in rapid time – it was responsible for an estimated 58 % of the increase in global emissions in the six years leading up to 2006 (in contrast, India accounted for 6 % of global emissions). China's desire to become the largest economy has put the world on a path towards increased global temperatures, which scientists at the United Nations International Panel of Climate Change (IPCC) warn would be catastrophic and irreversible.[11]

A Global Warning

By 2030, global pollution is expected to be more than 80 % above the limit the IPCC considers to be the tipping point for drastic climate change. The current aspirations of China and India in terms of lifestyle are not helping. The International Energy Agency (IEA) estimates that China, barring any major change in energy consumption habits, will emit two-thirds more pollution than the US in 2030 (International Energy Agency, 2007).

To provide us with the heat and light we desire, coal must be converted into electricity in a power plant. The process actually results in a major loss in energy since only about a third of the heat generated from burning the coal is converted into electricity. The same energy loss occurs when crude oil is turned into petroleum products such as gasoline, diesel and heating oil. Pollution levels are therefore a big problem.

International agreements that limit greenhouse gas emissions are not easy to reach due to the difficulty in accounting for emissions. China's emergence as the 'workshop of the world', for instance, has meant that thousands of factories around China are making goods in facilities which are actually owned by foreign companies, or producing goods under contract for foreign companies and brands. Wal-Mart – the US-based retail giant – alone imported about $18 billion worth of goods from China in 2007: a tenth of the US trade deficit with China.

The IEA – energy policy adviser to the developed countries – has estimated that more than a quarter of China's energy is used in the production of goods for export. This accounts for more than a third of the country's emissions. Energy consumption on exported goods has increased its share of China's total energy use – far higher than the proportion of energy expended on exported goods in the US, European Union and Japan.[12] In effect, developed countries are outsourcing not only their manufacturing capacity, but also a significant part of their energy consumption and greenhouse gas emissions.

Despite China becoming the world's largest greenhouse gas emitter, the average Chinese citizen emits less pollution than the average American or European.[13]

At present about one-quarter of the world's CO_2 emissions come from coal, but this share will increase if all the planned coal-fired plants go ahead, adding as much CO_2 over the life of the coal plants as that released by all coal burned in the last 250 years (Goodell, 2006). These estimates are based on the Chinese economy maintaining its current growth momentum. But growth has defied expert opinion for the last decade, and may continue to do so over the next ten years. 'China has become the goldilocks economy, it is always next year that it will slow down, but it never does,' said Mehdi Varzi, energy consultant and former Iranian diplomat.

Fatih Birol, chief energy economist at the IEA, believes that 90 % of China's new power supply will come from coal-fired power stations. 'They will be making CO_2 for the next 60 years and once they are built it would be impossible for them to be shut down. Therefore we may lock in our future and these plants will be with us for a long time,' said Birol. 'If we don't make big changes in the next ten years, it will be very difficult to change. Some of the things we are locking in are irreversible. Each year the situation is getting worse, we are burning more CO_2 using more coal and all we get is more talk, but nothing is done. The next decade is going to be very important for climate change.'

The Coal Conundrum

Coal is by far the most polluting fossil fuel compared with oil and natural gas. For every tonne of coal burned in a power station, 2.5 tonnes of carbon dioxide equivalent is emitted, and included in this are other nasty pollutants such as mercury, nitrogen oxide and sulphur dioxide; greenhouse gases that scientists attribute to global warming. It's not just coincidence that the increase in the CO_2 count in the atmosphere has coincided with the world burning more fossil fuels. Coal is the leading source of emissions in the world, overtaking even oil in 2004.

Coal deposits are remnants of plants which grew hundreds of millions of years ago during the Carboniferous period. The plants initially transformed into peat and then into coal when sufficient pressure and temperature squeezed out the remaining water. Oil and natural gas derive from plankton that dropped to the sea floor up to 140 million years ago (Lomborg, 1998). Biofuels also release large doses of CO_2 because they are essentially a plant containing carbon.

Carbon dioxide is the main greenhouse gas, accounting for more than three-quarters of all emissions. It actually fulfils a vital role in the world. Much of the carbon dioxide that is released into the air has already been breathed in by plants and trees – it is needed in order for them to survive – and released again once the plant decays. It plays another important role for the planet, keeping it warm by trapping some of the sunrays that bounce off the Earth and back into space: without this warmth Earth would be too cold and would be devoid of life. Like many things in life though, too much of a good thing is not a good thing: the more CO_2 released into the atmosphere, the more heat is trapped, hence the effects of global warming.

Pollution controls on coal have been around for centuries, but none have worked to halt the increase in pollution. Tighter air pollution controls were introduced in the 14th century to stop the black smoke from the coal that was used by English blacksmiths (Freese, 2003). In the 19th century, the British government introduced laws to reduce smoke from railways and factories. California became one of the first jurisdictions in the US to tighten air pollution control when it passed the Air Pollution Control Act in 1947, and in 1969, it was the first state to pass air quality standards for key pollutants, a move that was later followed by the rest of the US. The problem of coal pollution was the target of President Nixon's speech on the creation of the Environmental Protection Agency on New Year's Day, 1970. He declared that the coming decade was when 'America pays its debt to the past by reclaiming the purity of its air, its waters and our living environment. It is literally now or never.' Nixon's speech, almost 40 years ago, underlined the urgency of addressing environmental issues. Twenty years ago, in 1988, President George H. Bush talked about the 'White House Effect', whereby political power could be used to tighten pollution controls. Many regulations have since passed to no real effect.

The second George Bush used the White House Effect to dismiss the Kyoto Protocol, the international pact to limit greenhouse gas emissions, when he came to office in 2001. Barbara Freese, author of *Coal: A Human History* said that the election of George W. Bush owes much to the US coal industry. West Virginia, the traditionally Democrat stronghold, contributed to the Bush campaign fund, and was vocal in its opposition to Democratic contender Al Gore because of fears that he would tighten environmental controls.

The coal industry has been strongly averse to robust emission limits, and has been among the most outspoken against cleaner air policy. A former coal company executive once said that the Earth was deficient in CO_2 and that more coal should be burned to warm the planet so that plants could feed off the carbon dioxide, thereby making the planet greener.[14]

Shortly after the Bush–Cheney government took office, it launched a National Energy Policy. The report that accompanied its policy did little to suggest there would be any move away from coal (National Energy Policy Development Group, 2001). In fact it said that coal would remain the dominant fuel in meeting increasing US electricity demand.[15] Bush repaid the coal industry further by proposing financial incentives to develop clean coal in the Energy Policy Act of 2005.[16] The Bush–Cheney government gave $5 billion in subsidies to big coal, including $2 billion for research into 'clean coal' power stations, a technical process intended to reduce emissions from burning coal (Goodell, 2006).

Bush's support for the coal industry underlines his prioritizing of energy security over global warming. About half of all US electricity is generated by coal; the country burns more than 1 billion tonnes a year and most of that is met by local production. Almost two-thirds of US coal production comes from mines in Wyoming, West Virginia and Kentucky, with most of the coal moved by train across America. Many drivers that get caught by the red lights at a level crossing in America is often because they are waiting for a coal freight train to pass with dozens of carriages filled to the brim with coal.

Politicians talk about energy security and climate change in the same breath, but so far they have been proven to be largely contradictory objectives. Energy security has become a major focus under President Bush following the September 11 attacks, the wars in Iraq and Afghanistan and the sabre rattling between the Bush government and Iran. This has led the US to formulate its energy policy around securing supplies such as coal and corn for ethanol from domestic sources, and from friendly nations such as neighbouring Canada, which has one of the world's largest deposits of tar sands (an unconventional oil source that requires more energy for its extraction and is a bigger emitter of greenhouse gases than conventional oil sources). The Bush energy security policy has caused a ripple effect across the agricultural world with aggressive US mandatory targets for ethanol, which is made from corn grown in the US. The policy has been a significant factor in the worrying rise in global food prices.

James Connaughton, chief environmental adviser to President George W. Bush has long opposed mandatory emission cuts (which gives an idea of the advice Bush has received on the matter). When Connaughton – who was a lawyer defending industrial companies against environmental lawsuits before he got into politics – talks about the Bush government policy on energy and tackling climate change, he gives the impression that Washington is proactively seeking sustainable energy policies. But the Bush government has tried to stop California from setting a tougher fuel efficiency standard than the Federal government proposed in its 2007 energy bill,[17] and refused to pass the necessary law to set a carbon price in the US, which would provide an economic incentive to switch to cleaner fuels.

At the United Nations Climate Change conference in Bali in December 2007 Connaughton told an audience of journalists that the US was looking at technological solutions to reduce emissions from coal, rather than through a carbon price. 'One of the challenges we face when it comes to producing power from coal with lower emissions and having transportation with lower emissions, is that the technologies are very expensive,' Connaughton said. 'The traditional emission trading mechanism does not provide the price signal that would incentivize the switch to those expensive technologies, so what we have to do in the interim is we have to move as aggressively as we can to advance the research and deployment on low carbon coal power generation technology,' he said.

I Have a Cunning Plan

The US Energy Bill that President Bush signed in December 2007 aims to cut greenhouse gas emissions, bolster energy security and make the US more energy efficient. The US may achieve all of these goals in the future, but it is unlikely to be due to the Bush energy plan. US governments have never been shy of bold energy initiatives. Most have fallen by the wayside; market dynamics ultimately determine the supply and demand of energy sources. The Bush energy plan may well turn out to be no exception, because it is not an effective way to curb greenhouse gas emissions.

US government energy programmes launched in the 1970s fell short of their goals. President Nixon's Project Independence had the some-what optimistic goal of reaching energy self-sufficiency by 1980. In January 1975 President Gerald Ford proposed a ten-year plan to build 200 nuclear power plants, 250 coal mines, 150 coal-fired power stations, 30 oil refineries and 20 synthetic fuel plants (Yergin, 1991). President Jimmy Carter also unveiled a national energy plan within the first three months of his inauguration, though his bill resulted in the creation of the US Department of Energy. A common factor in the failure of the energy plans of the 1970s was the fall in the oil price due to the discovery of new oil reserves, as well as improvements in fuel efficiency for motor vehicles and the switch from oil fired power stations to gas and coal.

President George W. Bush espouses a similar goal to Nixon, how-ever, his energy policy doctrine was dismissed last year by a team of energy executives, policymakers and analysts, who make up the National Petroleum Council (NPC) in the US. 'Energy Independence should not be confused with strengthening energy security. The concept of energy independence is not realistic in the foreseeable future, whereas US energy security can be enhanced by moderating demand, expanding and diversifying domestic energy supplies, and strengthening global energy trade and investment,' the NPC said. 'There can be no US energy security without global energy security.' (National Petroleum Council, 2007).

Until cleaner energies become commercially viable, the world will continue to consume more coal and oil. With the end of the Bush–Cheney government drawing near, the legacy is a more polluted US and a country that is even more dependent on foreign oil. US oil imports now account for 60 % of the country's oil supply, compared with 55 % in 2001, the first year of the Bush–Cheney government, and US CO_2 emissions have risen over this period as the country's fossil fuel consumption is up more than 2 % (Energy Information Administration, 2006).

Clean Coal

Bush and Connaughton believe that clean coal technology is the way to achieve lower greenhouse gas emissions. Clean coal technology is a different process than conventional coal plants, and more costly to operate – hence it is not yet commercially viable.

Conventional coal plants burn coal in a big steel box, the heat driving the turbines that generate the electricity. One of the leading clean coal technologies is the Integrated Gasification Combined Cycle (IGCC), a process that involves 'cooking' the impurities found in coal, such as mercury and nitrous oxide. The cooking cleans the coal which is then converted into a synthetic gas, which is captured and finally burned in a turbine. The impurities and CO_2 are captured through another complicated-sounding process called *carbon sequestration;* a different technology to IGCC. In simple terms, carbon sequestration involves putting all the nasty pollutants into a big bag and shovelling them underground. Though the actual process is not quite as simple as that (for a start the impurities are gases, which cannot be put into a giant bag); the gases are funnelled into pipes that start at the IGCC plant and end in underground aquifers, a tricky process that could be susceptible to leakage.

The IGCC plants claim to be more energy efficient than conventional coal plants; 50 to 60 % efficient compared with 35 % for conventional coal plants. They use less water and reduce wastage – but they are more expensive to construct and operate according to studies by both the IEA and the US Department of Energy. This means that the cost of producing electricity from clean coal technology will be higher. The US does not have to pay for the pollution from coal fired power stations because it does not have a carbon price, but this will change.

The concept of IGCC is not entirely new. Gasification of coal has been used for more than 150 years, and many of the first street lamps in Europe and America were lit by coal gas. Commercial gasification for electricity generation is new though, and the combination of two unproven commercial technologies – the IGCC process and carbon sequestration – working together in the future is a big challenge. Research into the commercialization of the technologies has been taking place for decades. In the 1970s, there was an Office of Coal Research within the US Department of the Interior, which looks after government-owned land (including national parks) and administers Indian reservations. Most of the funding was given to projects controlled by companies with strong links to the oil industry (Ruttenberg and Associates Inc., 1973).[18] In the 1960s and early 1970s, six of America's largest coal producers were owned by oil companies, including Exxon, producing more than a fifth of annual US coal output. Today, the major oil companies have little or no interest in coal.

The federal funding of clean coal research has not always met with success. The US government report 'Lessons Learned in the Clean Coal Technology Program', released in June 2001, stated that, 'Many projects had experienced delays, cost overruns, bankruptcies, and performance problems.' It also identified some projects demonstrating technologies that might have been commercialized without federal assistance.[19]

With the world expected to use much more coal and emit far more greenhouse gases for the foreseeable future, achieving the diametrically opposed goals of continued coal-generated electricity expansion and greenhouse gas reduction may indeed rely on the success of clean coal technologies such as IGCC. But given the unproven nature of the technology and the focus on the bottom line, the coal industry is reluctant to spend the additional funds required for building new coal-based IGCC power plants.[20] The adoption of new energy technology such as wind and solar also depends on government assistance and policy. The US government has been generous in its assistance to the energy industry, giving about a third of the income it receives in taxation and royalties back to the sector, through research and development grants, government spending programmes and tax breaks. During the past 29 years, Congress has provided DOE with about $50 billion for R&D in renewable, fossil and nuclear energy technologies (US Department of Energy, 2006). The world is now facing its biggest energy challenge – providing clean energy, as opposed to running out of energy sources – and the spending on energy research and development has fallen well below the levels of the early 1980s.[21]

Liquid Coal

Coal is also promoted by some as a solution to the other great energy challenge – secure liquid petroleum supplies. There has long been a quest to use coal to make fuels for transportation. Nazi Germany converted domestically produced coal into synthetic fuel to power its Luftwaffe air force and its army, otherwise dependent on foreign oil supplies. Apartheid South Africa, subject to international trade sanctions, developed coal for use as a liquid; in fact the world's largest producer of this fuel is South African company Sasol. The technology may have helped Fascist regimes, but it has never fulfilled expectations as a widely deployed commercial fuel.

The following quote highlights the expectation surrounding turning coal into liquids. 'The development of synthetic liquids and gas will have a marked effect on competition in the energy market. Substitution of synthetic gas and oil from coal will probably reduce the naturally mined oil and gas. It could render obsolete hundreds of millions of dollars of refining plants and mining equipment. The threat to the oil industry is real' (Ruttenberg and Associates, Inc., 1973). These words were written in 1973, but it was not the first time such ambitious predictions were made. In his seminal book on the history of oil, *The Prize*, Daniel Yergin quotes from a story printed in the *New*

York Times in 1948 proclaiming that in the future gasoline would be made from coal, air and water (Yergin, 1991).

Turning coal into a liquid that can be put in a motor vehicle is unlikely ever to live up to this rosy forecast, largely because it is very energy intensive and the conversion process involves emitting almost double the CO_2 of conventional oil. That said, the US, Australia, China and South Africa are all investing in coal-to-liquids technology, with the aim to reduce their dependence on imported oil.

The Answer My Friend, is Blowing in the Wind

The drive to reduce greenhouse gas emissions has created demand for electricity generation that emits low or no emissions, such as wind and solar – known as renewable energies because they come from natural sources (as opposed to fossil fuels, which have a finite supply). Politicians all over the world are falling into line. It is now rare for any government anywhere in the world not to have a renewable energy policy; even the big emitters such as the US and China.

Hydrocarbon rich Russia also has a low emissions energy policy in that it is pursuing an expansion of its nuclear energy capacity and hydroelectric power; although on a global scale concerns about water supplies in parts of the developing world and environmental concerns about dam construction mean that hydroelectric power's share of the overall pie is likely to remain small. Even oil-rich countries in the Middle East are looking at cleaner energies. Abu Dhabi, the richest emirate of the United Arab Emirates, has a $15 billion plan to build a city that will be carbon neutral and will have no cars.

Renewable energy is the fastest growing energy sector in percentage terms, but in absolute terms the gains in coal and gas each year outweigh the additional power generation capacity from wind and solar. The growth of these markets has created new industries and made many 'eco-friendly millionaires'.

Wind power is not exactly revolutionary. Windmills were around when Cervantes was writing his classic *Don Quixote*; Senor Quixote charging at the windmills thinking, in his delusion, that they were giants. But recently, wind power in particular has grown enormously. Today, a long drive anywhere in the world will most likely take in the sight of these whirring giants of the energy sector. I've seen wind farms as far afield as Donegal in northwest Ireland on the very western tip of Europe; in the Alpujarras mountains south of the Andalusian city of Granada in southern Spain; in Iowa in Midwest America and south of Coimbatore in Tamil Nadu in southern India.

It is in India, though, where wind energy has become an essential part of the country's expansion. It started with the Indian Ministry of New and Renewable Energy in 1982 as a backlash against the high oil prices of the 1970s. According to Shri Subramanian, secretary of the ministry, wind has made the most advances because it can be installed at the local village level without building expensive transmission power lines to connect the village to the power grid.

India is the fourth largest producer of electricity from wind in the world and it has one of the biggest global producers of wind turbines in Suzlon Energy. Suzlon was formerly a textile business but shortages in the local electricity supply forced the owner Tulsi Tanti and his brothers to seek alternative power sources. They decided to buy some windmills, later ditching the textile business to focus on pioneering wind as an energy source. The Suzlon business was founded in Pune, which is in the western Indian state of Maharashtra. It was here that Enron built the giant ill-fated Dabhol gas-fired power plant to address India's power shortages and provide electricity to towns like Pune. In an ironic twist Suzlon has helped to address India's power shortages through a more modest solution: wind, a business model that has helped Suzlon expand internationally. Enron on the other hand, tried to go global with big projects such as Dabhol, but failed because its business model was ultimately flawed. 'The demand for wind power is driven more by shortages than by incentitives,' said Raghuraman Vaidhyanathan, an advisor to Suzlon.

Despite the growth in wind and other renewable energies – such as biomass which involves the burning of wood – collectively they still equate to about the same portion of the global energy pie as they did in the early 1970s, mainly because hydropower has remained static. Renewable energy needs not only government legislation, but also greater research and development to meet the future energy demands and lower greenhouse gases. In Denmark for example, the stimulation of renewable energy technology through government assisted programmes has resulted in wind energy accounting for 19 % of total electricity consumed in 2005. It's one of the few countries able to boast of economic expansion and falling greenhouse emissions, accomplished not only through the installation of wind turbines, but also through domestic energy efficiency measures, such as home insulation and better public transport.

One issue that has held back the wider adoption of wind or solar energy is that neither source is able to store power. This limits their ability to generate electricity to meet periods of peak demand. Wind does not blow at the exact moment when power is needed and the same goes for the sun – it shines during the day, but most solar power is actually needed when it gets dark and lights are switched on at home.

There are projects currently working on wind storage capacity. Just west of Des Moines, state capital of Iowa, amid the corn and soya bean fields, is the Iowa Stored Energy Park, which is using an underground aquifer as a test bed to store power from the wind farm located above. If successful it could radically change the dynamics of the wind power industry (and prove that Bob Dylan had a point when he sang, 'the answer is blowin' in the wind'). The project is backed by utilities in Iowa where wind power is becoming increasingly popular with farmers, who are installing wind farms as another potential revenue stream, selling electricity back to the power grid. But there's a long wait: demand for wind turbines is high. 'Worldwide there is such demand for wind turbines that prices have gone up significantly, and I will not be able to get them until 2009. I went out and bought ten turbines, but that is relatively small – manufacturers won't really work with you unless you are ordering 100 or 200 turbines,' said Philip Sundblad, a corn farmer and district director of Iowa Farm Bureau.

California is also embracing wind power. Arnold Schwarzenegger, the state's governor, is writing into law that a third of the Golden State's electricity must come from renewable sources by 2020 (California Energy Commission, 2007). To achieve this goal California plans to spend $2.2 billion installing solar panels on the roofs of more than a million homes, including low-income and affordable housing projects, to ensure that solar is adopted across the board. California is the most visible of government and local authorities around the world to have taken a proactive stance on climate change and energy security, partly because it is run by a former bodybuilder turned Hollywood star who is married to a member of one of the most famous American families. But visit any city around the world and chances are that the local buses will run on hydrogen, biofuels or liquefied or compressed natural gas. These buses are expensive; but they offer an opportunity for the local authority to demonstrate its green credentials.

With more proactive legislation on renewable energy and higher energy prices, the money people in the San Francisco area who backed the computer, internet and telecommunications technology start-ups in the 1980s and 1990s are turning their attention and dollars to renewable energy and energy-efficient technologies such as longer-burning light bulbs and electric cars. With the combination of dollars and brains, the proponents of renewable energy – also known as clean energy – are hoping that technological advancements will be made in the areas of solar, wind and biofuels in the same way that a mobile phone was turned from the electronic brick of the 80s to a slimline device that can send emails, take pictures and play music. The innovations from Silicon Valley have also led to computers light enough to carry around without dislocating your shoulder, with enough power and software to make telephone calls, download documents, book airline tickets, watch a video or listen to any radio station in the world.

Clean energy venture capital converts are optimistic that what they were able to achieve in IT they can repeat in energy. Vinod Khosla is a founder of Sun-Microsystems and a partner in venture capital group Kleiner Perkins Caufield & Byers, which helped fund Google and teamed up in 2007 with Al Gore to seek clean and green technology investments. The Indian-born entrepreneur has his own investment firm, Khosla Partners, which has a portfolio of renewable energy investments from cellulosic ethanol to solar technology, plastics, building materials and electrical efficiency. Google founders Sergey Brin and Larry Page are investors in Nanosolar, a solar-film technology group, and are promoters of plug-in cars as well as trying to make the company carbon-neutral. PayPal founder Elon Musk, who sold his electronic payments company to Ebay for $1.5 billion, has become the major financier of Tesla, the electric sports car. Craig Venter, pioneer of the human genome that cracked the DNA code first, is applying the same technique to plants in an effort to make biofuels from plants more effectively.

The two educational institutions in California credited with nurturing the brains and talent that spurred the tech revolution, Stanford and Berkeley Universities, have also established their own clean energy research arms. 'Energy was never an area for venture capital before, because it was considered a large upfront cost to get in,' said Guy Caruso, Administrator of the Energy Information Administration (EIA), a statistical arm of the United States Department of Energy. The barrier to entry is now pretty small, almost anyone it seems can set up an ethanol plant. The big thing would be whether this capital would bring investment of the scale that is needed; you are talking about a few per cent, if it stimulates technology that leads to bigger things.

Terry Tamminen, energy adviser to governor Schwarzenegger, displays a typical Californian-style confidence when it comes to technological solutions for the energy challenge. Tamminen describes thin-films of solar that can cover windows and roofs in the home and on skyscraper buildings, absorbing heat and turning it into power. He speaks of more energy-efficient solar panels, and wider deployment of other energy-saving technology such as LED (light-emitting diodes) lighting – known as 'intelligent lighting' because it is computer controlled to provide greater control of the lighting systems in large buildings. The art deco Empire State Building in New York (best known for King Kong's last stand) has installed this type of system in an effort to reduce carbon emissions and power costs. More research is being carried out on motion sensors which trigger lights when somebody moves from room to room inside the house.

Total investment (that is not just venture capital) in 'clean' or low-carbon technology was $74bn in 2007, according to Michael Liebreich, founder of consultancy New Energy Finance (Harvey and Allison, 2007). A more ambitious renewable energy programme that puts the aspirations of California and its venture capitalists in the shade is the Space-based Solar Power programme, directed by the Pentagon-based US National Security Space Office (NSSO). Its aims are like something out of a science fiction film: the idea is to put large solar shields in space, that can beam solar rays back to Earth (National Security Space Office, 2007).[22] The NSSO justifies its pursuit of an improbable solution by saying that, 'Every energy resource opportunity, including those from space, must be fully explored to determine its ability to contribute toward solving mankind's looming energy supply and security dilemma.'

The lack of widespread penetration by wind and solar energy because of the storage issues and the need for lower emissions has also led to the re-emergence of nuclear this decade.

The Nuclear Quandary

The nuclear industry has rebranded itself as an emissions-clean alternative to fossil fuels, without the energy security issues that dog oil and gas. One of the best examples of the changing political landscape for the nuclear industry was the reversal in the British government's position on nuclear. When the UK government, then led by Prime Minister Tony Blair, unveiled its energy white paper in 2003, the government had maintained its line from the previous decade on the decommissioning of nuclear energy plants. Within three years the government had released another long-term strategic review of its energy industry, putting the nuclear industry back in the frame.[23] This backtracking has been repeated around the world. Many countries that have been averse to nuclear in the past are reconsidering the nuclear option. Proponents of nuclear energy argue that the world would not be emitting so many greenhouse gases had nuclear continued on its trajectory of expansion in the 1960s.

In the 1950s nuclear was touted as the fuel of the future. A fuel that would be so cheap it did not need metering. President Eisenhower gave the go-ahead to commercialize nuclear energy in the wake of his 'Atoms for Peace' speech in 1953. Initially, there were optimistic predictions made about the technology, such as nuclear-fuelled cars, but a spate of catastrophic accidents beginning in the 1970s – culminating in the Chernobyl disaster in Ukraine in April 1984 – halted any further expansion of the nuclear energy industry. For almost 20 years nobody wanted to take the risk of building a nuclear plant for fear of further accidents and concerns about the storage of nuclear waste, which remains one of the biggest impediments to the growth of nuclear energy.

To overcome this negative perception, the nuclear industry maintains that it can still play a key role in reducing carbon emissions. Nuclear power stations around the world avoid what would otherwise be about 2 billion tonnes of carbon dioxide emissions each year.[24] Actual carbon savings, though, vary from country to country. Nuclear is not totally carbon-free, but comparable to the emissions from renewables such as wind power. Plus nuclear does not have the same security issues that confront oil and gas. Uranium – the metallic element that is turned into nuclear power – comes largely from politically stable countries such as Canada and Australia. Relatively little uranium is required to create the nuclear power that, in turn, produces electricity, therefore the volume of uranium required for the future is nowhere near the vast quantity of fossil fuels required. Like other commodity markets, it is the demand from China[25] and India that is really changing the dynamics of the nuclear industry.

The world's electricity capacity from nuclear power is expected to expand by about a fifth by 2030, according to the IEA (International Energy Agency, 2007). Most of that will be in China and India, with only a handful of other countries – the US, Russia, Japan and South Korea – also set to expand nuclear capacity. Over the next 20 years existing facilities built in the 1970s and 1980s will have to be replaced, since most nuclear plants have a lifespan of 40 years. New nuclear plants are estimated to cost more than double coal-fired power stations, and the industry relies to a certain extent on government tax breaks. Nuclear has received one of the biggest shares in research and development funding from the US government, which committed itself in 2003 to an ambitious research programme to develop nuclear fusion (the holy grail of nuclear technology) as it potentially eliminates the issue of waste management. The project funded through the International Thermonuclear Experimental Reactor (ITER) will see the construction of a pilot plant in southern France.[26]

The rate of nuclear expansion for electricity (as opposed to nuclear weapons) will substantially increase the demand for uranium.

Uranium-101

The World Nuclear Association estimates that the demand for uranium for the purposes of electricity generation will increase by 70 % from 2006 to 2030 (World Nuclear Association, 2007). In 2007 Canada and Australia produced more than half of the world's uranium, though Kazakhstan could challenge both countries as the world's biggest producer; the central Asian country has been rapidly expanding its output. The revival of the nuclear sector has prompted a worldwide search for new sources of uranium, after decades of negligible exploration activity (following a glut in supply from the uranium-mining boom of the 1970s). In the past five years more than 450 companies have listed their shares on stock exchanges in Australia, Canada, the United Kingdom and the US, promising to find uranium from all corners of the globe.

Uranium is actually a very common element on the Earth's surface.[27] It is mined like a metal, but unlike other metals, no objects or mechanical structures are made from it. Although it was used for the manufacture of ceramics and glass in the early 20th century (US

Geological Survey, 2001). Like other metals it also has to go through several stages of processing before it can be used. It's made up of different elements but only one very small element – uranium-235 – can be turned into a power source. Uranium-235 makes up only 0.7 % of all the uranium that is mined, and therefore it needs to be enriched to make it more commercially viable to use in power generation. Given that such a tiny proportion of the ore contains usable uranium from such a large volume of rock taken from the mine, the milling of the uranium from the rock is done close to the mine. It would be uneconomic to transport the ore away for processing. After milling it is turned into uranium oxide U3O8 – better known as yellowcake. The vast majority – around 99.3 % – of uranium ore is not used to generate nuclear power.

Making uranium into a more commercial fuel involves turning uranium into a gas – uranium hexafluoride UF6 – and then converting it back into an element again. The uranium now has an energy concentration of 4 %. Finally the uranium is burned into ceramic pellets and placed in fuel rods, which make up the fuel assembly that goes into the nuclear reactor. Like other mineral processing, the large volume of poor grade uranium left over is uneconomic to process unless the uranium price is high.

A tenth of the world's uranium supply has so far come from the plutonium (processed uranium) in decommissioned US and Russian nuclear warheads dismantled under the Megatons to Megawatts programme.[28] Lack of new supply combined with uncertainty over the future of the US–Russia pact means that the uranium price has more than quadrupled in recent years. Such is the demand for uranium that it has created tightness in the supply and demand equation.

There have been several previous attempts to commoditize the uranium market. In the 1980s and 1990s, Oren Benton (through his flagship company Nuexco Trading Corporation) bought Russian uranium and sold it into Western markets. The profits he made from uranium trading were used to build a business empire that included a controlling interest in the Colorado Rockies baseball team before the business imploded under a $500 million debt in 1996. Benton's legacy though, was that he created a spot market in uranium, previously dominated by long-term contracts. Given the fluctuations in prices, more uranium is being traded on the spot market now.

The New York Mercantile Exchange (Nymex), the world's largest energy futures exchange, launched a cash-settled uranium contract in 2007, but a physical uranium market is also emerging where utilities, producers and investors will be able to buy and sell uranium. They won't be able to physically move the material though. It's tightly controlled under an intergovernmental arrangement to stop uranium ending up in the hands of renegades who want to make nuclear weapons. What investors can buy and sell are the rights to hold the uranium, which is kept in registered warehouses. This is similar to the conditions for trading in base metals on the London Metal Exchange. There is growing demand from new players who want to make money from trading uranium. If this market takes off it will ensure enough trading volumes in the market for participants to buy and sell quickly, key to all successful financial and commodity markets (Raghavjee, 2006).

In the long term though, the potential of nuclear power is dependent upon the uranium resources available. Various studies have been done, some estimating up to 100 years of supply based on consumption levels seen this decade. Uranium, like other commodities we will examine in this book, is open to substitution if the price is high enough. Nuclear fuels can be made from thorium, another radioactive metallic element. It's similar to uranium but it doesn't have the waste issues associated with used uranium. Thorium was discovered in 1828 by the Swedish chemist Jons Jakob Berzelius, who named it after Thor, the Norse god of thunder. It can be found in small amounts in most rocks and soils, and it is about three times more abundant in the Earth's crust than uranium.

Thorium is also more energy efficient than uranium. Mined thorium is potentially usable in a reactor before it is enriched (compared with the 0.7 % of natural uranium). Thorium versus uranium is a bit like the betamax versus VHS debate that raged in the new era of video in the 1980s: VHS won out, but there are many who still argue today that Betamax was a better technology. Thorium-based nuclear reactors are a different technology to uranium, so unfortunately it is not a simple case of feeding a nuclear reactor in Europe or the US with thorium rather than uranium. A nuclear energy industry around thorium would involve an entirely new layer of infrastructure.

Burning the Midnight Oil

Of all the fossil fuels the role of oil in the global economy is the most vital. The world's primary modes of transportation are fuelled by petroleum products derived from oil, gasoline (petrol), diesel, jet fuel and bunker fuel. Without these liquids it would be impossible to travel by plane or boat or drive most cars. The fear about secure supply has triggered a race for viable alternatives to oil, such as hydrogen, liquid fuel from coal and gas and biofuels. The latter have gained much attention (and will be explored further in the second chapter). The search is now on for the second generation of biofuels, made from the backbone of plants and trees rather than from the fruit or seeds they bear. The desire for energy security has become more and more apparent. The demand for oil has not slowed down, in fact if anything it has accelerated with the unprecedented growth of China. The increase in demand comes at a time when oil supply from traditional sources in the North Sea and the Gulf of Mexico is declining – a trend that appears irreversible – leaving the world more reliant on oil supplies from the Middle East, Russia, central Asia and West Africa.

Most of the world's oil will come from supplies held by the Opec cartel, the group of oil producers whose de facto leader is the oil kingdom of Saudi Arabia, the world's largest producer.[29] Opec has been a major beneficiary of high oil prices this decade, recording record export receipts that have been used by some Gulf countries to acquire overseas assets to diversify their economies away from oil dependency. Other Opec members, such as Venezuela, have spent the dividends on large social programmes and a significant slice of Iran's oil earnings have been spent on importing refined oil products and subsidizing gasoline for its fast-expanding population. It is little wonder that both Iran and Venezuela have become the most vocal supporters of higher oil prices. Their oil production profile remains static, due to a lack of adequate reinvestment in the industry that provides both nations with their relative wealth.

Higher oil prices and increased demand have given Opec more leverage when it comes to its oil-production policies. Opec behaves more consistently like a cartel now than at any other time in its near 50-year history. When it was founded in 1960 most of the oil in the member countries was produced by Western oil companies. This arrangement changed through the nationalization of the respective oil sectors in Opec countries during the 1960s and early 1970s, which resulted in government-owned oil companies controlling supplies. The shift in ownership occurred around the same time as the Arab oil embargo in 1973, when oil-producing countries first exercised their power. The change in power and cohesion was relatively brief: two Opec members, Iran and Iraq, after the Islamic revolution in Iran in 1979, sent oil prices higher, only for them to collapse as oil demand fell due to the arrival of new supplies from the North Sea and the Gulf of Mexico, and the switch from oil power generation to alternative sources such as gas and coal.

In the 1990s the world faced an oil glut as Venezuela ramped up its oil production to increase its global oil market share. This policy of increasing market share was reversed when Hugo Chavez was elected in 1998. The election of the former army colonel marked a turning point in the oil price, which bottomed to less than $10 a barrel, leading *The Economist* magazine to predict in March 1999, a $10 barrel forever. The collapse in oil price hit the oil dependent economies of Opec hard. They responded by cutting oil supplies and adopting a more vigilant oil-production policy, meeting more regularly and fine-tuning supplies to ensure that consuming nations could not build up their oil inventories to the same levels again. Opec has been further aided by the succession of Vladimir Putin in Russia in December 1999, who became a de facto friend of Opec (Russia now has observer status at Opec meetings). Putin has also wrestled for control of oil production in Russia, which is the second largest exporter after Saudi Arabia. It is now back under state control following the privatization of the sector under President Yeltsin in the 1990s. The move to state control has coincided with a slowdown in Russian oil production growth.

Politicians from oil-importing countries have blamed Opec for high oil prices, but it is not that simple. If European politicians were really concerned about high oil prices, they could cut the taxes which make up about three-quarters of the retail price of petroleum products, and in the US, driving more fuel-efficient cars would go some way to reducing the country's demand for oil.[30] But that is not to let Opec totally off the hook; its members are increasingly addicted to higher oil prices to balance the government budgets. Some of the oil revenues subsidize telephone calls, water usage, and low or no personal income tax rates for local citizens, as well as financing the increasing cost of investment in new oil production. Opec oil ministers consistently talk down the cartel's importance in the oil market by blaming high oil prices on other factors such as a lack of refining capacity, the weaker dollar and competition from biofuels and speculators in oil markets. The first two reasons may have merit, but the latter two don't stand up under closer scrutiny, and will be discussed in Chapters 2 and 5 respectively.

For the oil-importing countries – the US, China, India, Japan and Europe – the increasing influence of Opec and Russia is a cause for concern on two fronts. Firstly, political risk: the troubles in the Middle East are well known – the Israel–Palestine issue, the rising influence of Hezbollah in Lebanon and the repercussions in terms of political stability, the rise of Sunni militant extremists across the Islamic world borne out of the puritanical ideology of Wahhabism in Saudi Arabia, the war in Iraq, the nuclear ambitions of Iran, the confrontation between Turkish troops and Kurds and the political instability of Pakistan, not forgetting the dynamics of Shia–Sunni relations in many countries of the Islamic world. These political issues are not going to disappear in the foreseeable future.

The second area of concern for consuming countries is longevity of supplies: the estimation of oil reserves is an opaque art that few outside the oil world understand. There is no global standard to measure oil reserves, nor is there any independent scrutiny. It comes down to the estimates by the oil host countries and the blind trust of the consuming nations that the guesswork is correct. This relationship is not a strong foundation for oil consumers to secure long term supplies of oil. Consuming nations are making alternative arrangements by looking at other energy sources. This ambiguity about global oil reserves has given rise to the peak oil theory.

Based on the number of recent large oil discoveries (not many), and the age of many of the existing oil fields in the Middle East (pretty old), the peak oil theorists may have a point. But the restrictions enforced by oil-producing nations on foreign companies and a desire not to maximize output has, for the short term at least, blurred the issue on peak oil. In his book *Twilight in the Desert*, Matthew Simmons, a Houston-based investment banker, warned that Saudi Arabian oil reserves – estimated to make up about a quarter of global oil reserves – could face serious and irreversible decline (Simmons, 2005). This prompted an angry response from Saudi Aramco, which dismissed Simmons's assertion. Nevertheless, concerns about the sustainability of high oil supplies linger.

Mehdi Varzi, the independent oil consultant who formerly headed energy research at Dresdner Kleinwort bank, wrote a report for them on Opec production. It took eight months to write and analyses supply field by field in each of the countries. Some of the fields were discovered 50 years ago, and Varzi found many were on their way to depletion. 'Opec production is depleting by 5 % a year, which means it has to find an additional 1.5 million barrels a day just to stay still,' he said, though he added that each Opec country has its own individual set of problems surrounding production and reserves. Whether the predictions about oil and other resource peaks are correct, we probably won't know until after the event. Right now, a higher oil price has resulted in exploration of other oil-containing resources, such as the oil sand deposits of Canada.

Catch 22

The wealth in oil-producing countries has provided more money to a rapidly growing population to spend on more and bigger vehicles. The Middle East is one of the fastest growing regions for oil demand, putting it just behind China and India. Iran's expanding population and its generous fuel subsidy programme has led to a rise in domestic oil consumption rates from less than 700 000 barrels a day in 1976 (when it was producing close to 6 million barrels a day) to more than 1.5 million barrels a day now (when it is actually struggling to produce more than 4 million barrels a day). This growing demand of course leaves less for export. In fact, Iran is importing more petroleum products from places like India, because of the lack of domestic refinery capacity to process its own oil (with Iranian drivers not paying much more than 42 US cents a gallon at the pump, it is little wonder they behave like racing car drivers on the wide roads of Tehran!)[31] The oil consumption and production trends for Iran pose a huge challenge for the country and for the global oil market, because they could lead to tighter oil supplies for importing countries.

Part of the reason Iran's oil production has not regained the levels last seen in the Shah's era is because some of its oilfields were bombed by Saddam Hussein during the eight-year war between the two neighbours. Rather naively, I first went to Iran during this period. Although I never saw any sign of conflict, hundreds of black and white photos of young men posted along the main roads of small towns and villages acted as a poignant reminder of who had died in the war. One of my memories of Iran at the time is the prevalence of Hillman Hunters on the roads. The Hillman was renamed the Paykan in Iran after the Shah government bought the rights to it and continued to mass-produce the car well after they disappeared from British roads. I travelled through war-torn Iran for five days on a bus, but the first time during this period that I saw a gun being fired was when we crossed the border into Pakistan and the border guard in his remote hut in the Baluchistan desert, got out his Enfield .303 rifle and challenged our bus driver to a target contest.

The unpredictability of the Middle East and large parts of south Asia has prompted energy-importing governments to respond. Energy policies now have the lofty aim of reducing their oil dependency from unstable suppliers and energy efficiency research programmes and alternative clean energy sources are being developed, as energy policy becomes entwined with climate change.

The difference between now and the 1970s is that there are no new conventional North Sea oil fields coming on, and the promises of the new supply from the Caspian Sea and central Asia have consistently failed to live up to expectations. At the same time demand for oil – predominately for transportation – remains strong due to the emerging mobile classes in China and India. The cost of cars is coming down, too. Tata Motors, the Indian carmaker, intends to sell its new Tata Nano for $2500 each, or about half the cost of the next cheapest car.

Today's equivalent of the North Sea oil fields – that is, oil supply from a politically stable region – is the Canadian tar sands, also known as oil sands. These are a combination of clay, sand, water and bitumen in a rock formation. Unlike conventional oil, which is drilled, tar sands near the surface are mined using open pit techniques, a common method normally used for large metal deposits. Once the rock is removed from the ground, the oil content, which is bitumen, has to be separated, from the clay, water and sand. The bitumen, a rather thick, gooey substance, is processed to make it more viscous so that it can be refined and turned into a liquid for use in our cars.

The extra processes required to extract and refine tar sand compared with conventional oil add significantly to its cost. Only in recent years has it been economic to commercially exploit the deposits of tar and oil sands, found mainly in Canada and Venezuela. The rise in Canadian petroleum production from oil sands has created an oil rush in the state of Alberta, which has become the Saudi Arabia of unconventional oil, and tar sands provide a new source of supply for American drivers. The US imports more oil from Canada than any other country. Given their political and geographical proximity, this is probably as close as the US may get to energy independence. Canadian oil sands production is estimated to account for most of the net increase in oil production from countries outside of the Opec grouping. By 2030, Canada is projected to produce as much oil as Iran does today. But it is a more energy intensive and costly process. It requires a lot of gas, another fossil fuel Canada exports to its southern neighbour; about 85 % of the US gas imports come from Canada. The oil sands sector is consuming so much gas that Canada predicts it will become a net gas importer in 20 year's time (National Energy Board, 2007), a fact that brings a whole new meaning to energy security, since most of the world's gas reserves are in the Middle East and Russia. At present the US and Canada account for more than a quarter of global gas demand.[32]

Not only do oil sands require a lot of gas for processing, but they are a big polluter. Oil sands production is estimated to release more than double the emissions of conventional oil, a major factor in emissions growth in Canada. Yet the Canadian government has signed up to the Kyoto Protocol, a pact to reduce emissions. Another factor contributing to the release of emissions from oil sands mining is deforestation in the area (which is bigger than the state of Florida) containing the oil sands deposits. The Alberta state government said that its greenhouse gas emissions from all sources have risen by 37 % since 1990, far more than the national average of 25 % for all of Canada. Although power generation remains the largest source for Canada's greenhouse emissions, oil sands and heavy oil production make up more than a quarter of all of the country's emissions, and more than 40 % of Alberta's (Alberta Government, 2007).

The US has its own unconventional oil resource, in the form of shale oil. This generally refers to any sedimentary rock containing a material called kerogen, which is like fossilized algae and was formed millions of years ago. Most of the US shale oil deposits are in the Rocky Mountain region.[33] Back in the oil crisis of the 1970s, Exxon embarked on developing shale oil, spending about $1 billion at the time on the Colony Project. After oil prices fell in the 1980s and the cost of extracting shale oil continued to rise, Exxon abandoned its plan (Yergin, 1991).

Even now, the commercialization of this resource is decades away according to the National Petroleum Council, headed by former ExxonMobil chairman Lee Raymond. Oil prices around $100 a barrel, it is still hard for shale oil to be economic. One of the factors inhibiting the exploitation of shale oil is the amount of water required to extract it – an estimated 1.2 barrels of water for each barrel of shale oil. The US shale deposits are in dry areas where rainfall is minimal.

Developers of oil shale projects would therefore need to buy water rights – a complicated affair in Colorado, and the demand for water is becoming even more competitive with the expanding population in the Rocky Mountain region.

US energy researchers have also experimented with the live form of algae. The US department of energy spent 20 years researching the prospect of turning algae into biodiesel, but found that it cost twice as much as making gasoline from crude oil (National Renewable Energy Laboratary, 1998). Large investments in the production of oil from natural gas have failed expectations. Qatar pulled the plug on one of the most ambitious gas-to-liquid programmes because of escalating costs.

The search for oil above all other fossil fuels can be explained by the fact that it is one of the most efficient. When discussing energy it is worth assessing the energy value for each source – it becomes clear why oil stands out among all fossil fuels and why it is going to be a tough job replacing it.

Here Comes the Science

Energy is measured in units called joules. A joule is a minuscule amount of energy, far smaller than the energy we expend drinking a drop of liquid or lifting a lettuce leaf. When people speak of joules they normally refer to them by the millions or billions: that is, mega-joules (MJ) or gigajoules (GJ). Energy can be measured by its physical characteristics – weight, volume – or in its nature – whether it is a solid, liquid or gas. Coal, for instance, has fewer joules per kilogram than the same weight in oil, making oil the favourite in terms of what you're going to get out of the effort of finding and producing it. In fact, oil is superior to all other fossil fuels, which is why it is the most strategic of all energy. The weight of oil is 43 MJ per kilogram compared with 25.5 MJ for ethanol from grain, 24 MJ for coal, 18 MJ for wood and 4.4 MJ for oil shale (the small content of energy power contained in oil shale is one of the factors that have limited its commercial viability).

In terms of volume, a cubic metre of oil contains 35 000 MJ of energy, a cubic metre of coal around 27 500 MJ, ethanol about 20 000 MJ, and a cubic metre of gas only 35 MJ. Another point in oil's favour is that it is a liquid, so it's easier to transport and store.

Shrinking Big Oil

As their conventional oil reserve bases shrink, the large Western oil companies have become major investors in projects like the Canadian oil sands, gas to liquids, shale oil and strategies for producing hydrogen. Back in the 1970s, US oil companies were also diversifying out of conventional oil and bought production, reserves and milling capacity in the uranium industry. In 1970, seventeen oil companies, including Exxon, controlled about 48 % of the known US low-cost uranium reserves (Ruttenberg and Associates, Inc., 1973).[34]

A major problem faced by the energy industry is a lack of skilled personnel who can develop large-scale oil and gas projects. The 1980s and 1990s saw fewer petroleum engineers coming out of universities – the industry was perceived as dirty and did not have the glamour of the technology, finance or communications sectors. Nearly half the personnel in the US energy industries will be eligible for retirement within the next ten years and a 'demographic cliff' is looming in all areas of energy industry employment. An American Petroleum Institute survey in 2004 indicated that by 2009 there would be a 38 % shortage of engineers and geoscientists and a 28 % shortage of instrumentation and electrical workers in the US oil and gas industry (National Petroleum Council, 2007).

The high price of oil today is blamed on the wastefulness of the finite resource when prices were cheap. The gains made in fuel engine efficiency in the wake of tighter standards in the aftermath of the 1970s energy crisis have largely been lost in the US through the sale of bigger cars; the increased weight and horsepower have meant that fuel economy levels have been flat for the past two decades (National Petroleum Council, 2007). 'You had a period of 25 years where the American public had a declining share of their personal income that would go to personal mobility and they chose to spend that gain in personal disposable income on heavier vehicles and higher horsepower,' said Guy Caruso from the EIA.'The fall in energy prices through the 1980s and 1990s has meant that energy costs for the household budget fell from 14 % in the early 1980s to about 7 % earlier this decade,' said Mr Caruso, who is in charge of one of the most comprehensive energy data-gathering bodies in the world and has been analysing energy markets for the past 30 years. Gains in energy efficiency in both residential and commercial buildings have been offset by the increase in the size of the average US home. The trend is mirrored in household appliances such as the refrigerator, where an increase in size has negated the gains made in energy-efficient design. 'The big difference with this energy challenge is that this is really driven by very strong economic growth,' said Mr Caruso, who told me that energy prices, particularly oil, are likely to remain high, which would underwrite the investment needed to commercialize cleaner and more sustainable energy sources.

On The Road

Terry Tamminen explained how California is gearing up for hydrogen cars and how the car industry is responding. Just days prior to meeting Tamminen near his Santa Monica office, Honda unveiled its fuel cell car at the November 2007 Los Angeles Motor Show. The Japanese car maker said a limited number of the FCX Clarity would be ready in the summer of 2008 in southern California at a cost comparable to the conventional car (based over the lifespan of the car when running costs and maintenance are factored into the equation). At the same show, General Motors announced that its Chevrolet Silverado hybrid pick-up truck would be available in late 2008. The truck will be one of its first passenger vehicles to go hybrid – long after its Japanese rivals Toyota and Honda launched their respective hybrids: the Prius and Civic have become market leaders in hybrid cars.

The unveiling of a clean energy car in a city noted for its traffic jams and pollution is welcome. The Pico Boulevard from the beachside suburb in Santa Monica to the convention centre in downtown LA is always clogged with traffic and introducing less-polluting cars will help clear the air (though it may not do much about the traffic jams). 'We will have 200 hydrogen stations by 2010, with thousands of vehicles, and we are in talks with governments up and down the coast from British Columbia to Baja (in Mexico) so that you can drive all the way in a hydrogen car,' said Tamminen, sporting a blue jacket with a logo for California's hydrogen highway.

The hydrogen initiative by California may represent just one of the 50 US states, but with 30 million motor vehicles, California is one of the world's top ten car markets. There are concerns about hydrogen storage at filling stations near residential areas. Hydrogen is highly flammable and the size of the storage tank in the car leaves little room for luggage in some prototype designs. California, though, has long been a supporter of cleaner energy cars. It supported the first modern electric car, which was built by General Motors and named EV1, short for Electric Vehicle 1. There were high hopes for the vehicle following California's well-intended Zero Emissions Vehicle (ZEV) mandate, but the project was abandoned after other car companies sued the state because they did not want to be mandated to produce electric cars, and the ZEV was subsequently dropped. The energy cleanliness of electric cars is also open to debate, since the vehicle is plugged into a network where electricity is generated from coal fired power stations. Toyota is looking to launch a plug-in Prius this year, which may stimulate more activity in the electric vehicle market.

America has become one of the largest markets for the sale of the Toyota Prius, which runs on a combination of electric motor (the part that gets the car started and powers the vehicle for low speeds) and the conventional combustion engine (the part that kicks in at higher speeds). Car companies have been designing more fuel-efficient gasoline and diesel cars as lower emissions and running costs become a key selling feature. That said, the era of cheap gasoline that Americans have enjoyed has led to more cars on the road. Getting millions of Americans to drive smaller, fuel-efficient cars will be key to determining the success of environmentally friendly cars.

Tamminen's view is that Americans have had subsidied oil for too long, as the true cost of oil is not factored into its price. A life-long environmentalist, he said it is not just the carbon cost which is increasingly becoming part of the energy market. 'People need to look at the true cost of oil, in terms of the war in Iraq and health care costs. Once people internalize that, then things start to change,' said Tamminen, who wrote a book on the subject: *Lives Per Gallon*. Tamminen is also a director of Vantage Partners in the San Francisco Bay area, which is investing in cellulosic technology to make the second generation biofuels. Proponents promise these will eventually be cheaper than the current biofuels made from sugar, corn and oilseeds.

Biofuels: The Next Generation

President Bush likes biofuels. He has boosted the emerging industry with generous tax breaks and frequently talked about them; most notably during his 2006 State of the Union speech, when he said: 'We'll also fund additional research in cutting-edge methods of producing ethanol, not just from corn, but from wood chips and stalks, or switch grass. Our goal is to make this new kind of ethanol practical and competitive within six years.' It's a timeframe that most energy experts consider optimistic.

Robert Brown, head of Biorenewables at Iowa University, said that there are four goals of the so-called 'second generation' biofuels, and economics is not one of them. The goals are: reduce US dependence on imported petroleum; reduce greenhouse gas emissions; increase opportunities for rural development in places such as Iowa; and increase and provide new opportunities for agriculture. Brown, who has worked on chemical lasers under the Reagan Star Wars Programme and on research projects to convert biomass into gas, acknowledges that cellulosic biomass is not the best material in the world to work with: it has moisture in it and therefore it has to be dried, and it is a solid material and not a more transportable liquid. It also has a lot of oxygen in it. One of the problems with making biofuels from woody or plant material, Brown explained to me, is how to break down nature's structure. It is a bit like the conventional oil production process versus the oil sands production process, in that there are a lot more costly steps involved.

All plants have an energy source, known as sugars. They're different to the one we put in our cup of tea, but they form the cellulose of the plant. This cellulose is bonded to the lignin, which is like the human equivalent of bones in the plant structure. Therein lies the problem: the separation of the two. Cellulose can be turned into ethanol, but lignin cannot and it makes up about a quarter of the biomass. Enzymes are used to break down these biological barriers to create an alcoholic liquid. The lignin cannot be fermented, but it does hold value in that it can be used as a binder for asphalt to build roads. Depending on the different processes, up to 70 % of the biomass could be converted into cellulosic ethanol. This biomass could be the native American grasses that once graced the prairies before European settlement, or the residue from corn plants, known as corn stover or wood waste. 'I don't think biofuels will be cheaper than gasoline was in its heyday, but there are other factors besides the selling price that will determine the success of cellulosic ethanol, such as cleaner or more secure fuel,' said Brown.

Brown believes that more money should be invested in cellulosic ethanol. 'When you think that the new Superman movie, which was made in Iowa, cost $350 million, and all we can put in is $500m (the budget of the US Department of Energy for cellulosic, biobuthanol research in 2007), there is room to do more,' he said. At the same time he warned that too much money could also create a problem. The US government has a mixed record on funding of energy research and development programmes. 'If we toss too much money at a problem, it won't be spent wisely, the same as what happened on the Manhattan project and the race to the Moon, so we have to be careful here.'

Not all are convinced about the take-up of cellulosic ethanol though, including Brown's colleagues at Iowa State University. Bruce Babcock, Head of Research at the Center for Agricultural and Rural Research Development at Iowa State University, said money would still determine the success of cellulosic ethanol. 'Each year the farmer in the Midwest has to decide whether to plant corn or soya beans, or a mix of the two depending on their selling price. But if he switches to grass or one of the other perennial grasses, then there is no need for all the farmers and the infrastructure that supports the corn industry, from the seed distributor to the John Deere dealership. These guys support the small towns across the Midwest – do you think all that is going to be given up for cellulosic ethanol?' said Babcock, who admitted that his views do not make him popular with energy policymakers. Babcock said the subsidies would need to be substantial in order for cellulosic ethanol to work. 'They are politically not palatable, and they are unaffordable,' he said.

Nevertheless, ConocoPhilips, the US oil company, has put $22.5 million into the Iowa Biorenewables wing. BP, one of the few other oil majors that is investing in biofuels, has put its money in a different pot. BP has teamed up with D1 Oils, a UK-based biodiesel producer. D1 is not using the traditional plants for biodiesel: it is using a non-food plant called jatropha. Together, BP and D1 have 200 000 acres of jatropha plantations across India, China, southeast Asia and Africa. Daimler also has a jatropha plantation in India.

Jatropha is not, strictly speaking, a second-generation fuel like cellulosic ethanol; it is a non-edible toxic oilseed that is part of the next stage of biofuels research. It moves biofuels away from the direct food versus fuel debate. Jatropha is thought to have originally come from Central America and is therefore suited to tropical environments. Since Portuguese traders took the plant to other parts of the world in the 16th century, it has been used mainly for medicinal purposes. Its potential as a biofuel was discovered only recently.

In comparison to other feedstocks for biofuels such as corn and sugar, relatively little research has gone into the plant. Yet many, including Goldman Sachs, the International Monetary Fund and the US government, are touting it as the next major biofuel that could be a cheaper replacement for biodiesel than existing feedstocks of soya oil, rapeseed oil and palm oil. What interests the plant breeders, biofuel promoters, governments and investors is the plant's ability to produce seeds with a high oil content of around 40 % (double the amount contained in a soya bean plant) and the fact that it can grow more plants per acre than soya beans. It is also seen as a plant that can be grown on dry marginal land in developing countries, thereby offering farmers an alternative crop to grow and a chance to cash in on the global biofuel boom.

Promoters say that jatropha does not compete with food crops because it can be grown on land that is not used for food production. However, for the plant to boost its yield it needs cultivation and that often involves using irrigation. If water is used for growing biofuel crops, critics will ask why it's not being used for growing food crops. There is little knowledge of growing jatropha for commercial purposes and therefore there are a great number of unknowns. Left to the wild, jatropha grows tall and leafy, and it grows with little maintenance, but plant breeders prefer a smaller, stocky jatropha plant that is full of seeds and to get it in this optimal condition it requires attention.

A factor which has prompted investment in jatropha is that it has good fatty acid properties that are necessary for transfercation (refining) into biodiesel. The research is very much a work in progress and there is no commercial production yet. All this is expected to change by the end of the decade. India is fast becoming a leading player in this emerging fuel. It not only faces a growing import bill for oil, but has one of the largest rural populations in the world, with the majority of its populace dependent on farming for their income. Because of the importance of farming, India has a large agricultural science research community, and, like the US, a desire to be energy independent.

Dr Jaap Vromans, a plant biologist who worked for D1 as a consultant, is one of the alchemists charged with turning this toxic weed into a fuel fit to power your car. He is based in Coimbatore in the southern Indian state of Tamil Nadu, the second largest in the state after Chennai, formerly Madras. The city is dotted with water tanks spouting like giant mushrooms above the palm trees that provide a welcome shade to the busy streets of this bustling town, better known for its textiles and automotive parts. Its links to the textile trade have given the town the title 'the Manchester of South India.' (though Manchester's link to the world of cotton is now ancient history).

Coimbatore makes an unlikely setting for the new frontier in the oil industry.

The D1 Oils' Product Development Centre can be found on the outskirts of Coimbatore. The centre is one of its key research centres for jatropha, with similar ones set up in Swaziland and Thailand, covering Africa and southeast Asia respectively. The centre has visitors from the biofuels and agricultural world. Jim Bolger, the former prime minister of New Zealand (who now heads up the World Agricultural Forum, a St Louis-based non-government organization) had visited the centre a few months before my arrival. 'We get lots of people coming to see what we are doing. Almost every week we have a visitor. Whether they are from D1 Oils or from government, agriculture or biofuels, they are all here to see and learn what we are doing with jatropha,' said Vromans, who is finding that his role is quickly becoming part tour guide, part educator.

Anyone hoping that there will be large-scale commercial biodiesel production from jatropha in the short term will be disappointed; Dr Vromans predicts that it will take five to six years for the tree to develop. The goal is to have about three kilograms of oil per tree, and 2000 trees per hectare, making 6000 kg per ha. The oil content per seed is about 30 to 37 % and the rest of the seed weight is the seed cake, which can be used for fertilizer to grow the crop or to go into animal feed, even though it is toxic. It could even go into biomass to use for power generation. But it could be another ten years before there is a track record with the seeds consistently producing the desired oil and before the breeding techniques for the plant are fine-tuned around the world.

The Energy and Resource Institute (Teri), the New Delhi-based research group headed by Dr Rajendra K. Pachauri, the chairman of the Intergovernmental Panel on Climate Change, is also conducting research on jatropha. 'We should not be debating whether there is land for fuel or land for food, we should debate what areas are suitable for non-edible crops,' said Dr Adholeya, director of biotechnology and management in Teri's bioresources division. His office was prone to intermittent power cuts during our discussions, a regular occurrence across India due to prolonged power shortages. Indians are used to the lights going out while they are at work; which is why India has an ambitious, programme to electrify the country. When added to China's ambitions, it creates an enormous energy challenge for a generation. Meeting this challenge will require energy to come from more varied sources. In effect it is more democratic because the world will not be reliant on one source. As Tamminen put it, 'It is the democratization of our economy by the democratization of the fuel that drives the economy. There is nothing democratic about an oil baron or a coal baron. It is totally democratic to get wind power or solar power because everyone has access to the sun and wind.'

Avoiding the Inevitable

To avoid the type of environmental catastrophe experts are warning about, significant changes in behaviour and habits will be needed. Swapping to energy-efficient light bulbs is one step, but more needs to be done in terms of government policies at local, regional and national levels. When energy prices hit the hip pockets, public awareness is greater and consumers will start to modify their energy consumption.

While energy prices are high, money will be attracted to finding more energy sustainable solutions. The expansion in global coal supplies will divide traditional government allies. Coal miners and farmers in the US and Australia will battle with each other over the expansion of coal mines into farming areas and the use of local water supplies. Forrest E. Mars Jr, whose family owns Mars Inc., the confectionery company, is fighting against the development of coal and gas in the Powder River basin near his Montana ranch, while Australian farmers in the upper Hunter Valley, home to some of the country's richest farmland, are concerned about plans to develop coal deposits in the region so it can be shipped to China to burn in power stations.

Right now we are heading into a phase of greater take-up of renewable energy, but it is still not enough to offset the increase in greenhouse gas emissions. The next chapter will look more closely at the growing link between agriculture, energy and greenhouse gases.

Notes

1. Kynge (2006) wrote that the Chinese economy in 1400 was larger than Western Europe based on 1985 dollars.
2. The IEA estimated that China had 37 million cars at the end of 2006, almost a seven-fold increase since 1990. China surpassed Germany in 2004 as the world's third largest car market.
3. The IEA estimates that China will build 750 gigawatts of power in the period to 2015.
4. Some 105 gigawatts of new power plants, almost all of which are coal-fired, were built in 2006 alone – a rate of increase for which there is no precedent worldwide (International Energy Agency, 2007).
5. The IEA says one of the most popular Chinese refrigerators with a volume of 220 litres uses on average 1.2–1.3 kWh per day, compared with around 0.8 kWh per day in Europe.
6. The EIA estimates that by 1885, coal had overtaken wood as the major fuel in the US (Energy Information Administration, 2006).
7. Coal supplied almost half of US energy demand by 1945, and oil was less than a third (Energy Information Administration, 2006).
8. The Gas Exporting Countries Forum (GECF) was set up in 2001 as a forum for gas producers. Its members include Algeria, Bolivia, Brunei, Egypt, Indonesia, Iran, Libya, Malaysia, Nigeria, Norway (as an observer), Oman, Qatar, Russia, Trinidad and Tobago, the United Arab Emirates and Venezuela. Collectively, these countries account for 73 % of the world's gas reserves and 42 % of production.
9. Jaccard (2006) estimates that coal-fired power stations have increased from 1 MW to 800 MW and stations as large as 1500 MW have been built.
10. Between 1950 and 2000, the world's population rose by about 140 %, fossil fuel consumption rose by almost 400 %.
11. The United Nations International Panel of Climate Change (IPCC) has said that stabilizing the global temperature increase at no more than 2 °C above the pre-industrial level is expected to prevent irreversible and potentially catastrophic changes in the global climate.
12. The IEA estimated that the energy embedded in China's domestic production of goods for export was 452 million tonnes of emissions (Mtoe)

in 2004, or 28 % of the country's total energy consumption. In 2001, the amount of energy embedded in exported goods was only 197 Mtoe, or 18 % of total energy use.

13. The United States, China, Russia and India contribute two-thirds of the projected increase in global emissions from 26.6 to 41.9 gigatonnes between 2005 and 2030. From 1900 to 2005, the United States and the EU countries combined accounted for just over half of cumulative global emissions. China accounted for only 8 % and India 2 %. China's share of emissions from 1900 to 2030 rises to 16 % compared with 25 % for the United States and 18 % for the European Union.

14. Freese (2003) wrote that these quotes were attributable to Fred Palmer who was head of Western Fuels, a lobby group set up by the coal and utility industry. She wrote that Palmer later joined Peabody Energy, one of the biggest coal producers in the US.

15. The National Energy Policy Development Group (2001) said that since 1989, electricity sales to consumers had increased by 2.1 % annually, yet transmission capacity had risen by 0.8 % annually, which created the need for more power stations. The President's energy taskforce recommended that the government spend $2 billion over ten years in clean coal technologies.

16. President George W. Bush said in his speech that 'When I ran for President in 2000, I promised to invest – or asked the Congress to invest – $2 billion over ten years to promote clean coal technology. So far, working with the United States Congress, we've provided more than $1.3 billion for research in the innovative ways to improve today's coal plants and to help us build even cleaner coal plants in the future. And the bill I sign today authorizes new funding for clean coal technology so we can move closer to our goal of building the world's first zero emission coal-fired power plant.'

17. California filed a lawsuit against the Environmental Protection Agency (EPA) over its refusal to allow the state to set its own vehicle-emissions standards. California's law would require vehicle emissions to be cut by a third by 2016 to 36.8 miles per gallon (mpg), which is tougher than the Bush inspired Federal plan to improve vehicle fuel-efficency standards to 35 mpg by 2020, four years after the Californian plan.

18. Ruttenberg and Associates Inc. (1973) said that of the proposed expenditure of $120 million between 1971 and 1975, the bulk was given to four research projects, which are to be 'concentrated in three firms whose relationship to the oil industry might be interpreted as something less than arms-length.'

19. United States General Accounting Office, Testimony Before the Subcommittee on Energy, Committee on Science, House of Representatives, *Fossil Fuel R&D Lessons Learned in the Clean Coal Technology Program*, Statement of Jim Wells, Director, Natural Resources and Environment, June 12, 2001.

20. The cost of constructing coal-fired power plants using new coal gasification technologies is about 20 % more than conventional coal-fired plants, and they carry higher perceived investment risk as new technologies according to the US Department of Energy (2006).

21. 'Given the scale of the energy challenge facing the world, a substantial increase is called for in public and private funding for energy technology research, development and demonstration, which remains well below levels reached in the early 1980s. The financial burden of supporting research efforts will continue to fall largely on IEA countries' (International Energy Agency, 2007).

22. The National Security Space Office in 2007 said that NASA and the Department of Energy have collectively spent $80 million over the last three decades in sporadic efforts studying this concept and, by comparison, the US Government has spent approximately $21 billion over the last 50 years pursuing nuclear fusion.

23. British ministers backed plans for a new generation of nuclear power stations on January 8, 2008.

24. A report by the World Nuclear Association (2007) says that US nuclear electricity avoids almost 700 m tonnes of CO_2, 1.1 m tonnes of nitrogen oxide and 3.3 m tonnes of sulphur dioxide.

25. The WNA estimates that China has the equivalent of 3170 megawatts under construction.

26. The ITER team includes the European Union (represented by EURATOM), Japan, the People's Republic of China, India, the Republic of Korea, the Russian Federation and the US. ITER will be constructed in Europe, at Cadarache in the south of France.

27. Uranium is more common than tin, about 40 times more common than silver and 500 times more common than gold. From Cameco website – http://www.cameco.com/uranium_101/.

28. In the 1980s, the markets were driven by liquidation of government and commercial stocks. The Megatons to Megawatts programme refers to a 1993 agreement between the US and Russia. This is an agreement to convert highly enriched uranium (HEU) taken from dismantled Russian and American nuclear warheads into low-enriched uranium fuel, which is suitable for civilian reactors. The future of this agreement after 2013 is uncertain.

29. The International Energy Agency forecast in its World Energy Outlook that Opec's global share of oil output would rise from about 42 % to 52 % by 2030.

30. Sport utility vehicles (SUVs), which are classified as light trucks and are deemed to be work vehicles, although the majority are driven by urban dwellers, are exempt from fuel efficiency standards and their popularity has negated any improvement in US fuel efficiency standards. A 2008 Ford Escape 4WD has a range of 11 to 13 miles to the gallon (MPG). The 2008 Toyota Prius hybrid car has a range of 35 to 56, more than three times the range. See http://www.fueleconomy.gov for further fuel efficiency comparisons.

31. According to FACTS Global Energy, the cost of Iran's oil imports is expected to reach $6 billion in 2007, more than double the level from 2005. According to PFC Energy, car ownership in Iran grew by 250 % between 1990 and 2006. The International Monetary Fund (IMF) estimated that energy subsidies accounted for 12 % of Iran's GDP, the highest rate in the world according to an International Energy Agency (IEA) study.

32. By 2028, Canadian domestic gas consumption is estimated to be equivalent to Canadian domestic gas production and Canada's position as a net gas exporter would potentially come to an end.

33. A US Geological Survey report showed that the global oil shale resource base is believed to contain about 2.8 trillion barrels, of which the vast majority, about 2 trillion barrels, is located within the United States. The most economically attractive deposits, containing an estimated 1.2 to 1.8 trillion barrels (with an oil content of more than 10 gallons/tonne), are found in the Green River Formation of Colorado in Piceance

Basin, in Uinta Basin, Utah and the Green River and Washakie Basins, Wyoming.

34. Ruttenberg and Association, Inc. (1973) said, that in 1970, seventeen oil companies, including Exxon, accounted for about 55 % of the drilling and controlled about 48 % of the known US low-cost uranium reserves, with about 28 % of the uranium ore-processing capacity.

2

Agriculture

'Although man does not cause variability and cannot even prevent it, he can select, preserve, and accumulate the variations given to him by the hand of nature almost in any way which he chooses; and thus he can certainly produce a great result.'

Charles Darwin

Bread for Oil

A drive through the heartland of America in the summer would typically take place on a long road lined with endless rows of long-leafed plants stretching, and often extending several kilometres from the edge of the highway, as far as you can see on the flat horizon. The plants are most noticeable along Interstate 57 from Chicago towards Champaign, which, like its more famous namesake Champagne in France, has a reputation for high quality local produce. Instead of premium wines, Champaign, Illinois is growing crops for another type of alcohol – the type you put in a car, not the type you drink.

The dark green leaves of the plants by the highway provide shelter for the most lucrative crop for American farmers: corn. The local counties of McLean, Champaign, Macon, Piatt, Sangamor and Christian are among the best corn-growing areas in the country. Vintners boast about the quality of their grapes, but in the cornbelt, it's all about yield. Corn here grows more than a fifth above the national average per acre; the rich soils and near perfect combination of regular rain and heat make it an ideal spot.

While I was there during the summer of 2007 though, the famous US cornbelt – which is largely based in Illinois and Iowa, the two biggest producers of the grain in the world – was suffering its driest June in almost 20 years. I must have brought the English weather with me because my visit was accompanied by dark grey clouds that spilled heavy rainfall, thunder and lightning. It was an unwelcome element on my first drive into the US Midwest, but it was good for the farmers, whose fate and fortune is determined by the weather.

Corn farmers love to talk about the weather and swap rainfall statistics with each other. And little wonder; they all want to know what their corn yields are going to be like and what impact the weather will have on them. Corn thrives on water and heat, and in the right quantities, these provide the food and drink for the plants to grow to more than two metres within six months – that's more than a centimetre a day on average. In the US cornbelt they say they can hear corn grow during July and August when nights are hot, humid and windless (Walden, 1966). I'm not sure I could hear it, but I swear I could see the corn growing in the fields as I drove towards central Illinois with the warm rain pelting down around me.

Driving along this flat stretch of road through the heartland, there's little to look at besides the corn and occasional field of soya beans. The soya bean plant by comparison looks like little more than ground cover; the height of the heart-shaped leafed plant was barely off the ground, though by the time it is harvested in the autumn it will be protein rich and knee-height. Corn reaches this height within its first two months of planting. The other noticeable sight on the road is the size of the vehicles; the 'Land of Lincoln' number plates are as ubiquitous as the SUVs they're attached to. The reference to Abraham Lincoln – the first US president from the Midwest – is apt: Lincoln was highly influential in the opening up of the cornbelt (Crabb, 1947).[1]

The All-American Hero

Corn's profligacy in the right conditions has made the yellow cob the all-American hero of the US agricultural industry. It is literally all-American; in its various forms it's been grown all over the western hemisphere from the southern tip of Chile to Canada (Walden, 1966) and it was also cultivated by the Inca and Aztec empires. Its historic journey is one that has emerged from a humble start in Mexico, to the creation of a new empire in the Midwest of the United States.

Today the empire is built on the perception that corn is a sustainable energy fuel. On my drive through the Midwest farmers were showing their support for this belief with the occasional placard placed beside the corn stalks bearing slogans such as 'Home Grown Energy Independence' or 'We Grow American Energy.' Independent gasoline stations also like to reinforce the association between corn and fuel: on billboards along the highway are images of giant corncobs for nozzles at the end of the gasoline hose, or an even bigger juicy corncob that is the gasoline pump stand.

The advent of ethanol, mainly used as a blender in gasoline (petrol) cars, is not just a US phenomenon – it's a global one. It has changed the dynamics not only of America's largest crop, but of agriculture globally as countries turn to biofuel industries to lessen their dependence on foreign oil imports and boost their domestic farm sectors. Concerns remain as to whether this notion is sustainable and economical, and whether it really is as green as the proponents of the fuel portray. The emergence of biofuels also connects the family of grains, oilseeds and fibres through the competition for land, and forces farmers to choose whether to grow crops for fuel or food.

This chapter takes a look at how the US came to view the humble corn plant as a solution to its domestic energy deficiencies. We will examine how the vegetable overcame the biological odds to be a major beneficiary of government subsidies (much like a father looking upon a favoured son) and how it has eventually come to be viewed as a transport fuel. The corn-ethanol push comes at a time when the food industry is dealing with its own changing dynamics, triggered by a burgeoning middle class in China and India who are eating more grain-fed meat. The strong demand for meat has raised issues about land use and deforestation, as well as competition between arable and grazing land use and the environmental impact of this. The demand for grain is also causing tension between the ethanol and food industries, with higher food prices and food scarcity been blamed on the diversion of corn and grains for ethanol production.

Sounds Corny

The concept of corn as a fuel alternative is a rather strange one. People mainly associate corn with a steaming yellow cob, with butter melting over its softened surface at a barbeque, or as a box of popcorn at the movies. But popcorn and sweetcorn are actually both niche variations of the world's largest grain crop, accounting for a very small proportion of global corn supplies. The main bulk of corn produced is known as field corn, used mainly as feed for the cattle, pigs and chickens which provide the milk, cheese, beef, pork and eggs on our kitchen tables.

Corn kernels are used far and wide. Hundreds of millions of people eat them each day in one form or another, there are 10,000 corn-containing products found on supermarket shelves,[2] including ice cream, frozen desserts, salad dressings, hot dogs, cold meats, chewing gum, jams, jellies and bourbon whiskey. Derivatives of corn are used to prevent foods from going stale, which is why they are often found in processed foods from instant meals to puddings, in the form of the food additive, monosodium glutamate. Traces of corn are even found in penicillin and other antibiotics.

One of the biggest developments for the multitalented, fingernail-sized corn kernel is its use as a fuel in millions of cars, motorbikes and buses, mainly in the United States – a country that until 1976 could boast that it was the world's largest oil producer (Energy Information Administration, 2006, Table 11.5).[3] Proponents of ethanol like to talk about the alcohol one day replacing oil: comparatively, their resource base differs greatly. Oil lies in vast reservoirs dotted around the world waiting to be tapped, while corn has to be grown each year, relying upon weather, land availability and the ability to dodge the constant threat of insects and weeds for a good yield.

Corn is primarily a source of starch – a carbohydrate – which puts it in the same food family as the potato, peas, lentils and bananas. The American Indians knew all about corn's versatility and would grind it with a mortar and pestle to turn it into flour for bread. Or they would burn it as fuel, and the silks (the skin) would be smoked.[4]

The term 'corn' is confusing for many Europeans, who generally refer to the plant as maize, and use the word 'corn' to refer to a field crop such as wheat or barley. My father used to tell me he grew corn as a teenager, but he was actually referring to wheat, barley and oats. At the time of Adam Smith, reference to corn was meant as a generic term for the dominant grains, but in the United States today the word corn is now only used for maize, (Indian) corn being by far the most dominant crop on the US agricultural landscape.

Fill Her Up with Corn

The concept of ethanol as a fuel is not new, but previous attempts to promote the industry have never received anything like the widespread political and business support it received this decade. It has brought together a coalition of supporters from agribusinesses and biotechnologists to farmers and politicians. Under President George W. Bush the ethanol industry has collected generous subsidies, and benefited from high tariffs on competing imports and favourable environmental rulings, which have propelled the US into the role of the biggest ethanol producer, and the most committed biofuel producer in the developed world. In Bush's America, the latest reincarnation of biofuels is based on a concoction of intentions; from providing jobs in rural communities to becoming an oxygenate for petrol, increasing energy security and improving air quality and the environment.[5] It has created many jobs and has been successful as an oxygenate, but the latter two goals are highly questionable.

The US and Brazil are the global powerhouses of the biofuels world. Their combined output is bigger than the oil produced by Oman in the Persian Gulf and on a par with India, but only enough to substitute a fiftieth of the oil that is consumed each day (BP, 2007). Their net impact is even smaller: for every litre of 'green fuels' produced, the equivalent of three quarters of a litre of energy is required to make it.[6] Even this tiny amount added to the global energy supply has raised concerns about the impact of biofuel production on food prices, land usage and the environment, though it has not stopped governments around the world developing their own biofuel programmes, under the broader agenda of tackling climate change.

For the farmer, biofuels are great for business. The farmer is at one end of the food supply chain and the supermarket is at the other end. The global consolidation of supermarket retailing has given the retailers greater buying power and they have exerted this strength on suppliers; the pressure on prices trickling down from the food manufacturer and processor to the farmyard. Prices of crops such as corn, wheat, soya beans and sugar have not kept pace with the inflation rate over the past 30 years, while living expenses, seed, fertilizer and diesel costs have all risen sharply. Now farmers have a new customer for their goods – ethanol producers. And another major customer means that the supermarkets' power to dictate prices has been reduced.

The prospects for ethanol and the American farmer are best summed up by the following quote: 'As energy prices rise, grains, oilseeds, forage crops, crop wastes and forest products will become increasingly attractive as sources of liquid fuels. This additional demand on the agricultural sector will further alter resource and production decisions. More importantly, it will bring food demand into close competition with energy and industrial demands in the US economy. This factor alone will change agricultural investment and returns to agricultural resources significantly, which will further redistribute income within and beyond the agricultural sector.' This is no contemporary thought; they are the words of a group of economists at the United States Department of Agriculture (USDA) almost 30 years ago (Meekhof *et al.*, 1980). The US ethanol strategy pioneers hope for a change in the economics of agriculture, which is tied into Bush's mantra of energy independence. It's a tough ambition for a country that imports 60 % of its oil consumption and accounts for almost a quarter of daily global oil demand.

Fuelling Ethanol

Ethanol emerged on the US political agenda in the 1970s in reaction to the first oil shock, when several Arab nations, angered by the US support of Israel in the Arab–Israel war, responded with an oil export embargo to the US and the Netherlands. Concerned about security of supply, the US, along with Brazil, started ethanol programmes as part of an energy independence strategy.

Ethanol in the US has a history stretching back to the American Civil War. Henry Ford was an early supporter of fuels made from alcohol. He designed a quadricycle in the 1880s to burn alcohol, and his Model T was built with a carburettor that could be modified so the engine could use pure alcohol (Meekhof *et al.*, 1980). 'A beautifully clean and efficient fuel which can be produced from vegetable matter-waste products of our farms and even garbage of our cities,' was the way the alcohol was described by Alexander Graham Bell, pioneer of the telephone (Meekhof *et al.*, 1980). After the First World War sales of fuel alcohol (or alcogas as it was then called) reached 1.5 million barrels a year, surviving even Prohibition. The fortunes of alcogas took a dive after the Second World War as materials were rationed. It was relaunched in the 1970s under the name gasohol, which was a blend of gasoline with at least 10 % alcohol and became a replacement for lead in gasoline because of the metal's poisoning capabilities. President Carter's government gave 40 cents a gallon subsidy for making the blend.[7]

The industry was slow to get started. Then the Soviet Union invaded Afghanistan in December 1979, prompting President Carter (who, with an election looming and the Iranian hostage crisis more than a month old, was under considerable pressure) to retaliate through a 'food weapon' – the imposition of an embargo of corn, wheat and soya bean sales to the Soviet Union. The embargo came into play on January 4, 1980.[8] It is ironic that Afghanistan plays an indirect role in promotion of ethanol today, since current concerns about energy security are linked to the battle between Islamic militants and Western forces in Afghanistan.

The grain embargo forced the US Commodity Futures Trading Commission (CFTC) (regulator of the US futures markets) to take the rare step of ordering the suspension of grain trading on futures exchanges for two days. The loss in exports left farmers holding on to more grain and oilseed stocks, and grain prices plummeted. Farm groups reacted to the embargo by calling for further assistance, setting up stalls on the Mall in Washington near the US Capitol Building and the United States Department of Agriculture (USDA) headquarters (which is at the other end of the Mall near the Smithsonian Institute) to demonstrate the practicability of gasohol (Bowers, 1981). Farmer power won out, and Congress responded with the biggest boost for the nascent industry – new legislation, including tax benefits for ethanol producers and blenders. The 1980 Energy Security Act allowed the government to offer loans for small producers and imposed an import tariff on foreign produced ethanol, which was largely aimed at Brazil. The tariff is still in place today.

Further ethanol friendly legislation was passed in the early 1980s to increase the subsidy on ethanol; but the generous tax breaks, loans and tariffs could not prevent the collapse of the US ethanol market, which followed a sharp decline in global oil prices, and little more than half the 163 commercial ethanol plants remained in operation by the end of 1985 (Meekhof *et al.*, 1980).

The ethanol industry was to get another revival through the Clean Air Act of 1990, which created a tighter emissions standard, with the aim of burning cleaner gasoline in the large cities by using an oxygenate. Instead of choosing ethanol though, the petroleum industry (which has a history of opposition to ethanol) chose methyl tertiary butyl ether (MTBE), a chemical made from methanol. But by the late 1990s MTBE (as it was more commonly known) was classified as potentially carcinogenic by the US Environmental Protection Agency. The additive was found to dissolve easily in water and was hard to filter out, plus it left a nasty taste and smell. But gasoline still required an oxygenate by law, and ethanol became the preferred choice, its proponents promoting its clean, green credentials. The September 11 attacks on New York and Washington combined with the rise in oil price this decade prompted President Bush to seek energy independence: ethanol came to his assistance. Within a few years, ethanol had been transformed from a cottage industry to one that was high on the US government's energy agenda: it was the key to making air in the big cities cleaner and drinking water safer.

Concerns about global warming went from being an environmental niche to a mainstream issue, further enhancing the perception of ethanol as a clean energy. Ethanol had become even more political: Bush beat the energy independence drum as hard as he could with the support of a patriotic America, reeling from the tragic terrorist attacks in 2001, and together they kick-started the biggest ethanol expansion in US history. Its knock-on effects for agriculture were global.

President Bush (ordinarily a teetotaller) appeared intoxicated with the alcohol at his State of the Union address in January 2007. He called for a mandate of 35 billion gallons by 2017; a target that raised eyebrows and caused even some of the most ardent supporters of biofuels to doubt whether this could be achieved. They were right: the target was revised to 36 billion gallons by 2022, and US biofuel output in 2008 was expected to be 9 billion gallons. Under the current US renewable fuel tax regime, each billion gallons of ethanol costs the American taxpayer at least $500 million. This does not include the multitude of state-based financial incentives also aiding the industry. Since biodiesel production is far smaller than ethanol, renewable fuel in the US is predominately ethanol.

The New Deal for Corn Communities

With the backing of generous tax breaks, farmers and ethanol producers claim that the business is sustainable, and that it creates skilled

jobs in communities which have seen families torn apart by rural decline and the lack of career opportunities. 'Ethanol has changed the
dynamics of the Midwest,' said Philip Sundblad, a corn farmer and
district director of Iowa Farm Bureau, at the Albert City ethanol plant
in northwest Iowa where we met. The 100 million gallon a year facility was opened in December 2006 and has provided a huge boost
to local corn farmers, including Sundblad, along with many others in
the town of 700 people (the plant employs engineers, maintenance,
quality control, marketing and sales staff). The plant juts out of the
blanket of cornfields covering the local landscape, and the distillery
is wrapped in a layer of stainless steel pipes, transporting the corn on
a long, complex journey, from slurry to a transparent 100 % alcohol
liquid – the strongest moonshine in the country (a drop of oil placed
in the ethanol before it is transported renders it undrinkable, to deter
any thirsty workers).

The Albert City plant is one of many that have sprung up in rural
communities across the Midwest, where three new ethanol plants
opened every two months between 2004 and 2007. Most of the industry's expansion has taken place in Iowa, which produces a sixth
of all US corn and as much corn as the whole of the European Union.
Iowa is to corn what Saudi Arabia is to oil; it is the key player, and the
corn grown in this midwestern state is shipped all around the world
to feed hundreds of millions of people and animals.

The Ethanol Boom

Iowa has been at the forefront of the US ethanol boom, which has
seen nationwide capacity double to about 6.5 billion gallons in the
three years running up to 2007.[9] Between 2004 and 2007, the number of US ethanol plants doubled to 119, with a further 86 under
construction or expanding.[10] One of the biggest groups of lenders
to the ethanol industry is the regional banks, which come under the
umbrella of the US government-owned Farm Credit Administration,
created as part of President Roosevelt's New Deal for Agriculture in
the 1930s.

In 2007 ethanol distillers consumed a quarter of the corn supply. In the previous year ethanol plants had accounted for less than a fifth of total supply and in the 2008 marketing year they will account for a third. The rising demand from ethanol is chewing into US corn exports, and growing at a faster rate than supply, which has caused global maize stockpiles to fall. This is a trend repeated across the grain world; the grain mountain of the 1980s has turned into a mole-hill, with global wheat stockpiles falling at the start of 2008 to their lowest level in 60 years. Iowa had an ethanol production capacity of two billion gallons in 2007 – the amount the entire country was producing five years earlier. But Iowa has big plans, and wants to reach a five billion gallon capacity by the end of the decade. The Hawkeye state had 27 plants in January 2008 and another 17 under construction or in the planning stage[11] with a range of new energy players from local farmer cooperatives to foreign-based investors,[12] as well as the bigger players like Archer Daniel Midland (ADM) and Verasun.

Nevertheless, five billion gallons of ethanol sounds like a lot of alcohol. It sounds less once it is converted into the parlance of the energy industry, where they speak in terms of barrels a day and a barrel is 42 gallons. A quick calculation gives an answer of 326 157 barrels a day – about 3 % of daily US gasoline consumption (it's not quite as straightforward as that though, as ethanol has a lower energy content, so if a car were to be filled purely with ethanol, it would only go two-thirds the distance of conventional gasoline). To compare apples with apples (or in this case, ethanol with gasoline), a further calculation is needed. Measuring on energy content value therefore, the ethanol refining capacity is closer to 250 000 barrels a day – far more than the amount of fuel that the drivers in Iowa use in their trucks, sports utility vehicles, cars, motorbikes and buses each day, leaving a big surplus of ethanol to be transported around the country. 'We are an energy exporter; we are producing more than enough ethanol to meet our needs,' said Sundblad, whose family have been farming in Buena Vista County (where Albert City is located) for generations.

Beside the Albert City refinery sits an 80-car train that stretches for about a mile. It takes about nine days to fill all the cars (which have a total capacity of 30 000 gallons) before it starts its journey west to California, the biggest ethanol-consuming state in the US. Train or truck is the only way ethanol moves out from Iowa. Oil travels through pipelines, criss-crossing America from the Canadian oilsand fields to the refineries and storage farms in Louisiana, but unlike gasoline or diesel, ethanol cannot be carried through pipelines, as its corrosive properties would damage the pipe (the same reason it can't be put straight into a car engine). Even if ethanol was blended with gasoline and then transported through the pipeline, it would separate from the gasoline because ethanol is water-soluble and gasoline is not. Given the volumes and distances involved it's more economical to use rail freight (and, to a lesser extent, river barge) than it is to use road freight. So any increase in ethanol production will largely be dependent on rail capacity. The US government warned in a report last year that further expansion of ethanol production could create transport bottlenecks: 'Currently, biofuels are transported primarily on the freight rail system, and this system has limited capacity to transport greater amounts of biofuels if production significantly increases' (US Government Accountability Office, 2007a).

To make five billion gallons of ethanol Iowa will require a lot of corn, even by their standards. 'Corn flow from Iowa used to go out and then down the river to the Gulf, now you are seeing the prospect of Iowa becoming a net importer of corn because of all the ethanol plants,' said Sundblad, highlighting the changing industry dynamics he had eluded to earlier. The change in the corn world would be equivalent in the oil world to Saudi Arabia becoming a net importer of oil. Such a change would have ripple effects throughout the grain industry. Iowa is the biggest corn producer within the US, and its exports of the grain are the single biggest export earner for the state. It supplies grain to countries all around the world, which rely on it to feed their people and livestock, and in terms of agricultural export per state, it is the second biggest earner in the US. Now those countries may have to look elsewhere for their corn, raising issues about food security that have emanated from the US's concerns about energy security. If Iowa does become a net importer of corn, it could find that the grain is hard to come by. Its neighbouring cornbelt states, Illinois, Minnesota and Nebraska, have much the same idea about expanding their ethanol industry, and they too will be consuming much of their own corn production.

But Iowa is even more committed to ethanol than just making it for other US states – it wants to consume more of it, too. Last year, the Iowa state government approved one of the most aggressive renewable fuels programmes in the country. It wants a quarter of gasoline retailers' sales to be in ethanol and biodiesel by 2019.[13] To achieve this, the state's gasoline stations will have to install new pumps that can tolerate fuels with a higher ethanol content, otherwise known as E85, which (like its name suggests) has an 85 % ethanol content, as well as new tanks that will be needed to store this fuel (it cannot be kept with conventional gasoline). This process is costly, and has so far been met with reluctance from the large petroleum retailers such as ExxonMobil, ChevronTexaco, ConocoPhilips, BP and Shell. A US government report showed that only about 9 % of the fuelling stations offering E85 came under the brand of one of the five main oil companies, highlighting the reluctance of the oil industry to embrace biofuels. None of the major oil companies have built a corn-based ethanol plant during the industry's recent boom (US Government Accountability Office, 2007a).

A Presidential Concern

Ethanol has been marketed very well to consumers; its environmental and patriotic credentials emphasized to a public that is increasingly concerned about global warming and energy security. But the economic viability of the industry remains reliant on government subsidies and favourable regulatory rulings. President Bush's successor is just as likely as 'Dubya' to be enthusiastic about ethanol, regardless of what side of the political fence they sit. Barack Obama, the Democrat candidate from Illinois – the second biggest corn-producing state – backed The Biofuels Security Act, which called for 60 billion gallons of renewable fuels by 2030. Even Hillary Clinton and John McCain, the Arizona Republican, have reversed their previous opposition to ethanol. 'I was never against using ethanol,' said Clinton, though she had voted against pro-ethanol initiatives after she arrived in the Senate in 2001. McCain had been more vocal against ethanol, describing it as 'a giveaway to special interests in corn-growing states.' Campaigning in the Midwest last year, he voiced his new-found support for the industry (Lambrecht, 2007).

With many swing states in the Midwest, presidential hopefuls don't want to upset potential voters, particularly farmers who like high corn prices. Even though Iowa is not the most populous state in the US, politically it punches well above its weight. Iowa held its state caucus in January 2008, the first real test for both Democratic and Republican candidates in the race for the White House. Six months before the Iowa caucus, I had flown out of Iowa from Des Moines International Airport (which, despite the name, has no scheduled flights outside of the country). Hillary and Bill Clinton were in town to spend the July 4th holiday week in Iowa campaigning. Mr Obama and Republican Mitt Romney, both of whom are advocates of energy independence, visited ethanol plants on their campaign trails in Iowa.

Despite all the enthusiasm politicians are showing in the run up to the elections, and all the tax advantages and friendly government rulings, the expansion of the US corn-based ethanol industry is limited by the amount of economically viable land, and the amount of corn that can be physically grown on that land. It's a constraint of nature that humankind cannot overcome. The US Department of Energy (DOE) estimated that the maximum amount of ethanol that could be produced from the US corn supply was between 15 billion and 16 billion gallons (US Government Accountability Office, 2007a). Proponents of ethanol, the Renewable Fuels Association and the National Corn Growers' Association, however, do not want to put any cap on the potential of corn. To meet the DOE estimate, about 5.4 billion bushels of corn (or 137 million tonnes) are needed, based on current yields of converting corn into ethanol. This is about the same amount of corn grown in 2006 in China, the world's second largest corn producer.

It Is Not all About Alcohol

Inside a shed the size of a football pitch are two mountains of golden yellow grain. They continue to quietly grow as granules pour from a pipe attached to the metal framed ceiling onto the pile of distillers' dried grains with solubles – or DDGS as they are known in the trade. This is a by-product of ethanol-making plants. Pete Krull, general manager at BioEnergy – owner of the Albert City ethanol plant – explained that during the process of turning the billions of corn kernels into ethanol, the carbohydrates in the corn are turned into sugar, which is then fermented and distilled.

Krull, a veteran of the pet food industry, said that of the 56 pounds (25.45 kg) of corn in each bushel, 2.8 gallons of ethanol are made, 17 pounds of distillers' grains are produced, and another 17 pounds of carbon dioxide are emitted into the air. Protein accounts for about 11 % of each corn kernel, none of which is used in the ethanol production, leaving a high concentration of protein over. This excess is used to produce distillers' grains with a protein content of about 30 % that can be mixed with animal feed for cattle, pigs and chickens. This is far too high a protein content for cattle, which tolerate only up to 12 % protein – anything more and the cattle dispose of nitrates either through manure or urine onto the soil (because protein contains nitrogen). As a result, the distillers' grains have to be mixed with other feed for cattle.

The trend for using corn in cattle feed can be dated as far back as the early American settlers, who gave the corncob to their cows. Modern animal nutritionists developed new diets with grain and oilseeds to boost protein and energy for cattle, pigs and poultry, in order to boost their weight and growth rates, and in the case of dairy cows, milk production. Feeding grain to livestock became more widespread in the 1950s in North America, extending to Europe, the former Soviet Union and Japan in the 1960s and 1970s. It is now common in the rest of the world, with the exception of southern Asia and sub-Saharan Africa, where livestock is still reared on local food. This trend increased grain demand, which was met by improving yields (Food and Agriculture Organization of the United Nations, 2006).

Today's animal feed diet includes other grains too, such as wheat, barley, sorghum, oilseed by-products such as soya meal, linseed meal and cottonseed meal, peanut meal and fishmeal. There are about 100 different ingredients in animal feed, including various trace minerals such as salt, iron and zinc. The animal feed and breeding industries are entwined and their development marked another layer in the industrialization of agriculture. The switch from a largely grass-based diet to one with a significant amount of grains gave birth to another industry where farmers had to pay. Grass, on the other hand, they had traditionally attained for nothing.

The distillers' grains are also an alternative to soya meal, a protein-rich feed for animals. Soya bean demand is, in effect, a de facto indicator for global protein demand, a nutrient that is mainly consumed via meat, dairy products, fish or pulses. The creamy coloured soya bean is about the size of a thumbnail. Comparatively it ends up in as many foods, ingredients and industrial products as corn; including tofu, soya burgers and soya milk. Soya oil makes salad dressings, cooking oil and biodiesel, which has a by-product – glycerin – a substance found in soaps and hair care products.[14] Soya meal accounts for 80 % of the soya bean, oil making up the remainder, and 97 % of the soya meal is used for animal feed. The projected rise in the output of distillers' grains will take more of the soya meal market share, and reduce the impact of a decline in American soya bean production.

Gregg Doud, chief economist at the National Cattlemen's Beef Association, the marketing organization for the country's 740 000 beef farmers, said, however, that there is enormous variability in the quality of the distillers' grains, with only small proportions going into chicken and hog feeds. There is a side effect to consuming too much of the grain made in ethanol plants. 'The problem with the distillers' grains is that it is high in sulphur, and sulphur acts as an appetite suppressant in ruminant animals: the more by-products you feed them, the more sulphur they consume and then the animal quits eating. It reduces their energy and the animals can get sick,' said Doud. With the volumes of ethanol Iowa plans to produce, it will be making more distillers' grains than the animals in the state can consume. New markets will have to be found.

The volume of distillers' grains coming out of Iowa's ethanol plants would not be suitable for Iowa's 14 million pigs. The pigs outnumber the state's residents by five times, though it would be hard to know this just from driving around Iowa: the pigs are nowhere to be seen among the corn and soya bean fields. The flat horizon is occasionally interrupted by the towers of the grain storage buildings (known as elevators), ethanol factories and the occasional town. The low-rise pig factories in Iowa, which house a quarter of America's pigs, are harder to see.

About half of the world's hog production originates from industrial systems, along with more than 70 % of global poultry meat. This means there is a very strong chance that chicken breasts or pork chops bought at the supermarket have come from a factory. The factory method of meat production has changed the rural landscape; pigs are now rarely seen roaming in open fields. Iowans are proud of their status as the biggest hog producers in the US, a position they have held for more than a century. You get the sense that there is a lot of pork around; bacon and sausages are abundant at breakfast time and Iowa hog steaks are a favourite dish at dinner. The two-inch thick steaks are generally served with either chips or potatoes, but no vegetables: Iowa does not grow much fruit or vegetables. Fewer and fewer Iowans are now raising hogs, a reflection of the broader industrialization of the industry. In 1980, about 65 000 farmers in the state raised hogs, with 200 hogs on average on each farm. By 2002, the number of farms with hogs had fallen to around a sixth of the 1980 total, but with seven times the number of hogs on each farm (Herriges *et al.*, 2005).

So if the high fibre content in the distillers' grains makes a large proportion of it unsuitable for pigs, what's the answer? Bringing more cattle to the state, it seems. 'Ethanol plants can't exist without live-stock, they go hand in hand,' said Sundblad from Iowa Farm Bureau. 'We want cattle production coming back to the Midwest,' he said. Nebraska and Texas are the largest beef producers in the US and California has the biggest share of dairy farming. A shift of cat-tle to Iowa would represent another significant structural change in America's agricultural industry. The link between grains, oilseeds and livestock is an important connection to highlight. Livestock has been the main driver for the increase in corn and oilseed demand over the past three decades, whereas biofuels have only been a serious factor for the past three years. Animal feed accounts for more than half of the corn crop, whereas ethanol, food and industrial use accounted for a third of the US crop in 2007. In 2006, feed for hogs and poultry accounted for 75 % of all the soya bean meal consumed in the US; beef cattle and dairy cows consuming about 10 %.[15] The livestock in-dustry, therefore, feels a direct impact when corn or soya bean prices rise and this impact is passed on to consumers at the checkout till.

Chicken Out

Until the early 1980s, diets that included milk and meat were largely confined to breakfast or dinner tables in developed countries. When I was growing up, the Sunday roast was the most anticipated meal of the week. Today more and more people eat meat, in more countries, and more often, and it is no longer considered a luxury item in devel-oped countries. In the past three decades there has been a 'livestock revolution' around the world.[16] Once again, China has been in the driving seat of change. Its economy has boomed over the past 30 years following economic liberalization in the late 1970s, and meat is one of the first consumables that Chinese workers have spent their increased disposable income on. Economic growth in developing countries tends to see a higher proportion of the rise in income spent on food than that which is spent on food following an equivalent increase in wages in developed countries.[17]

There was a doubling of meat consumption per capita per year in developing countries between 1980 and 2002, to 28 kilograms. The consumption of steaks, chops, burgers, chicken wings and meat products tripled from 47 million tonnes to 137 million a year, due to the large population increase in the developing world. China alone accounted for 57 % of the increase in meat consumption in the developing world. The Chinese prefer to eat chicken and pork, resulting in poultry and pigs accounting for more than three-quarters of the increase in meat supply (Food and Agriculture Organization of the United Nations, 2006).

Like so many statistics on China, they follow a different pattern after the economic reforms of 1978. Between 1949 and 1979, Chinese annual per capita meat consumption amounted to less than 5 kg and increased to 39 kg by the end of the 1990s (Food and Agriculture Organization of the United Nations, 2007). With such a rapid increase in chicken and pork consumption, the developing world has been eating more meat than the developed world since 1996.

China's increase in demand for commodities has had ramifications for a range of industries; from oil to gas, metals, grains and poultry, which is having a knock-on effect for the dynamics of the meat industry. Chicken and turkey are known as poultry, and if you add pigs into the equation they are referred to as monogastric, or white, meats, often perceived as being healthier than red meat. From a meat producer's point of view they are also easier to deliver to the consumer, as they take less looking after than a herd of cows or a flock of sheep. It is important to understand the difference between white and red meat demand because it has a huge bearing on land usage, as well as on grain demand. In 1970, the world ate virtually equal portions of white and red meat; by 2010, there will be about two and a half times more white meat produced than red meat (Sansoucy, 1995).

Due to the way poultry is produced, chicken is often cheaper to buy than red meats. The life of a chicken has radically altered from running around the farmyard to remaining in a confined space in a crowded factory, often not ever seeing daylight. Poultry production can be mechanized most easily and industrial production lines are now commonplace; the baby chick sees a conveyor belt soon after hatching and the slaughter, plucking, gutting and cutting of the chickens is all done by machine.

Mechanization of the meat industry has its origins in the Chicago meat stockyards of the mid-19th century. This type of poultry farming is a world away from the days of my childhood in the 1970s, when I remember the chickens and hens running around my uncle's farmyard; 'as free as a bird', you could say. The saying is far from the truth for the battery-farmed chicken of today. Awareness of these farming methods has heightened among conscientious consumers and many are now demanding free-range farming techniques. Television stars such as Pamela Anderson and UK TV chefs Hugh Fearnley-Whittingstall and Jamie Oliver have also raised awareness of the issue of factory farming through high profile campaigns.

Tyson, the world's largest meat producer, proudly boasts that improved animal diet, selective breeding, production technologies, equipment development and better management practices have enabled the industry to speed up meat production (Tyson Foods Inc., 2005–6). 'A 3.5 to 4.5 pound chicken can now be produced in six to seven weeks compared with 16 weeks in 1935,' Tyson claims. The company boasts further that, 'feed conversion is now two pounds of feed per pound of live broiler, compared to more than four pounds of feed in the mid-1930s', adding (rather ominously) that chicken is the most efficient of the meat proteins in feed conversion. A broiler is a chicken raised for meat products; poultry is fowl raised for meat and/or eggs.

Such is the 'efficiency' in chicken and egg production that it now only takes 44 days from when a chicken is hatched from the egg to grow into a 5.25 pound chicken ready for slaughter, to appear on the supermarket shelf as sliced luncheon meat, pizza topping, in part or in whole in the meat aisles or at a KFC outlet. Eighty years ago, it took

112 days for a chicken to grow to 2.5 pounds on 4.7 pounds of feed for each pound in weight; now it's 1.90 pounds of feed for each pound in weight. Left to their natural life, a chicken can live up to 15 years.

Herding Cattle

While chickens have moved from the farmyard to the factory, cattle have been more stubborn. This is mostly to do with their genetics; there are more breeds and therefore they are harder to 'standardize' in the way that poultry and hogs are bred. However, cattle are put in industrial feedlots in the final stage of their life (about two years old) before they are taken to the slaughterhouse (Food and Agriculture Organization of the United Nations, 2006). This is an important distinction: cattle still require vast land to thrive on, whereas poultry and hogs can be raised inside. The need for cattle land will determine land usage; conversion to arable farming or retaining it for grazing. The growth in meat and milk consumption has increased the need for land, which in turn has been a major factor for deforestation – responsible for about 18 % of carbon emissions – the key contributor to global warming (Stern, 2006). About 70 % of the total area of deforestation in the Amazon has been turned into pastures for cattle farming (Food and Agriculture Organization of the United Nations, 2006).

Since domestication thousands of years ago, cattle and sheep, known as ruminant animals, have largely lived off grass and other pasture-based feeds, such as hay and silage. The area of grazing land has expanded six-fold since 1800, covering 3.4 billion hectares of the world's surface, much of it in semi-arid or arid lands in the US, Australia and Argentina. Another 0.5 billion hectares are used for growing crops for animal feed. As a result, livestock accounts for 78 % of all agricultural land use, though it should be made clear that much of this land would not be appropriate for intensive farming practices, such as the Australian outback, which is little more than scrub. The rise in meat consumption has created two trends for livestock and land use, one being the overall need for more land for more cattle and sheep to live on. Simultaneously, the industry is adopting more intensive farming practices. This may ultimately slow down the rate of new land required following the trend for people to consume more white meat produced in factory settings.

Milking It

The developing nations have not only increased their appetite for meat, but also their thirst for milk. In volume terms the taste for milk has been far stronger than for meat, with consumption more than doubling to 222 million tonnes in the developing world between 1980 and 2002. With population growth in the developed world rising at a far slower rate, milk consumption rose by a more moderate 37 million tonnes to 265 million.

Much has been written about the success achieved by the green revolution of crops in the developing world, but the increase in livestock output appears to be at least as impressive. Most notably, egg production has increased by 331 % over the last two decades, compared with 78 % for cereals (Sansoucy, 1995). The livestock industry accounts for about 40 % of the total agricultural industry in terms of sales, and provides about one-third of the protein intake of the world's population (Delgado, 2000).

The growing demand for meat and dairy products has coincided with an increase in the number of people living in cities throughout the world. 2007 will be remembered for marking the first time in human history that the majority of the world's population have lived in cities. About 3.3 billion people live in cities and this is expected to swell to five billion by 2030 (Food and Agriculture Organization of the United Nations, 2006). Urbanization means people have greater access to power, refrigeration and supermarkets, so they can consume more perishable goods, such as meat, milk and cheese. The popularity of supermarkets has boosted the sales of convenience foods, snacks and pre-cooked foods, many of which are frozen, thanks to additives

derived from corn. Together with the spread of fast-food chains –
McDonalds, Starbucks and Pizza Hut – around the world, an increasing proportion of people's earnings is now spent on food away from
the home. It also marks a convergence of diets globally, as the same
fast-food outlets are established around the world.

With more people living in cities, incomes have risen, and food
prices, in real terms, have fallen since the 1950s. This is partly due
to the rise of the supermarket and an increase in buying power,
which in turn have driven prices down – much to the detriment of
the grower and farmer. In China alone the number of supermarkets has risen from 2500 in 1994 to 32 000 in 2000. The rise of
supermarkets has grown in tandem with the emergence of global
agribusinesses, the companies that process grains and oilseeds into
foods or animal feeds, oil products and processed meat; such as the
likes of Cargill, ADM, Bunge and Louis Dreyfus. This reflects the
trend for processed food; foods are branded and marketed and 'value
added', further distancing the relationship between the farmer and the
consumer.

Agricultural Alchemy

Much of the food on the supermarket shelf have been brought about
by technological change. Research by chemists and biologists in the
19th century found that corn is made up of about 72 % starch, 10 %
protein and 4 % oil, with the remainder consisting of fibre and gluten.
One of corn's relatively recent innovative by-products is high fructose
corn syrup (HFCS). The evolution of the HFCS industry is also largely
thanks to luck and the US government's sugar policy – another legacy
of corn-breeding pioneer Henry Wallace (Gardner, 2002).

Part of the 'New Deal' under Franklin D. Roosevelt's government
in the 1930s was the sugar programme, which has kept US sugar
prices above the world price for the majority of the past 80 years.
The interference with the market has given sugar 'the most distorted
policy of all commodities', with a history of protection dating back

to at least the 1800s (Mitchell, 2004). It was mainly designed to protect sugar beet producers in Europe, Japan and the United States, where production is more costly than the sugar cane grown in tropical countries, particularly Brazil. The consequence of this artificially high US sugar price has stimulated the supply of alternatives to sugar, in particular sweeteners. In effect this has subsidized the corn sweetener business, which is dominated by a handful of companies.

Since its introduction in the early 1970s, HFCS's share of US caloric sweetener consumption rose from 2 % in 1973 to 36 % by 1987 (Gardner, 2002). By 2000, Americans consumed an average of 32 teaspoonfuls of sugar and sweeteners a day, according to the Economic Resource Service (ERS), the economic forecasting arm of the USDA. That's more than three times above the USDA's recommended level (US Department of Agriculture, 2001–2). Both Coca-Cola and The Pepsi Company use HFCS in their soft drinks.

Fast-paced lifestyles have much to do with the increase in the consumption of sweeteners, which can be found in pizzas, hot dogs, luncheon meat, spaghetti and flavoured yoghurt. The popularity of corn-based sweeteners has coincided with the rise in obesity over the past three decades. The sweetener is not directly to blame for the prevalence in the condition, but it has nevertheless put the spotlight on diets and a greater scrutiny on the intake of sugars and sweeteners. The factors for the obesity endemic are more complex than the intake of a single form of sugar, and involve issues of exercise, diet, sedentary lifestyles and the reliance on cars.[19]

Life Is Sweet

The US sugar price support programme and its tariff on ethanol imports also affect Brazil, which is by far the world's largest producer of sugar. Brazil is the only other country that compares with the US for making ethanol. To put the US corn-based ethanol industry into its economic perspective, a comparison with Brazil's ethanol industry is needed. An acre of sugar cane in Brazil produces about 650 gallons of ethanol, whereas an acre of corn in the United States yields 400 gallons (Hofstrand, 2007). Sugar cane grows in a tropical climate; the hotter temperatures and rainfall allow it to grow faster than any crop grown in a temperate climate. The 6.2 million hectares of sugar cane plantation in 2006 represented a little more than 2 % of Brazil's arable land or a fifth of the US corn-growing area. Yet, from that amount of land, Brazil was able to supply almost a third of global sugar production, about 40 % of global sugar exports and still have enough left over to boost global sugar stockpiles. Brazilian corn acreage was twice the size of its sugar plantations, and soya beans grew on an area more than three times larger than its sugar cane plantations. As a consequence of the rise in sugar stockpiles, sugar prices have halved from their 30-year peak in 2005 of almost 20 cents a pound. This price fall negates the argument that all biofuel production has led to higher food prices (Valdes, 2007).

Sugar is superior to corn for making ethanol as it contains sucrose, which is converted straight into ethanol (corn requires an extra processing step as it is refined into starch prior to being turned into sugar that is then made into ethanol). This makes ethanol from sugar more energy efficient, as it requires less energy to produce. About 6500 kilocalories are needed to produce a gallon of sugar cane-ethanol; 4.3 times as much energy is required to produce the same volume of ethanol from corn (Hofstrand, 2007). Furthermore, waste from the sugar cane, known as bagasse, is used to process heat and electricity for ethanol plants, making many of Brazil's 300 plus sugar cane processing plants and distilleries relatively energy self-sufficient whilst reducing carbon emissions.[20] Despite the high tariffs, Brazil accounted for the lion's share of the 653.3 million gallons of ethanol imported into the US in 2006, or 12 % of total US demand.[21]

The sugar and ethanol industries have helped turn Brazil into the world's largest net exporter of agriculture and food items over the past decade, bigger even than the US. Brazil is also the biggest producer of coffee, orange juice and tobacco. It is the world's biggest exporter of soya beans, beef and poultry, and the expansion of its livestock industry has been blamed for the deforestation of the Amazon forest. Brazil is also the world's fourth biggest corn producer (Valdes, 2006), and this, together with its role as the major soya bean exporter, reflects the fact that the US has allocated more of its arable land to growing corn for ethanol use, prompting Brazilian farmers to plant more crops to satisfy the export markets the US is giving up in its rush for ethanol.

Since the launch of Brazil's National Alcohol Programme (Programa Nacional do Álcool) in 1975, its national oil company Petrobras has made a number of oil discoveries in deep water off the Brazilian coast. This has reduced Brazil's oil imports from 80 % of domestic oil requirements in the mid-1970s to almost zero. Brazilian oil output supplies 85 % of the country's total petroleum demand and the balance has been met by sugar-ethanol. The oil discoveries and the growth of the ethanol industry have helped Brazil achieve energy independence. A goal set at the launch of its ethanol programme, which was in response to the large Brazilian sugar stockpiles in the early 1970s (Sandalow, 2006) when the country's industry was a smaller sugar producer than Fidel Castro's Cuba.[22] The US set a similar goal around the same time and is further away than ever from achieving this.

The success of the Brazilian ethanol programme is down to the popularity of the flex-fuel cars, which are vehicles that can run on gasoline and other fuels, such as ethanol. Aided by favourable tax breaks, Brazilian drivers have quickly taken flex-fuel cars to the road. The flex-fuel car acts as a safety valve for fluctuating commodity prices. The driver of the flex-fuel car chooses the balance of the mix between the two fuels based on the relative price: if the sugar-ethanol price is higher than gasoline, then more gasoline will be chosen, which will, in turn, moderate the demand for sugar-based ethanol until supply catches up and prices fall. To ensure that a proportion of ethanol is used, the government has maintained a minimum requirement for the amount of ethanol to be blended with each gallon of gasoline consumed in Brazil. This is what the US wants to emulate with E85 cars.

The emergence of Brazil as an agricultural powerhouse highlights a wider trend – that the developing countries are now accounting for a greater share in the world trade of agriculture, with China taking much of the agricultural exports from South America. Agribusinesses and farmers interpret these trends to imply that Brazil has the potential to produce more food, ethanol and fibre. For agribusiness, Brazil's vast swathes of savanna-like scrubland, also known as Cerrado, are seen as future soya bean or grain fields, or as more land for grazing livestock. For environmentalists, the Cerrado is a great source of biodiversity, supporting 4000 different species. At the current rate at which agriculture is advancing into the area, the Cerrado's vital ecosystem could be gone by 2030, according to estimates by Conservation International (Food and Agriculture Organization of the United Nations, 2006).

Environmental issues will continue to surround the biofuel industry, but concerns about the Cerrado and the Amazon are unlikely to deter Brazil's sugar cane and ethanol expansion. Like the US, there is an ethanol rush in Brazil, where the sugar cane area is estimated to expand by 3 million hectares, or 50 %, by 2012 (Valdes, 2007). Most of this expansion will take place in the state of Sao Paulo, home to one of the world's biggest cities and a vast number of its car drivers. It is a long day's ride on Brazil's bumpy roads to the Amazon; so the industry's planned growth is not directly leading to destruction of the rainforest.

Together with Indonesia, Brazil recorded the largest net loss in forest area between 2000 and 2005, due mainly to the increased demand for agriculture and timber. Indonesia is the world's largest producer of palm oil, accounting for almost half of global output of the oilseed, which produces more oil per hectare than any other oilseed – making it an attractive feedstock for biodiesel production. The 50 % increase in global palm oil production since the early 1990s has mainly occurred in Indonesia and Malaysia (Stern, 2006). Indonesia and Malaysia export much of their palm oil to Europe where it is turned into biodiesel. European biofuel producers like palm oil as more of the oilseed can grow on an acre of land than rapeseed, the main feedstock grown in Europe for biodiesel. Rapeseed has become a familiar part of the northern European landscape in late spring, its yellow flowers brightening up the scenery. However, the European Union has tightened its requirements for biofuels, stating that they must save 35 % in carbon emissions and must use 'best practice' in the cultivation of palm oil, because the EU finally acknowledges the inextricable link between rainforest destruction and agriculture (and therefore biofuels).

Brazil welcomes the new EU plan, as it favours the more emission-friendly sugar-ethanol over other biofuels. The ascent of Brazil's status as food basket for the world has occurred without the level of subsidies given to American or European farmers, a fact that has given them considerable political muscle when it comes to agricultural trade talks. Brazil demonstrated this clout when it came up against the US through the World Trade Organization (WTO) over US subsidies on cotton. The action forced the US to drop one of its financial assistance programmes to its cotton farmers, who have since turned their farms over to corn production. Brazil has joined other developing nations to form the G20 to speak with a single voice at the Doha round of trade talks under the WTO.

Nevertheless, the primary role of agriculture is to provide food for the world's 6.6 billion people. This is more than double the world's population in 1960 and is projected by the United Nations to reach 8.2 billion by 2030. The rise in global population has been accompanied by increased affluence around the world this decade, following the strongest period of economic growth for years. This has provided more people with more disposable income, which in turn has increased demand for food at a time when the world's arable and grazing land is under threat from urbanization as well as the vagaries of the weather events that cause crop damage from floods and droughts.

Land Factory

World population growth is putting more pressure on land and resources. Proponents of biofuels believe there is enough land to grow crops to feed people and grow ethanol crops. This push is part of a long-held philosophy to use the land as a factory for a range of industries. The US government has always supported industrial diversity in agriculture: the seal of the USDA is, 'Agriculture is the foundation of manufacture and commerce.' It is emblazoned on the USDA flag that was first designed in the late 19th century.

It was not until the late 1930s that the USDA built regional research laboratories to find new uses for farm products. The construction of the four USDA centres was a reaction to the creation of the Chemurgic Council in the mid-1930s. Henry Ford and Thomas Edison supported the new body which had the aim of creating new industries from the fruits of the land (Finlay, 2004, p. 35). Ford was an enthusiastic supporter of farmers, taking the view that they were his potential customers and for them to afford to buy his cars they needed to be able to sell their produce for a good price. He was particularly interested in soya beans. There is a short film of Ford striking the back of a car with an axe and showing that there were no dents from his blows to a panel made from a resin produced from soya beans. Ford researchers also made synthetic wool and panels for the interior of the car from soya beans (Time, 1940).[23]

The Chemurgic Council was founded in the wake of the Depression and focused on self-dependence of resources, echoing the philosophy of the contemporary biofuel movement, declaring: 'When in the course of the life of a nation, its people become neglected of the laws of nature ... necessity impels them to turn to the soil in order to recover the right of self-maintenance' (Finlay, 2004). The mobilization of industry and raw materials for the Second World War extinguished the high aims of the chemurgic movement. In more recent times, the idea of self-reliance has lived on. In the late 1980s when farmers were reeling from high interest rates and low prices, there were moves by the sector to diversify from agriculture, as a way to improve the rural economy through the production of bio-based products (Conway and Duncan, 2006).

A US report from the New Farm and Forest Products Task Force in 1987 recommended that a new array of farm products and forest products be commercialized over the next 25 years, utilizing 150 million acres, or almost half the arable land in the US. The report prompted Congress in 1990 to approve the creation of a body called the Alternative Agricultural Research and Commercialization Corporation (AARCC) to expedite the development and help bring to market the new bio-based products.[24] The AARCC did not live up to expectations. Ten years later Congress stopped funding for the government-run venture capital group after an audit found AARCC's investment selections were not adequate because applicants had not displayed any reasonable basis for prospective success. One of the cases involved a dispute between AARCC and a manufacturer over incontinence pads made from starch.[25]

Undeterred by AARCC's failing, the USDA has set up more bodies to promote new industries from agriculture, in particular from corn. Corn has been a favoured crop by the USDA, underlined by the fact that it is the only crop featured on the shield at the centre of its flag.

Coming to America

The question is – can corn supply all these competing needs? The answer (like many things in life) depends on the weather and on genetics.

The Indians that roamed the prairies before the arrival of Columbus in the 15th century would barely recognize the modern corn plant. It stands taller and the stalks are more densely spaced, allowing more corn to grow per acre than ever could have been imagined centuries ago. But none of this would have been possible had the local Indians not taught the early settlers how to grow corn. Columbus came looking for the New World, envisaging vast treasures, but I doubt he thought they would be of the food or fibre variety. Corn, cotton, potatoes, peanuts, strawberries and tobacco all came originally from the Americas (Day-Rubenstein and Heisey, 2003).

The origin of corn is still the subject of some debate, but the most accepted view is that it came from Mexico and spread throughout the Americas over thousands of years. Maize was domesticated from a wild plant called teosinte in Mexico. The evolution from teosinte to corn is quite dramatic. Jared Diamond wrote in his book *Guns, Germs, and Steel* that teosinte's value as a food crop would not have impressed hunter gatherers: it was less productive in the wild than wild wheat and it produced much less seed (Diamond, 1997). For teosinte to become a useful crop, it had to undergo drastic changes in its reproductive biology . . . Diamond even suggests that the virtues of wheat and barley and the difficulties posed by teosinte may have been a significant factor in the differing developments of the New World and Eurasian human societies.

'A key step in the domestication process from the wild plants was picking seeds off the plant and planting them for a new harvest,' said Stephen Smith, who has a doctorate of philosophy on the evolution of corn from the University of Birmingham, UK.

Maize, wheat and barley are all part of the same biological family, Poaceae (Gramineae), which also includes rice, oats, sorghum and sugar cane among its relations. It is thought that they came from a common ancestor within the last 55–70 million years, near the end of the reign of dinosaurs (Buckler and Stevens, 2006).

Jumping forward millions of years, maize arrived in the south-west of today's United States around 3500 BC, and by 1000 AD it was growing in the upper northeastern state of New England. The Indians throughout the Americas had already developed thorough crop-breeding techniques and had preferred varieties for boiling, roasting, popping, milling and brewing. By the time Columbus arrived in the New World, it was already an important part of the diet (Smith *et al.*, 2004).

The arrival of Columbus in the Americas, and the subsequent returning ships from his voyage, brought corn to Europe, Africa, India and parts of the Far East by the end of the 16th century (Smith *et al.*, 2004). Columbus is also credited with taking sugar to the Americas; planting it in Santa Domingo in the Caribbean.[26]

When the English colonists arrived in modern-day Virginia more than 400 years ago, corn was not really at the forefront of their minds. 'The settlers at Jamestown, Virginia in 1607 had little intention of engaging in agriculture. None of the settlers in the first expedition appears to have known all that much about farming. They came expecting to make their fortunes quickly and looked to the 'London Company', under whom they were operating, to furnish them with food and other necessities from England' (Carrier, 1923). In order to survive, the colonists had to rely on the benevolence of the local Indians, the Powhatan. It is important to highlight the early exchange between the Indians and the settlers, as it gives birth to today's modern corn industry. Anyone who has a young child will be familiar with the Disney film *Pocahontas*, which depicts the fictional love story between the local Indian princess and the English sea captain, John Smith, and includes scenes of the Indians' corn fields as a backdrop. But there's another, less well-known, angle to that story.

Settling for Corn

The real John Smith was put in charge of seeking out local tribes willing to swap corn, fish and game for English copper and glass beads. Smith's success at negotiation helped feed the young colony, although he was prone to gunboat diplomacy (Deans, 2007). 'It pleased us God to move Indians to bring us corn ere was halfe ripe to refresh us,' and in September they 'brought us great store both of corne and bread ready made,' Captain John Smith is quoted in Carrier's 1923 publication. The colonists eventually took a farming lesson from the Indians (Warman, 1988).

Another Indian who plays a role in the early adoption of corn cultivation by the English colony on American shores (though there were many more that are unrecorded) is Squanto (Warman, 1988). Squanto gave lessons in growing corn to the Pilgrims, religious dissidents from cities who knew very little about farming. After the success of the first harvests by the Pilgrims in Virginia, they would thank the local Indians for help. This was the forerunner to Thanksgiving Day, one of the most important holidays in the modern US calendar. It was also a tradition that the indigenous people upheld, and 'differed only in details from the rites enacted long before by the Mexican and South

American Indians, for it was an expression of gratitude to God for the corn harvest and ensured food for the coming winter' (Walden, 1966). The significance of corn for the modern US festival is underlined by its symbolism on Thanksgiving Day, along with the turkey, pumpkin, cranberry and beans. The holiday, which occurs in late November, traces its roots back to a harvest festival, as it was the time of year when the corn harvest was in and farmers knew how much they had in store for the year ahead (Warman, 1988).

Corn was an important part of the settlers' diet as it could be eaten off the cob and turned into corn flour to make bread. The leaves were used as fodder for cattle, and the corn husks were used to make mattresses, rugs and twine. Fermented corn mash became beer and whiskey and any left over corn was used for animal feed to fatten up the cows, pigs and chickens, which in turn produced more milk, eggs and meat. Once the colonists had learned from the Indians the techniques of crop rotation and planting of the seeds, they no longer needed the farming skills of the indigenous people.

Go West

The westward shift of corn from the east coast to the Midwest is a significant reflection of the expansion of the US at that time. At independence in 1776, about 90 % of the population of 2.8 million were in agriculture, and the tobacco from plantations in the south was the biggest commercial agricultural export (Warman, 1988). The journey of corn from its tropical origins to the prairie lands of the US Midwest marked one of the most rapid changes in the history of corn. By the 1830s, the American cornbelt was centred in Tennessee, Kentucky and Virginia, but it was set to move further west and also north following the defeat of Black Hawk, chief of the Sac and Fox nations in 1832, which opened up the potential of the rich farmlands of Illinois (Walden, 1966) and Iowa (Schwieder, 1996).[27] Illinois quickly emerged as a major corn producer, and with the railway boom of the mid-19th century, Chicago was establishing itself as the major corn and livestock capital of the US. This led to the creation of the Chicago

Board of Trade in 1848, which was set up specifically to trade grains (Walden, 1966).

The invention of the steel plough by a blacksmith called John Deere helped further expand the farm population of the Midwest. Deere went on to establish the eponymous company, known for its green and yellow coloured farm equipment.[28]

Then the Homestead Act was signed by President Lincoln on May 20, 1862. This provided 160 acres of the Midwest to Union soldiers, and any other American who wished to qualify, by proving they had been living on the land for a year and had put a building on the vast public lands in the west and Midwest (Crabb, 1947).

By now corn had become the biggest crop in the US, but its political and international economic muscle was much smaller than cotton, which remained 'King of the South'.

By 1866, just a year after the end of the American Civil War, US corn was planted in 30.02 million acres (just less than a third of the 2007 acreage), with average yield a sixth of what it is today. It was about the same yield as barley, but lower than oats (US Department of Agriculture, 2007) (today's corn yields are 2.5 times greater than barley and oats). Once the US completed its stretch from the Atlantic to the Pacific coast, the country was linked by rail. The network created new opportunities for farmers, as their grains could now be transported around the country and to the ports for the export market. The competing rail companies saw agriculture as an important freight customer; they even went to the extent of educating farmers on the new technique: 'There were trains going around the Midwest to show people how to grow corn,' said Smith, from Pioneer. Corn plantings soon reached their peak of 102 267 acres in 1910, when it accounted for a third of all arable land in the US (Fowler, 1994), which is still more than the area dedicated to corn in 2007 and 2008.

By this time farming was undergoing rapid technological change in the early part of the 20th century, with the introduction of the revolutionary diesel tractor, pickers, mowers, sprayers and choppers, all of which became part of the farm furniture (Gardner, 2002). By acquiring a tractor, farmers gave up their status as independent power suppliers on their farms, moving from horsepower to tractor power and from hand harvest to mechanical maize pickers (Duvick, 2001). The replacement of animal power by mechanical power radically altered land use. An estimated 93 million acres of US cropland (or 27 % of total harvested acres) were used to grow feed for horses and mules in 1915, but by 1960, this acreage had dropped to four million, freeing up about a quarter of the country's cropland for other uses (Gardner, 2002). This use of land for feeding horses is actually an early form of biofuels, since more than a quarter of the land was not being used for growing food. It was also a greater proportion of US farmland dedicated for fuel than is allocated this decade. The sons of farmers were being educated in agricultural science through land colleges, set up in the mid-19th century following the Land Grant College Act, which was signed by President Lincoln in 1862 (Crabb, 1947).

With no further land expansion by the US government, increases in production were only going to occur if yields themselves improved, through better breeding, crop rotation, tillage, use of fertilizers and insect control (Gardner, 2002).

Seeds of Growth

After the end of the Civil War, corn yields improved at a slow and steady rate. Corn was grown from open-pollinated seeds, without any intervention from farmers – a process still used for wheat, oats and barley. The rate of yield growth improved in the 1930s with the introduction of new seeds that changed the way corn had been grown for hundreds of years.

In the early 20th century, the thrust of corn breeding was basically to take seeds from the prettiest ear, plant them and watch them grow. Corn, like wheat or barley, self-pollinated, which meant that the pollen from the tassel (the flower at the top of the corn stalk) would blow in the air until it either hit the ground or landed on a silk (the thin hairy part that juts out of the ear). Each of the hundreds of silks is linked to a seed on the cob and acts as a tube to take the pollen down to the seed, which then impregnates and produces a kernel.

Plant reproduction research has evolved radically. Gregor (Johann) Mendel is seen as a pioneer of plant breeding following his work in the mid to late 19th century on the inheritance of characteristics (Fowler, 1994).[30] Mendel's research was not followed for another 50 years after his first experiments. By this time a new generation of US plant breeders had come along, who found that putting the male and female seeds together produced hybrids, shown to improve yields. It marked a significant turning point in the evolution of corn breeding and for the corn industry. Families of corn breeders even made their own varieties, including the Wallace family of Iowa (Crabb, 1947).

Henry A. Wallace, a student at Iowa State College (now Iowa State University), started to question the rationale for conventional corn breeding. Wallace, who at the time was still a teenager, was inspired by George Washington Carver, son of a slave, who had become one of America's top botanists and was researching at Iowa College.[31] Wallace concluded that there was no control on quality in the breeding techniques of the day.

The young Wallace did a further study in his backyard in Des Moines and discovered that if you crossed two unrelated weak in-breeds, it provided much better yields than those attained through the conventional self-pollination process. His garden-plot experiments grew when the family bought land in Johnston, near Des Moines, where he formed a company, the Hi-Bred Corn Company (Brown, 1983), the headquarters of which are still located there today (the company is now called Pioneer Hi-Bred, a unit of DuPont). The farming community greeted the new type of seeds with scepticism. To overcome this resistance, Wallace gave the hybrid seeds to the sons of the farmers who were more prepared to try them, and after a number of years the senior farmers found that their sons were yielding more corn than they had through the conventional means. This triggered a greater acceptance by the farmers, resulting in huge growth in hybrid corn seed sales. Corn hybrid seeds did not pass on their enhanced attributes to their offspring, requiring farmers to purchase new seeds each year to maintain the higher yields (Warman, 1988).

The introduction of hybrid corn also took away one of the most fundamental traditions of farmers: the keeping of seeds for the next growing season. It meant that farmers could no longer know what inbred lines had been used to produce the hybrid – now hybrid corn is a proprietary product, protected by patent laws (Fowler, 1994). Hybrid seeds brought great success to the fields. The US corn-growing area devoted to hybrid corn grew from 1 % in 1933 to 78 % by 1943 and to more than 90 % by 1960. US corn yields doubled to more than 55 bushels an acre in 1960 from their average prior to the introduction of hybrid corn.

Corn's high productivity is a reflection of solar power at work. The sun's rays (solar energy) are used to transform the energy from the corn plant's leaves to the rest of the plant through photosynthesis, which is the process of making carbohydrates from carbon dioxide and water.

The change in the seed business also affected government activities in agriculture. Until the emergence of hybrids, government funding was the primary source of seed research, mainly through land colleges (farm subsidies had not yet become a major feature of Washington's involvement in the industry), but the research gradually transferred to the private sector as speciality seed companies evolved from family-run businesses. The sector is now dominated by a handful of companies with a large team of researchers, patent specialists and lawyers (Morgan, 2000).

Wallace did not remain in the seed business. He went on to become Secretary of Agriculture in 1933 under President Franklin D. Roosevelt; the same position his father Henry C. held under President Warren Harding a decade earlier.[32] Wallace did much to help farmers through his innovation of corn hybrids. As a politician he helped them through government initiatives of price support programmes, farm credit, housing, soil conservation, rural electrification and food stamps (Schlesinger, 2000) as the depression of the 1930s hit American farming hard with about a quarter of the nation working on farms.[33] He oversaw the introduction of one of the most sweeping programmes of government assistance to farmers with the New Deal Farm Laws.

Seeds of Change

US seed makers were empowered by changes in intellectual property which gave their seeds protection under the Plant Patent Act of 1930 (Fernandez-Cornejo and Caswell, 2006). This legislation was the first of many that have since been passed in Washington to provide businesses with a high degree of certainty and power. Armed with intellectual property rights, seed breeders were able to keep information on the seed lineage, and therefore control of seed supplies.

The mechanization of farming and the hybridization of corn helped bring in a new era of industrialization and productivity in American farming. Farmers found that stalks from hybrid seeds were (literally) no pushover, even for a very heavy tractor; they had a hardiness that was not found in the open-pollinated varieties. Greater yields on the same area of ground meant more corn to be picked and machines were more effective than humans for the job (Duvick, 2001). The hybrids were also more tolerant of higher quantities of nitrogen fertilizers, which in turn contributed to more groundwater pollution.

From 1960 until the mid-1990s, hybrid corn yields doubled again to about 120 bushels per acre. By this period all but a minority of corn acres were covered by fertilizers or herbicides (Fernandez-Cornejo, 2004). In comparison, cotton yields improved almost four-fold, soya bean yields rose three-fold and wheat yields were up 2.5 times from the 1930s to the mid-1990s. More than half of the yield gains are attributed to genetic improvements achieved by plant breeders; fertilizers and better soil management account for the rest (Fernandez-Cornejo, 2004).

From Hybrids to GM

The constant search for higher yields by large seed companies with deep pockets was helped by the protection of patent laws and supportive government, as well helped as a desire by farmers to improve productivity. The industry conditions were ripe for the next generation of seeds. In 1996, the US became the first country in the world to introduce genetically engineered seeds, also known as genetically modified organism (GMO) seeds. As with hybrids, corn farmers were relatively quick to adopt GMO seeds, as were cotton and soya bean farmers (Fernandez-Cornejo and Caswell, 2006). With US production of corn, cotton and soya beans representing about 40, 20 and 40 % of global output respectively in 2006 (US Department of Agriculture Advisory Committee on Biotechnology and 21st Century Agriculture, 2006), that means a sizeable amount of global agricultural production is now grown by GMO seeds.

The introduction of GM seeds also marks a departure from traditional plant breeding, including the hybrid revolution, and alters plant traits in a way that cannot be done via traditional methods. Researchers like to refer to this as *gene shuffling* (Fernandez-Cornejo and McBride, 2002).

The first generation of GM crops focused on the input traits of the corn plant such as herbicide tolerance and insect resistance, to reduce the amount of chemicals sprayed on the crop. Major agricultural producers China, Argentina, Canada and Brazil for soya beans, have embraced GM seeds, but on nothing like the scale of the US. GM's acceptance has differed widely around the world, consumer groups in the European Union being particularly anti-GM, causing US corn exports to the EU to drop drastically. This also marks the fact that Europe is becoming self-sufficient in cereals again following the post-World War II period when it depended on US grains.

'It is all very well to talk about buying non-GM food, but what that really means for the farmer if he wants to grow non-GM soya (beans) or corn, he is going to have to go out in 90 degree heat with overalls, gloves, spray mask and there are lots of flies around,' said John Robinson, a farmer in central Illinois, as he waved away several flies while standing by his fields of corn. 'It gets very hot in the cornbelt, and spraying the crops full of insecticides and pesticides is a very hazardous occupation. I think the consumer who feels good about buying non-GM food has got to understand what the farmer has to do to grow crops.' Robinson's latest crops of corn were already chest high in late June, making a mockery of the old saying 'knee-high by the fourth of July'. Whether that is the effect of GM or the deluge of rain the crop had just received is open to plenty of debate.

The extensive laboratories of the large seed companies – Monsanto, Pioneer and Sygenta – have spent vast sums of money developing new GM seed traits; not only to prevent new strains of weeds and insects, but increasingly to develop drought tolerance traits as corn-growing expands into areas where annual rainfall is far less than in Iowa or Illinois. They are also looking at modifications intended to increase the nutritional value of corn for the feed industry, and to meet the output needs of the pharmaceutical and bioenergy industries.

Seed Diversity

The choice of seeds has proliferated. Farmers can wade through 80-page seed catalogues – thicker than an Ikea catalogue. The *Seed Resource Guide* is focused on one thing only though, and that's seeds for corn and soya beans. The pages are filled with extensive tables of statistics on yield, height, weight and growing periods for the corn seeds. Pictures of cornfields are interspersed with captions about strong roots and moisture content, all accompanied by the seed marketer's magic phrase 'high-yield'.

Despite the choice of seeds and the pursuit of yield there are concerns that diversity may ultimately narrow as researchers work on a core number of super seeds; all-combating GMO corn seeds that will fight off insects and weeds, consume less water, produce higher yield and be more nutritional and which are more suitable for the bioenergy and pharmaceutical industries. This evolution of hybrids and GMO seeds has worried the US government; the congressional watchdog has warned about lack of diversity in the US crop gene pool. The US General Accounting Office found that relatively few wild relatives of domesticated varieties are held in gene banks and not all collections have sufficient diversity (US General Accounting Office, 1997).

Also noted in the report was that all the major US field crops relied on germplasm, the part of the cell in a plant that carries hereditary traits, transferred from generation to generation of the plant (in much the same way that the genetic cells of humans are carried through the generations), originating from wild relatives of the plant; that is corn from Mexico, wheat and barley from the Middle East and soya beans from China. Research on developing new seeds for the major crops in the US will therefore depend on cooperation with other countries like Mexico and China through the International Treaty on Plant Genetic Resources for Food and Agriculture.[34]

Genetic uniformity increases the likelihood that a mutation could prove harmful to a crop. Proof of this came in the form of southern corn leaf blight, which reduced the US corn crop by 15 %, or 710 million bushels, in 1970 (Day-Rubenstein and Heisey, 2006), and the infamous Irish potato famine in the 1840s. The potato had become Ireland's staple food after its arrival from South America in the 18th century, but farmers were growing just a single variety, which increased its vulnerability to disease. This came in the form of the potato blight, which devastated a number of successive potato harvests, leading to the famine and Ireland's population decline from more than eight million' from which it has not fully recovered since (Stationery Office, 2006). Academics have also warned that uniformity ultimately poses a risk from pests and diseases that may overcome the initial resistance, which is a feature of GMO plants. 'Widespread adoption of genetically uniform crop varieties makes the crop population more susceptible to a widespread disease or pest infestation,' Kelly Day-Rubenstein and Paul Heisey wrote in 2006.

David Bubeck, research director of crop genetics research and development at Pioneer Hi-Bred, is all too aware of the need for diversity in agriculture, and the dangers that gene uniformity may bring. Bubeck grew up in the 1970s on a farm in north central Iowa, where the family grew oats, alfalfa, corn and soya beans, as well as raising sheep, hogs, cattle and chicken. Now the farm just grows corn and soya beans. He believes the seed industry is addressing the diversity issue. Pioneer has kept data on the inbreed lines from the past 80 years, and has a genetic bank of seeds from the 1930s, 1940s and 1950s. They are able to make new hybrids from their early breeding lines as a safety valve to ensure genetic diversity. Opposite Pioneer's headquarters in Johnson, Iowa, lies a field of corn. In front of the stalks are labels of all the different corn seed types; there are 40 varieties for the state of Iowa alone, and about 250 across the United States. 'If you took a variety from Illinois to Iowa it would not work, the traits grown in the south are different to those grown in the north, and seeds used in the west where the climate is drier are different to the ones in the east where it is more humid,' said Bubeck.

Whether via conventional or genetic engineering, the evolution of plant breeding is focused on improving yields. None of the improvement has come from the plant producing more corn though, but instead from planting more seeds in the same area of ground; more corn plants therefore grow per acre. Researchers at the Iowa State University estimated that to get the optimum yield, 35 000 seeds per acre are required. In the 1960s, 16 000 seeds were planted per acre (Elmore and Abendroth, 2006). In fact the hybrid plants on an individual basis, do not yield any more than they did in the 1930s.

'If you get any semblance of stress, those old hybrids just give up the ghost,' said Smith. The newer hybrids and GM corn seeds produce a higher density of plants, which share a relatively smaller proportion of local resources, such as soil and water. Smith explains that the newer varieties are still better equipped to deal with adverse weather conditions.

The real question is how closely the seeds can be planted to one another, as this will have a major bearing on future yield increases. Monsanto, the world's largest seller of GM products, has said there is potential to double corn yields to 300 bushels an acre by 2030 (Fraley, 2007). In the US, corn yields have increased by about 1.77 bushels an acre per year over the past forty years. A trajectory that the industry still uses as a marker for future growth, which implies corn yields at more than 190 bushels an acre by 2030. The gap between the Monsanto and the long-term growth rate is wide and has dramatic implications for the scale of the industries that can be built around corn production.

The expansion of the US corn acreage in 2007 was the biggest in 100 years and has raised issues about crop rotation, and the knock-on effect on the environment. Corn is deficient in nitrogen, a key nutrient for growth: in the way that humans need a healthy mix of protein, carbohydrates and essential vitamins, plants need nitrogen, phosphate and potassium. Corn yield enhancement over the last 50 years has been attributed to the use of nitrogen fertilizer; a continuous high use of nitrogen can deplete the natural nutrients in the soil and affect long-term soil fertility. This factor has been a major reason for farmers in the US Midwest switching their land use each year between corn and soya beans.

Farmers welcomed the soya bean. Unlike corn it contains nitrogen and it does not need the levels of fertilizer that corn does. Farmers often grow the two crops and rotate their field allocations. The growing seasons for corn and soya beans are complementary: corn is often planted in April and soya beans are planted from early to mid-May because they respond better to the warmer soil. They are then harvested in September just before the corn harvest in October, so farmers would use the soya bean harvest as a chance to fire up the combine that had been sitting idle in the shed since last autumn. The switch between corn and soya bean growing abides by the traditional farming method of crop rotation, which was one of the tenets of one of the founding fathers of America, Thomas Jefferson, third president of the United States. Crop rotation is practised widely around the world. My grandfather used to do it by growing hay one year, followed by barley and then turnips to feed the cattle.

Ultimately though, the crop decision comes down to potential price and financial return for the next season. This competition provides a price linkage throughout the cereal and oilseed world. It means the farmer has to judge prices at least six months out. Here he uses the futures market as a price guide. The drivers of price are also influenced by the myriad government payments, loans and marketing programmes.

The USDA has warned that the rush for corn-based ethanol leads to corn-on-corn planting, which leads to lower yields, which will have a bearing on future corn production. 'The corn–soybean rotation is shifting more to a corn–corn–soybean rotation, even though most producers know that they are losing yield by planting second year corn' (Singer, 2006).

Gulf Syndrome

The increase in nitrogen use has been attributable to more corn planting, leading to the increase in run-off of nitrates into rivers in the Midwest. The rivers feed into the Mississippi, which runs through the heart of the corn-growing country and has for decades carried corn down the river to the ports in Louisiana where they are loaded onto ships destined for all corners of the globe. The Mississippi also carries all these excess nutrients from agricultural run-off, as well as from other sources such as household and industrial waste. At the end of the river, it dumps them all into the Gulf of Mexico.

The high level of nutrients creates a 'dead-zone', an area devoid of oxygen that cannot support marine life in waters that used to be full of fish, crabs and shrimp. It's posing big problems for commercial fishermen in Louisiana; the southern coastal state catches a quarter of US seafood each year.[35] The loss of oxygen is caused by nitrogen, boosting the rapid growth of large populations of algae and plankton. When they die, they sink to the bottom of the water, and their decay causes the depletion of oxygen in the water (Ribaudo, 2003).[36] In 2007, the dead-zone was estimated to be the largest since records began in 1985, covering the size of New Jersey.

A report by the US government in 1999 said that fertilizer use was the biggest contributor of nitrogen and phosphorus into the Mississippi. 'The global nitrate problem is most apparent in the North Central region of the United States where 83 % of the nation's corn is produced and 53 % of the commercial nitrogen fertilizer is used,' said the report from the National Oceanic and Atmospheric Administration (Mitsch et al., 1998). The report found that the nutrient concentration was higher from cornbelt cropland, than from urban residential run-off or confined animal feeding operations.

Farmers tend to use nitrogen like an insurance policy: too little could affect yields, too much does not affect yield or quality, but increases costs. It also has environmental consequences, estimated to be up to 60 pounds of fertilizer an acre (Sawyer, 2007).[37] The deadzone, known as a hypoxia zone, is an annual phenomenon during the spring and summer. Another deadly factor is the excess run-off of phosphate, one of corn's three main nutrients. It drifts into the water mainly through sediment loss from the soil, which occurs after heavy rain or when the soil has been dug up at harvest time.

Richard Cruse, a professor in the Agronomy Department at Iowa State University, said the loss of sediment has been happening at a steady rate over the past 15 years, but that this is now changing. High corn prices mean that land that had been previously taken out of farming under the US Department of Agriculture's Conservation Reserve Program (CRP), is being lured back into production. The CRP was originally set up in 1985 to protect erodible land.

Cruse, who conducts research on soil and crop management and soil fertility, said that much of the CRP land is not great quality. This is why farmers readily took the money from the government to put the land into conservation. It is often sloping ground close to rivers and – with high rainfall in the region each year – prone to erosion, which increases the likelihood of further phosphate run-off. The cost for reducing farm run-off in Iowa was more than $600 million a year, according to economists at Iowa State University, or about half the amount of Federal farm payments the state received in 2006 (Brasher, 2007).

'Land ownership is important (for farm management practice), because if I own the land and want to hold onto it, to pass onto my children and their children, so it can be kept in the family for the next hundred years, then I am going to do something about it, whereas if I am in some short-term agreement with a neighbour or a friend, I might think differently about the way I deal with the land,' said Cruse, who has been monitoring water run-off and soil erosion losses from each township in Iowa. Cruse added that there are a significant number of hectares managed by land management companies, which get paid on gross return. The motive is to earn as much as you can, and there is no reason to add to the costs by investing in conservation measures. 'If we want to produce the quantities of ethanol and biomass to meet the targets that have been set by government, we simply cannot degrade our soil and resources, because our productivity is dependent upon a healthy soil and water ecosystem,' he said.

To underline the amount of nitrate in Iowa's rivers, the state has one of the world's largest nitrate removal facilities in the state capital Des Moines (Burkart and Jha, 2007). The city receives its drinking water from the Raccoon River, which drains some of Iowa's richest farmland and feeds the Des Moines River that joins the Mississippi. Kendall Lamkey, professor of agronomy at Iowa State University, said the effect on water quality and soil erosion from a change in farming practices needs addressing to ensure sustainable agriculture. 'Iowa has some of the richest soil in the world, we have a rain fed system, we have plenty of sunlight, the soil is Iowa's most valuable resource, it is a matter of how long we can sustain that,' he said. 'Every downfall of civilization has been due to failure to use land properly,' referring to the fact that much of modern agriculture started in the region known as the Fertile Crescent, which stretched from the eastern Mediterranean towards modern-day Iran. That land region today is either desert or semi-desert unsuited for agriculture, following centuries of clearing the land for agricultural expansion (Diamond, 1997).

Quality is not the only issue with water and corn; water quantity is also an issue. Corn-growing accounts for 19 % of US irrigated land, which, together with hay, soya beans, orchards and cotton make up more than half of irrigated land in the US. Nebraska, which borders Iowa's western side, grows about half of its corn crop through irrigation, with the water coming from the High Plains aquifer, known as the Ogallala aquifer, one of the largest freshwater aquifers in the world.

Nebraska is the third largest producer of corn after Iowa and Illinois, and the second largest ethanol producer behind Iowa. One of the reasons for Nebraska's high corn productivity is irrigation; the corn yields grown on irrigated land are double those on non-irrigated land (Farm and Ranch Irrigation Survey, 2003).[38] In 2007, Nebraska planted more acres than it had since 1936, which has increased its water consumption – but from a depleting water resource. The Ogallala aquifer is vital to US agriculture, supplying about 30 % of all the ground water used for irrigation in the US. Much of it is in semi-arid west-central United States, also known as the Plains region and covering the western parts of Nebraska, Kansas, upper Texas and Colorado. The expansion of corn and wheat since the 1950s has contributed to a decline in the water table – more than 30 metres in some areas (Gurdak, 2006).

The environmental impact on water is not just down to corn – the intensification of farming in general is a major factor. As urbanization spreads, food has to be produced from fewer resources and there is less farmland. Agricultural production is aided by government subsidies that distort the economics. In effect they subsidize the true cost of food production for consumers. Agriculture accounts for about three-quarters of water use in the US, but water charges do not reflect the cost of production and supply of water; that is, the funds invested in water infrastructure and maintaining water quality.

By encouraging ethanol production with tax breaks, which stimulate more corn production, the US Government is effectively subsidizing pollution of the Gulf of Mexico. (In order to grow the crop it needs more nitrogen, and this is found in high levels in the rivers near the cornbelt, that ultimately discharge into the Gulf.) Farmers are concerned about the environment, but right now they are enjoying their best income in a generation. This, too, has raised its own issues.

A New Era or Another Cycle?

High grain prices, the strong demand for dairy and meat and the burgeoning ethanol market have given farmers renewed confidence in a new era of prosperity. America's two million farmers are earning more than $70 billion a year, thanks to high commodity prices and generous government subsidies (most of which go to the already wealthy farmers), and this decade farmers have taken their biggest earnings ever.

Sundland explained to me that the increase in farmer income did not reflect the complete picture. 'Anyone that wanted to start in farming would have to find $1 million of cash to start an operation. It's very capital intensive and to find land to farm is hard; either it has been locked up in a family for generations or it is getting too expensive to rent,' he said. 'You've seen rents go up, land values double in the past five years, property selling for $9000 an acre, just Northwest of here that five years ago would have cost $3000,' he said. The biofuel boom and the growing demand for food have pushed up the price of farmland from Iowa to Argentina, with values rising faster than the price gains for apartments in Manhattan and London in 2006 (Wilson, 2007). The credit crisis in the US housing market has not affected the value of rural properties.

Higher corn and meat prices do not go entirely in to the farmer's pocket. 'Since the 1930s and 40s farmers have typically given back 80 % of their new found profits into what they are going to pay in rent and other costs,' Sundland said. The fortunes of arable farmers are tied to the price of crops, and these prices are one of the more volatile segments of the commodities market. Energy and metals are finite whereas corn, wheat and soya beans grow each year, their supply and demand contingent upon unpredictable events from the weather to the spread of diseases. Making predictions about agricultural conditions is based on shaky ground.

Forecasts are also based on sentiment, and in the cornbelt faith is high. Perhaps with good reason; the debt crisis that plagued farming communities in the 1980s is a distant memory, but a painful one for the hundreds of farmers who left the land because they could not meet the high mortgage repayments after interest rates rose above 15 % (as the then Federal Reserve chairman Paul Volcker tried to tame inflation.) It was the sub-prime debt crisis of its time. The debt crisis in rural America of the mid-1980s became a mainstream issue with Jane Fonda, Jessica Lange and Sissy Spacek starring in separate Hollywood films about it.[39] Willie Nelson, the country musician, organized Farm Aid to raise money for struggling farmers (Dudley, 2000). Farm debt is no longer an issue: the level of farm debt to the value of the farm is at historic lows, and the asset values of farm households are larger than the average household in urban America (Collins, 2007).

There are parallels between the start of the last farm crisis and the optimism of the late 2000s. The 1980s farm debt crisis followed the expansion of farms in the 1970s when farmers were told by Earl Butz, the US Secretary of Agriculture under both President Nixon and President Ford, 'Low prices are a thing of the past,' and 'Plant fencerow to fencerow' (Eagleton, 1978; Critser, 2004). Low prices came back to bite in the late 1970s, a time when costs were rising due to higher oil prices, this led to higher interest rates on loans taken out to finance the purchase of land based on the optimistic outlook.

A Rich Business

The very large, family-owned farms (those with 2000 acres or more) represent 4 % of America's 2.1 million farms and received 31.9 % ($7.75 billion) of the 2005 total payments, while small farmers (those with 100 acres or less), who represent 51.3 % of all farms, received 4.5 % of all payments, and more than half of this was for farmers, not farming, as it was payments for land in the conservation programmes.[40]

The USDA made no secret of the method of the payment system when it said, 'Generally, the size of the farm is directly correlated with the value of sales. Larger farms receive more payments and payments increase with the size of the farm.' The government payment system appears even more skewed to the rich farmers – it is essentially based on profitability (Hoppe and Korb, 2006). Nearly 90 % of all subsidies go to growers of just five crops: wheat, cotton, corn, soya beans and rice, and until 2007, no American fruit and vegetable growers could receive a payment. Dead farmers were eligible for government subsidies though: the government paid $1.1 billion in subsidies to 172 801 dead individuals between 1999 and 2005 (US Government Accountability Office, 2007b).

Farmers' income and net worth is higher than the average American household. The median income for a US farmer was $53 779, compared with $46 326 for the average American household, and a farmer's net worth was five times more than the average household (Covey *et al.*, 2005). Together with tax credits and other subsidies, American farmers are well looked after. So in fact are farmers in Europe and Japan: global agricultural subsidies total more than $200 billion a year worldwide, which equates to a sixth of the $1.2 trillion 'value added' agricultural sector (US Congressional Budget Office, 2005).

Nevertheless, agricultural subsidies are politically expedient. Each state has an agricultural industry, and American presidents often have a connection with the land. President Carter was a peanut farmer from Georgia, President Reagan liked to spend as much time as he could at his Californian Rancho del Cielo (Ranch in the Sky) and President George W. Bush strongly promotes himself as a Texan ranch owner, far from his east coast upbringing. Hillary Clinton has made money from trading in cattle futures (Babcock, 1994).[41]

The Golden Age?

It's a golden era for farming it seems at the moment. But while hailing the biofuel industry as good for farmers and good for business, politicians could rapidly change their tune if there is a persistent sharp increase in food prices. To satisfy the demand for both ethanol and food has involved an intense debate about the competition for land, deforestation, carbon emissions[42] and hunger. All issues are linked, but the rise in food prices in 2007 and 2008 cannot be put down entirely to biofuels. The floods and droughts that simultaneously occurred in different parts of the United States last year significantly affected wheat crops, and the production of the grain was also affected by droughts in Ukraine, Australia and India and by floods in the UK. The drought in Australia also caused a drop in milk production, which had a knock-on effect around the world, with a rise in dairy product prices. Floods in China affected great areas of farmland, causing food prices to rise. And a freeze in the sunshine state of California – the biggest fruit and vegetable grower in the US – wiped out large quantities of its fruit and vegetable harvests. The freeze impacted food prices across the US.

These price hikes were down to the weather, not biofuels. The rise in oil prices pushing up the cost of crop production, transportation and food processing didn't help either. The biofuels industry is partly implicated in the rising cost of food though; after all, the demand for biofuels is putting more and more pressure on land resources. Keith Collins, former chief economist of the USDA, has a chart of the wheat price going back to 1790. The direction of the line tells the story of a long-term decline in agricultural prices, productivity having managed, by and large, to outpace demand over the last 218 years. 'I am not going to fly in the face of history, but what I would say is that we are in a period where there are a number of factors working together . . . that suggest that we are moving towards higher market prices than we have seen in the past, which is digestible: we can pay a little more for our food,' Mr Collins said. US spending on food has halved to about 9 % of total income over the past 20 years, but in countries like Mexico, Indonesia and Pakistan, where food spending accounts for a greater slice of the family income, there have been protests over rising tortilla prices (Mexico), wheat shortages (Pakistan) and soya bean shortages (Indonesia) and food riots (Haiti).

Food supply and price is a sensitive and complex issue. There are almost as many people in the world that are classified obese as there are malnourished (about one billion each). The use of agriculture as a solution for energy security is not sustainable because the demand for food is ever increasing given the growing world population and rising affluence in developing countries, at a time when global water supplies are under stress due to changing climate conditions.

Farming is an industry that has long been neglected by government, and market conditions have not been in its favour for most of the 1980s and 1990s, so it's no surprise that farmers want more competition for their produce. But the pro-corn ethanol policy has knock-on environmental consequences which need to be monitored closely and addressed. International trade, self-sufficiency, food miles and animal welfare are issues that form part of government food policy (though they're beyond the ambit of this book) but also significantly affect the supply and demand of grains, oilseeds and livestock.

The prevalence of government subsidies for agriculture is another issue that ultimately impacts food prices and demand. They are unlikely to be removed despite the best efforts to move to a free-trade environment. A positive development of higher food prices is that they have focused world attention on agriculture. Just as high energy prices have stimulated energy-efficiency measures, the same is now happening with food. Surveys have found that up to a third of the food that is bought at supermarkets is thrown away because it has gone off: this produces methane, a greenhouse gas that contributes to global warming. Better monitoring of our food intake may lessen wastage as well as the waistline, which in turn may influence the supply and demand equations of agricultural markets.

Creating a biofuel industry has stimulated research into second generation biofuels that may provide some breakthroughs in the future and further diversify the world's sources of transport fuel. It may also result in the eventual closure of existing corn-based ethanol plants: not the first time this has happened in the farming sector.

I am reminded of farming cycles and the use of land for more than just food production when I visit the family farm in Ireland. Dotted around the hilly countryside of South Armagh and the North Louth border area, are many dilapidated stone buildings. They were flax mills; a relic of a major industry of the first half of the 20th century when many farms in the area, including my grandfather's, grew flaxseed. The linen industry in Northern Ireland declined after the second World War and flax was no longer grown in the area, as cheaper materials such as nylon and polyester replaced the demand for linen. Will today's ethanol plants be tomorrow's empty flax mills?

Notes

1. Lincoln was born in Kentucky; his family moved to Indiana before settling in Illinois. Lincoln also founded the United States Department of
   Agriculture (USDA). In Lincoln's day, 58 % of the 'people' were farmers.
   Today, 2% of the US population are farmers.
2. See the Ontario Corn Producers' Association website – http://www.
   ontariocorn.org/envt/envcanad.html.
3. Although the USSR was a bigger oil producer than the US in 1976,
   the amount in Russia was estimated to be smaller (Energy Information
   Administration, 2006).
4. Corn refiners' association website – www.corn.org.
5. An oxygenate is a liquid that contains oxygen, which helps gasoline
   reduce emissions from motor cars as its reduces sulphur in the gasoline.
6. In 2002, the USDA conducted a study to estimate the net energy value
   of ethanol and to identify the cause of variance among studies. The
   USDA's analysis determined that corn ethanol yields 34 % more energy
   than it takes to produce it – considering the entire fuel cycle of growing
   the corn, harvesting it, transporting it and distilling it into ethanol –
   when using the assumptions that the fertilizers used in growing the corn
   was produced by modern processing plants, the corn was converted in
   modern ethanol plants and farmers achieved average corn yields (US
   Government Accountability Office, 2007a).
       Moreover, ethanol is not a gallon-for-gallon replacement for gasoline
   because it contains only about two-thirds of the energy of a gallon of
   gasoline. While ethanol combusts more efficiently than gasoline, drivers
   nonetheless experience about a 25 % reduction in miles per gallon in
   vehicles using high blends such as E85. In addition, although DOE,
   the US Department of Agriculture (USDA) and most other researchers
   maintain that a gallon of corn ethanol contains more energy than it takes
   to produce a gallon of the fuel, a small number of researchers believe
   that corn ethanol has a negative energy balance, meaning that it takes
   more energy to produce than it contains.
7. The four components of Carter's National Energy Plan were: the Public
   Utilities and Regulatory Policies Act, the National Energy Conservation
   Policy Act, the Powerplant and Industrial Fuel Use Act and the Natural
   Gas Policy Act. For biomass energy, the Energy Tax Act introduced the
   excise tax exemptions for alcohol fuels, the business energy investment

tax credits, and the tax-exempt bond provisions to provide financing incentives (Lazzari, 1994).

8. President Carter suspended eight million tonnes of grain guaranteed under the terms of a 1975 bilateral agreement. A pact that was signed following the Soviet grain purchases of the early 1970s following poor harvests.

9. The 2007 US ethanol production estimate is based on the projection by the International Energy Agency's medium-term oil market report, July 2007.

10. Based on statistics from the Renewable Fuels Association – http://www. ethanolrfa.org/industry/statistics/ accessed on January 10, 2008.

11. Iowa statistics are taken from the Des Moines Register of Iowa biofuels database – http://data.desmoinesregister.com/ethanol2/index.php.

12. Global Ethanol is based in Brisbane and funded by Investec, a South African-based bank.

13. Iowa Renewable Fuel Association – http://www.iowarfa.org/PDF/Iowa_ RFS_Provisions_2ndVERSION.pdf.

14. Many of the soya bean plant's new uses were discovered by George Washington Carver, the mentor of hybrid corn pioneer Henry Wallace. Until he started studying the soya bean, the plant was mainly eaten straight by cattle.

15. American Soybean Association website – http://www.soygrowers.com/ soymeal/Default.htm

16. Nobody is credited with coining the phrase Livestock Revolution, but it is referred to in a paper written by Christopher L. Delgado, Mark W. Rosegrant, Henning Steinfeld, Simeon Ehui and Claude Courbois as a background paper for a conference run by the Commission on Sustainable Development between 24 April and 5 May 2000 in New York.

17. In a speech by Keith Collins, chief economist at the USDA, at the Agricultural Outlook Forum 2007, he said 'In high-income nations, consumers spend less than 10 cents of each additional dollar on food. In developing countries like Indonesia and Vietnam, each additional dollar of income increases food purchases by between 30 and 40 cents.' See full speech at http://www.usda.gov/oce/forum/2007%20Speeches/PDF%20speeches/ KCollins_doc.pdf.

18. The 2002 Economic Census undertaken by the US Census Bureau showed that the processing of corn for sweetener, thickening agents and food additives equated to 'added value' of $17.9 billion in the six

years to 2002. The earnings were mainly shared by a small number of food companies, Archer Daniels Midland, Cargill, Corn Products International and Tate & Lyle of the UK.

19. The link between obesity and HFCS was acknowledged by Philip Reeves at the Grand Forks Human Nutrition Research Center, which is part of the Agricultural Research Center – another arm of the USDA. Reeves wrote in a guideline on fructose consumption and health on October 23, 2006, that some health care professionals believe that the connection between high fructose consumption and obesity and type-2 diabetes involves the way fructose is broken down in the body. 'After fructose is absorbed into the body from the intestine, it is carried to the liver and made into smaller sugars that can readily form fats. Thus, the more fructose you consume the more is forced into fat. As the fat builds up in the blood, it begins to impair the actions of insulin, which normally signals the body to use glucose to produce energy. It is thought that such suppression over time makes the body resistant to insulin. As a result, glucose builds up in the blood, initiating type-2 diabetes.'

The cost of obesity is estimated to cost overweight or obese people 37 % more in annual health care costs than for people of normal weight, adding an average of $732 to the medical bill each year.

20. It is possible to generate 288 megajoules of electricity from one tonne of sugar cane. Of this amount, 188 MJ are needed to provide energy for the plant, leaving 100 MJ to be sold back to the grid. Burning the sugar cane waste has allowed Brazil to become energy self-sufficient in electricity (Hofstrand, 2007).

21. Renewable Fuels Association website – http://www.ethanolrfa.org/industry/statistics/#F.

22. The ethanol movement in Brazil, like the US, has a long history. The country created the Sugar and Alcohol Institute (Instituto do Açúcar e do Álcool) in 1933 to implement the sugar sector's industrial policy.

23. See the Ford Motor Company website – http://media.ford.com/newsroom/feature_display.cfm?release=18754.

24. Testimony of W. Bruce Crain, Executive Director of the Alternative Agricultural Research and Commercialization Corporation before the Committee on Agriculture, Nutrition, and Forestry. The United States Senate March 20, 1997.

25. Statement of Roger C. Viadero, office of the inspector general, US Department of Agriculture before the House Appropriation subcommittee

on Agriculture, Rural Development, Food and Drug Administration, and related agencies. February 17, 2000.

26. British Sugar website – http://www.britishsugar.co.uk/RVEe24abbb33b 93496a9b07a5dee9c82270,,.aspx

27. Wisconsin Historical Society website – http://www.wisconsinhistory. org/. Lincoln was an officer in the Black Hawk wars.

28. John Deere website – http://www.deere.com/en_US/compinfo/history/ johndeerestory.html.

29. The institutions were funded by the funds raised from the sale of public lands.

30. Gregor Mendel did pioneering work on the theories of heredity, he also became a priest. In his research he used simple pea pod plants. Mendel studied seven basic characteristics of the pea pod plants and discovered three basic laws which governed the passage of a trait from one member of a species to another member of the same species. The first law states that the sex cells of a plant may contain one of two different traits, but not both of those traits. The second law states that characteristics are inherited independently from one another (the basis for recessive and dominant gene composition). The third theory states that each inherited characteristic is determined by two hereditary factors (known more recently as genes), one from each parent, which decides whether a gene is dominant or recessive. In other words, if a seed gene is recessive, it will not show up within the plant, however the dominant trait will. Mendel's work and theories later became the basis for the study of modern genetics, and are still recognized and used today.

31. http://www.nal.usda.gov/outreach/carver2.pdf – National Agricultural Library. Carver was one of the first black botanists to be educated in the US; he was an orphan and overcame racial prejudice and helped improve farming practices in the south, including developing 400 products from the sweet potato and peanuts.

32. Wallace was the Secretary of Agriculture for seven years until he resigned, having been nominated for Vice President under Roosevelt for the 1940 election and served through most of the second World War as arguably the second most powerful man in the country. However, he was not renominated for the 1944 election, and served as Secretary of Commerce from March 1945 to September 1946 under Harry Truman following Roosevelt's death in April 1945. Wallace had higher political ambitions; he campaigned to become the US president in the 1948 election as the

candidate for the Progressive party, a political force that withered away. He advocated an end to segregation and full voting rights for blacks, which did not happen until two decades later, and universal government health insurance.

33. Iowa State University website – http://www.wallacechair.iastate.edu/ wallacechair/henry_bio.html.

34. International Treaty on Plant Genetic Resources for Food and Agriculture – http://www.fao.org/AG/cgrfa/itpgr.htm#text.

35. South Louisiana Business Council website – http://www.slec.org/ site75.php.

36. The estimated size of the dead-zone was 8543 square miles or 22 126 square kilometres (Ribaudo, 2003).

37. The amount of nitrogen fertilizer on corn following soya bean rotation is about 125 pounds an acre on average and can range between 105 to 145 pounds an acre; for continuous corn it is 175 pounds an acre, ranging between 155 and 195 an acre.

38. Some of the best corn yields are found in unlikely places in the United States, such as the arid regions of Arizona, and the highlands of the states of Washington and Colorado. Neither state is a significant grower, but they have counties with consistent water supply from the local aquifers via the irrigation systems. For instance, the average yield of corn in the state of Washington was 210 bushels an acre in 2006, but it only grew 75 000 acres of corn. In Colorado some counties produce 300 bushels.

39. Jessica Lange was nominated for an oscar for her role in *Country*, Jane Fonda appeared in *The Dollmaker* and Sissy Spacek was in *The River*.

40. USDA, Economic Research Service, Farm Income and Costs: Farms receiving government payments http://www.ers.usda.gov/Briefing/ FarmIncome/govtpaybyfarmtype.htm#specialization.

41. Hillary Clinton made about $100 000 in trading cattle futures on the Chicago Mercantile Exchange.

42. The EU unveiled its emissions strategy from 2013 to 2020 on January 23, 2008.

3

Climate

'When one tugs at a single thing in nature, he finds it attached to the rest of the world'

John Muir

Climate for Change

The traffic slows to a snail's pace along Jalan Pratama, and the restless Balinese motorbike riders weave their way through the crowded bending street. Children – in their pristine white shirts and blue uniforms – and women carrying fruit on their heads compete for the small space on the edge of the busy street. The air is thick with exhaust fumes. The cause of the congestion is a sea of taxis ferrying delegates, government officials and journalists in their thousands from hotels and the airport to attend a conference on how the world should lower greenhouse gas emissions.

About 15 000 people flew from all corners of the globe to the Indonesian island of Bali – which the tourism industry usually promotes as a tropical paradise – for the United Nations Framework

Convention on Climate Change (UNFCCC) in December 2007. Government representatives from 189 countries, Al Gore – the former US vice president turned businessman and environmental campaigner – and a myriad of industry lobbyists, environmentalists, lawyers, bankers, students, journalists and hundreds of television camera crews flood the spacious Bali convention centre for the two-week talkfest. The conference's wordy title is typical of the lexicon of titles, agreements and groupings that characterize the travelling circus of climate change talks.

The carbon footprint of the 2007 event was astronomical; 137 000 trees[1] would need to be planted to offset all the emissions that were generated – from the flights to Bali to the air conditioners to cool the sauna-like temperatures. Not to mention the thousands of laptops, mobile phones, cameras and battery chargers needed to photograph and record the event for television, radio, print and the internet – this is just some of the vast amount of electrical consumption that the event required. Photocopiers and printers also whirred day and night, drinking up electrical juice, to churn out the numerous agreements reached at the discussions – in the six official UN languages.

Despite the slow pace of the discussions (which generally resulted in an agreement by negotiators to meet again for more talks at another location)[2] given the timing of the conference (following more scientific evidence that human impact is responsible for climate change), there was high expectation that an agreement would be reached among the world's biggest polluters to lower greenhouse gases.[3]

It is not only government officials and environmentalists who are talking about climate change. The issue is at the forefront of people's minds. Hardly a day goes by without some reference to global warming in the news or weather report. Previously you would only worry about the weather when deciding what clothes to wear. In London, it is always advisable to take an umbrella to work, preferably one that can be stowed in a briefcase or shoulder bag, as there is always a high likelihood of a shower of rain. The concern now, however, is not so much about what the weather will be like today or tomorrow, but the long-term forecasts. We're more interested in rising sea levels, floods, the spread of the deserts, hurricanes and cyclones and the melting ice caps. This chapter will examine how market-based mechanisms are evolving to help address these worrying climate trends.

Ages of Weather

Long-term climate changes are nothing new. Thousands of years ago, all of modern day Canada and large swathes of the United States lay under ice. During medieval times, London enjoyed Mediterranean summer temperatures and viticulture was common.

Since the Romans first introduced the vine to Britain there have been various periods of viticultural renaissance, from King Alfred to the Normans[4] (French vintners are back in the UK as warming temperatures are making the British Isles more suitable for wine growing) but by the mid-16th century the River Thames in London was so frozen in winter that stalls were pitched on the ice, an event known as Frost Fairs, that the diarist John Evelyn recorded, 'Streetes of Boothes were set upon the Thames . . . all sorts of Trades and shops furnished, & full of Commodities . . . '.[5]

While some scientists have disputed these more recent climate change assertions, it is accepted that the planet has been warmer in the past few decades than at any time during the medieval period and is possibly the warmest it's been for 6000 or even 125 000 years.[6]

My personal experience of a modern-day 'Frost Fair' in London is rather less picturesque-sounding than in the days of yore. The main difference to the fairs of the 16th century is that there is no frost, no snow and no freezing of the Thames. But there is a winter theme with an ice sculpture and some husky dogs giving kids rides up and down the wet tarmac outside the Tate Modern. I tried explaining to my young daughter that the Thames had once frozen over. But she thought I was making it up, as she found it hard to believe London was ever that cold. Snow – common every winter in my childhood during the 1970s – has become a rarer event in England over the past two decades. My childhood winters may well have been the tail end of a mini-global cooling period, although the world was still warmer in the 1970s than it was 100 years previously.[7]

The debate around these long-term climate changes is whether we are accelerating the process through human activity – in particular the carbon emitted from power stations, cars, homes, farms and the cutting down of rainforests.

Emissions Daily

Each of us has a carbon footprint. We emit carbon whenever we switch on a light, turn the radio on for the morning news or boot up the computer to check our emails. Even having a cup of tea or a slice of toast releases emissions, because these daily acts use electrical power, which, in most parts of the world, is generated by burning coal and gas. We can minimize our individual carbon output by switching from conventional light bulbs to compact fluorescent light bulbs, turning off the tap when brushing teeth, cutting down on car trips, walking more or taking the bus or train, and by replacing plastic shopping bags with reusable ones.

The food we eat each day is also responsible for emissions; not just from the gas or electricity we use in cooking but from the production of food itself. Environmentalists are calling for people to eat less meat in order to save the planet. The world's increased livestock population is belching more methane and excreting more manure, accounting for a little over 5 % of global greenhouse emissions per annum. All of which is in the form of methane (Stern, 2006). This is more than triple the amount of emissions from air travel (which attracts far more attention) and is still more than the emissions generated by all plane, train and ship journeys taken each year.

So, are those innocent looking cows more dangerous to the environment than air travel? Cows spend most of their time munching grass or animal feed in a field. They smell too, but often it is associated with fresh country air. Planes, on the other hand, are noisy and leave a visible trail of pollution that is becoming bigger each year, cheap air travel and (European) city breaks being more popular than ever.

When I was a child flying was associated with the wealthy – it was expensive and out of the reach of many parents taking their families on holiday. Today, holidays with family or friends often involve a long car journey or flight to an overseas destination – these journeys emit tonnes of carbon. Air travel is one of the fastest growing areas of CO_2 emissions, and although not the biggest culprit, it has become one of the focal points of the global warming debate because it's highly visible: planes are noisy and pollution is very apparent near airports. Greenhouse gas emissions from air travel account for about 1.6 % of the world total each year (Stern, 2006), planes also emit water vapour that eventually forms heat-trapping clouds.

One of the reasons for the expense of air travel in the 1960s was that the industry was highly regulated, which discouraged competition. Deregulation has led to greater competition, lower prices and a huge increase in air travel as it became more affordable. The deregulation of industry in general (including banking, telecommunications, steel and transportation), which has taken place since the 1970s, combined with the removal of price controls, has contributed to the boost in trading volumes on equity and commodity markets (see more on commodities markets in Chapter 5). This has shifted the global economy from being highly regulated in the West and centrally planned in developing nations, to a global market-based economy. Prices are now determined by supply and demand rather than government controls. It's this free-market approach which is also increasingly being used to tackle global warming.

Green Giants

It seems that everyone is an environmentalist these days. Al Gore is now far more popular than the man that defeated him, President Bush. He may have lost the presidency but his film *An Inconvenient Truth* won him an Oscar and the Nobel Peace Prize for the awareness it generated about global warming. Arnold Schwarzenegger, the former Hollywood star turned senator of California, is also battling other politicians to become the green political warrior, and although he still owns gas-guzzling Hummers, he has been one of the more proactive US politicians addressing the issue. Hollywood, too, has started to recognize that climate change films sell. Leonardo DiCaprio, for example, recently starred in an environmental documentary *The 11th Hour* (though with film studios relying heavily on transportation and energy, it is an industry comparable with the more polluting ones such as petroleum refining) (Institute of the Environment, 2006).[8]

But environmental awareness is not a new thing, nor just a 'celebrity thing'. At the time of writing this book, a group of local people are protesting about the construction of a third runway at Heathrow Airport in London, one of the busiest in the world. A commendable idea, but will it be effective? Our world is now completely dependent on international movement, from goods and services to humans. Many people visit family and friends in different parts of the world, more people are taking long haul holidays too, so the movement of people around the globe is immense. Do people really embrace the concept of flying less? What is the alternative? Going by boat perhaps, but then more boats would be needed and ports would have to expand to cater for the extra traffic.[9] The solution lies in technology. The innovation that has taken place since the Industrial Revolution has transformed our lives beyond recognition. It is unlikely that in order to save the planet people are going to go back to some pre-Industrial Revolution society.

It's a Gas

The key to global warming, scientists have said, is the increase in carbon dioxide emissions, and the media-hyped predictions of global warming, including floods and droughts of biblical proportions, are often reminiscent of the prophecies of Malthus warning that uncontrolled population growth would lead to mass starvation (Malthus, 1798; Ehrlich, 1968).

The gases of most concern to scientists, politicians, environmentalists and businesses are carbon dioxide (CO_2), methane (CH_4), nitrous oxide (N_2O) and so-called F-gases such as perfluorocarbon and sulphur hexafluoride – both of the latter produced from agriculture and waste and industrial processes, including cement and chemical production. These gases are known as greenhouse gases (Stern, 2006).

Carbon dioxide is the main greenhouse gas, accounting for 77 % of global emissions. It comes from burning fossil fuels to generate power for industry, transport, and to heat and cool buildings. Methane accounts for 14 % of global emissions and comes from burning gas, those eructing cows and, to a lesser extent, from landfills and waste. Nitrous oxide makes up 8 % of emissions and largely comes from burning coal and from agricultural soils when crops are cut, which also produces CO_2.

Coal burnt at a power station to generate electricity emits twice the amount of carbon dioxide for each megawatt hour of electricity than natural gas does for the same amount of power produced.[10,11] However, this ratio is not so straightforward. James Lovelock warned in his book *The Revenge of Gaia* that it is not a simple equation that natural gas is half as polluting as coal (Lovelock, 2006); natural gas emits more methane than coal, and methane is a more potent greenhouse gas, although it does not remain in the air as long as carbon dioxide.

The release of CO_2 into the atmosphere is a concern because it traps an increasing amount of the sun's rays that rebound from Earth back into space, which in effect traps heat – hence the term global warming. It is also known as the greenhouse effect, as it functions just like the greenhouse in the garden. Most of the sun's rays are absorbed on the ground and provide the heat for growing vegetation, enabling Earth to be the only known planet in the solar system to support life.

All greenhouse gases are converted to carbon dioxide so that there is a common measurement for all gases. Scientists forecast that greenhouse gases will have doubled from pre-industrial levels between 2030 and 2060. A rise of this amount is very likely to mean an increase of between 2 and 5 degrees in global temperatures. This might not sound a lot – a movement of this magnitude occurs each day – but it is a big concern. 'A warming of 5 degrees centigrade on a global scale would be far outside the experience of human civilization and comparable to the difference between temperatures during the last ice age and today,' said the Stern Review in 2006, which was commissioned by the UK government.[12]

The amount of CO_2 being trapped in the atmosphere is measured in parts per million (ppm). The United Nations body set up to monitor global warming, the International Panel for Climate Change (IPCC), released its latest assessment of climate change in 2007 and warned that, 'Warming of the climate system is unequivocal, as is now evident from observations of increases in global average air and ocean temperatures, widespread melting of snow and ice, and rising global average sea level.'[13]

The Stern Review also relied on IPCC data, repeating their forecast that: 'The warming effect due to all greenhouse gases emitted by human activities is now equivalent to around 430 ppm of carbon dioxide or CO_2 and rising at around 2.3 ppm per year. Current levels of greenhouse gases are higher than at any time in at least the past 650 000 years.' The report warned ominously that if we did nothing and continued to pollute at the same rate, the 'world would experience major climate change.'

Weathering the Change

If the tipping point is 2030, then we don't have much time left to deal with the issue. During the time I have researched and written this book there have been some very significant weather events. I was in the United States in the summer of 2007 when there were major floods in Texas and Oklahoma, while in the adjoining state of Arkansas there was a drought. Missouri, Tennessee, Mississippi, Georgia, Alabama and South Carolina also experienced 100 degrees on the thermometer.

The lack of rain has put pressure on the regions' water supply. It was the driest summer in the southeast since records began in 1895, making it the sixth warmest US summer on record (National Oceanic and Atmospheric Administration, 2007).[14] In contrast, Texas had its wettest summer.

I was also in London when England and Wales had their wettest May–July period in more than 200 years. The rain lashed down outside as I typed away, while news footage showed scenes of flooded towns and people knee-deep in water wading through their damaged homes. Europe was also split by extremes in weather; floods in Germany and Poland contrasting with the heat wave in southern Europe where Italy and Portugal sweated and Greece fought off savage forest fires. This pattern of summer weather differs from the last big European heat wave in 2003 when hundreds of people died from heatstroke, and the soaring temperatures were felt as far north as Scotland, and east to Poland. Both the 2003 and 2007 weather events were explained as global warming, even though they had entirely different patterns. Little wonder people are confused.

When I flew from New Delhi to Coimbatore in the state of Tamil Nadu in southern India, to research this book, all I could see below from the plane was very dry land with pockets of green vegetation. Admittedly it was before the Indian monsoon season.[15] My subsequent trip to Australia coincided with torrential rain and lightning – a break in one of the worst droughts since European settlement more than 200 years ago. Only a week before, then Prime Minister John Howard had prayed for rain – he couldn't really do much else. Howard was a sceptic of climate change for most of his 11 years as head of Australia, a country that emits more greenhouse gases per person than any other developed country. Their drought in 2007 has, however, been attributed to climate change.[16]

Returning to England's floods after my somewhat sodden trips to Sydney and to the US cornbelt, I felt a bit like a rain god, bringing wet weather to wherever I travelled. After my visit to Asia, the floods in India and in Bangladesh during the June to September monsoon were described as the worst in decades. More than one million people were affected by floods in the Sahel region of Africa too, including Sudan, which had been ravaged by drought. Snow fell in Buenos Aires for the first time in a century and parts of South Africa had snow for the first time in decades.

The turning point for the US and climate change was probably the devastating hurricanes of 2005. Katrina wreaked havoc on New Orleans and, not four weeks later, Hurricane Rita trashed parts of the Louisiana and Texas coastline, causing yet more death and destruction and bringing home to millions of Americans the power of Mother Nature. In the two years since 2005, there have been hurricanes – causing much damage in the Caribbean and Central America – but not on the scale of Katrina or Rita, confounding expectations of strong and frequent hurricanes at the beginning of the 2006 and 2007 Atlantic season. This doesn't, however, imply that Katrina was a one-off. Hurricanes are indeed becoming more frequent in North America; in the late 1990s, the US endured more than twice the number experienced annually during the 20th century (Flannery, 2005).

Costing the Earth

The hundreds of scientists who participate in the IPCC have released four major assessments of climate change since 1988, each report more grave than the last. Despite the threat, Stern, a former World Bank chief economist, was hopeful that the world could tackle the problem of global warming. He quantified it in economic terms – the first major document on the subject – and concluded that it would 'not cost the Earth', so to speak. The economic conclusion was that if the world does not act, then the economic impact will be the equivalent of losing 20 % of gross domestic product (GDP) – the measurement of the economy – if the wider risks of global warming are taken into account. By taking action early it will cost only 1 % (Stern, 2006).

Consumers are already paying for climate change through higher insurance premiums. Extreme weather events have caused more damage than expected to insured property, which in turn has led to higher payouts by the insurers (who in turn recoup the costs from increasing premiums to their customers). This goes for all types of insurance, including property, motor and health. The estimated insurance loss from Hurricane Katrina was $60 billion.[17]

Insurers have, in effect, taken the lead among the business community in raising awareness of global warming. Limiting CO_2 emissions will force the world to be more economical with its resources and invest in technology which will clean fossil fuels or harness more efficient natural resources such as the wind and the sun. In the 1970s the surge in oil prices after the Arab oil embargo spurred innovations for more efficient use of oil. Once again the world is conducting more research on efficiencies in the use of all fossil fuels.

Car makers are designing vehicles that use less petrol per mile. Energy efficiency is paramount in the construction of new buildings in parts of Europe, and power stations and fossil fuel producers are looking at deploying technology that will restrict the emissions of carbon dioxide, known as carbon sequestration. This is an additional cost for power stations – they have never had to pay for polluting the air before – which has added to the cost of generating electricity, meaning higher power bills for consumers.

Pricing the Environment

The negative impacts of climate change are costly but so is the funding of preventative measures, far in excess of any government budget. This is why people look to financial markets to help address climate change. The simplest way to create financial incentives for private investment in cleaner energy technologies is to put a price on carbon, the main pollutant. Like any other commodity, price determines behaviour. If a price is high, fewer people will pollute. In effect, a carbon price puts a price on clean air. It is global and is more effective than a carbon tax, which requires each country to introduce its own tax – a more complicated and convoluted procedure.

Some who are concerned about the environment find the concept of a price on air difficult to digest. In 1990, British comedian Ben Elton wrote a play called *Gasping* about the discovery of 'designer air' where oxygen is extracted from air, compressed, stored and sold, leading to its privatization. In the play, the rich countries buy Africa's share, starving the world's poorest continent of its air. I remember seeing it when it first came out and, although it was a parody of excessive market capitalism, I thought that the idea of a market value on air was an exaggerated theme. Today I can see its important role in tackling CO_2 emissions.

Herman Daly, former senior economist at the World Bank, said the environment is increasingly being made a commodity, priced to reflect the cost of economic activity. 'The economy is the subsystem of a biosphere. The economy used to be very small, as it (the planet) was relatively empty of people and their stuff, but it was full of other (natural) things. As there are more and more people, they have taken over more of the planet, so while they have grown in numbers, the biosphere hasn't,' said Daly, adding that the increase in population has put more strain on the natural world.

'The commodification business is necessary and good, but it is misleading if it is described as free-market environmentalism,' said Daly, former Professor at the University of Maryland, School of Public Affairs, who has spent the past 30 years advocating sustainable development. Daly, co-founder and associate editor of the journal *Ecological Economics*, said that pollution has to be included as an economic production cost. Pollution is part of the metabolism of the economy. Production starts with the depletion of resources and ends with pollution.

'In order to put an economic value on the environment, it has to become a commodity through government legislation, by creating property rights that entitle the holder to ownership of the underlying asset and permits allowing the right to pollute,' said Daly. Peruvian economist Hernando De Soto writes in his book *The Mystery of Capital* that the use of documents to prove ownership is one of the main conditions for the success of capitalism in the West. In developed nations, writes De Soto, every parcel of land, every building, every piece of equipment or store of inventories is represented by a property document. These documents reflect an asset that can then be turned into collateral for credit and are the foundation for creating securities such as equities or mortgage-backed bonds that can be sold in secondary markets, which in turn generates capital (De Soto, 2000).

Professor Ian Swingland, founder of The Durrell Institute for Conservation and Ecology at the University of Kent, said property rights are key to the conservation of the ecology. Swingland, who is also a founder of Sustainable Forestry Management, said the transformation in Russia from a communist era to a market-based economy is an example of how ownership can make a difference to behaviour. 'A visit to a Russian hotel 20 years ago would have found an old woman sitting in each corridor doing nothing in a hotel that was falling apart. Now those same hotels are smart, the food is fantastic, the bedding is fresh and clean, the lifts will work and the staff will be friendly and courteous. The difference? If you own it, you look after it and take care of it ... the problem for many on Earth is that they don't have rights, so they can't earn any money from those rights, and they remain poor.' Having visited Moscow in 1989 in the era of Perestroika, I can concur with Swingland's view of Soviet-style hotels.

Tradable carbon permits allow the emission of a defined amount of CO_2. Other environmental rights and entitlements, such as water rights for example, permit the holder to use a specified volume of water, and fishing permits allow the owner to take a specified quantity of fish from the ocean. These permits become the commodity – they are limited in number and therefore their relative scarcity adds value. Now that they are commodities, they are assets which have monetary value. They can be bought and sold under a robust legal system.

Reliance on government legislation or voluntary agreements distinguishes environment markets from other commodity markets like oil, gold or copper – all tangible materials that experienced the evolution of their respective markets through their physical trade. Carbon, on the other hand, is not tangible; nobody knows what a tonne of carbon looks like, and it cannot be traded physically. However, the trade of CO_2 in the futures and the over the counter (OTC) markets is no different to trading oil, copper or corn; they are based on contracts that detail a specified quantity of the underlying commodity.

There are differences, but also important parallels between environmental markets and physical commodities. The carbon market is evolving like the oil market, in that there are a number of regional markets that are interchangeable; the carbon market in Europe and the voluntary carbon market in the US. In the case of oil it is the Brent in Europe and the West Texas Intermediate in the United States, and also the local oil markets for Dubai in the Persian Gulf and Tapis for the Asia Pacific. Each has its own rules and contracts, but all reflect the relative price of oil.

Market-driven solutions are not universally welcomed. Environmentalists blame industry for the world's environmental ills. They view the market as a 'licence to pollute' – another way for city traders to make money rather than addressing the source of emissions, which they say is unsustainable economic activity. At the same time many environmentalists have come to accept the market-based approach as a mechanism to address climate change.

In the Markets for Clean Air

The philosophy of cap-and-trade systems for dealing with environmental issues is not a result of unrestrained market capitalism, but rather the refinement of an academic debate which has lasted almost 50 years. It can be traced back to an article in 1960, 'The Problem of Social Cost' by Ronald Coase. The British-born economist (and Nobel Prize winner for economics in 1991), suggests that well-defined property rights could control 'externalities.'[18] (Latterly this has been taken to mean the effects of economic activity on the environment.) Coase refutes the work of Arthur Cecil Pigou, who, in 1920, recommended corrective taxes to discourage activities that generate 'externalities' (Hahn and Stavins, 1992)

Coase's work was followed by more research when Thomas Crocker in 1966 and John Dales in 1968 each wrote papers about the prospect of using transferable permits to allocate the pollution-control burden between emitters. David Montgomery concluded in his 1972 paper 'Markets in Licenses and Efficient Pollution Control Programs' that tradable polluting permits would provide a cost-effective policy for pollution control. It wasn't long before the first environmental markets were launched.

The first cap-and-trade system was established by the US Environmental Protection Agency (the federal body set up to oversee the protection of the environment and human health) in 1974 with the Emissions Trading Program for local air pollutants, as part of the Clean Air Act Amendments. States were not required to use the system, and uncertainties about its future made companies reluctant to participate. Even so, substantial savings were achieved over the life of the programme.[19] Undeterred the EPA launched another cap-and-trade system in 1982, when it authorized inter-refinery trading of lead credits.[20] The purpose of the scheme was to allow gasoline refiners greater flexibility to meet emission standards at a time when the lead content of fuel was reduced.

In 1990, legislation to allow permits to emit sulphur dioxide (SO_2) and nitrous oxide (NO_x) was enacted through the US Acid Rain Program (ARP) as part of the Clean Air Act Amendments (Stavins, 1998).[21] This paved the way for the futures market in environment markets for the first time.

The EPA selected the Chicago Board of Trade (CBOT) to administer the auctions of SO_2 and NO_x permits to reduce pollution emitted by US power stations in the Midwest, which caused damaging acid rain in the north and in Canada (Napolitano et al., 2007). The spiralling cost of pollution was one factor prompting the US government to seek market-based solutions. By 1990, US pollution control costs had reached $125 billion annually, or 300 % above the 1972 levels in real terms (US Environmental Protection Agency, 1990; Jaffe et al., 1995). The sulphur dioxide and nitrogen oxide markets were seen as a success. Not only had SO_2 and NO_x prices fallen, but also, more importantly, the amount of sulphur dioxide released into the atmosphere had shrunk. By the end of 2006, annual sulphur dioxide levels had fallen by more than 40 % and nitrogen oxide emissions by almost 50 % (Napolitano et al., 2007). Much of the decline was credited to the market mechanism.

As SO_2 and NO_X emissions declined, so did the associated environmental problems, leading to cleaner waters in streams and lakes.[22] There were health benefits too, which far outweighed the cost of the electric utilities complying with the new regulation. 'The annual ecological and health benefits resulting from the ARP emission reductions are estimated at $142 billion by 2010 compared with annual compliance costs of $3.5 billion. The majority of these benefits come from the expected avoidance of nearly 19 000 premature deaths' (Napolitano *et al.*, 2007).

This was also the first time that an environment related futures contract had been traded on an exchange; traders could now buy and sell SO_2 and NO_X futures alongside pork bellies, corn and ten-year US government bonds. The ARP led to the launch of more cap-and-trade systems devised by the EPA,[23] including endangered species and water quality. They became a template for today's carbon dioxide markets around the world. The biggest test bed for trading CO_2 emissions is Europe, but it was not the first. The UK had a voluntary emissions market before the EU scheme started in 2005[24] and a voluntary market has existed in the United States since 2003.

All legislation for CO_2 markets can trace its origin to the Kyoto Protocol (an intergovernmental agreement to a market solution to climate change and a commitment to reducing greenhouse gases). Under the protocol, the legal framework for an emissions market is created through the conversion of emission targets into allowances, which can be traded among signatory countries.

The market approach sits alongside technology and energy efficiency as the protocol's key mechanisms for reducing emissions. The Kyoto Protocol agreement, drawn up in 1997 – under the auspice of the UNFCCC, pledged to cut emissions of greenhouse gases by an average of 5.2 % from 1990 levels.[25] However, the level of cuts was not uniform for all signatories to the pact. Some eastern European countries, where emissions were already well below 1990s levels, were not required to cut their CO_2 emissions at all.

The IEA – the energy research and advisory group for developed countries – estimated in 2005 that Eastern Europe and other 'economies in transition' (from command control economies of the Soviet era) were in a position to sell their pollution credits. This meant that the industrialized countries that were signatories to the Kyoto Protocol could essentially buy back the levels they required (International Energy Agency, 2005).[26] They would not have to physically cut emissions if they bought the excess permits from the former eastern bloc. This rendered the pact meaningless in terms of actually reducing emissions, but it has succeeded in focusing attention on a very important issue.

The slow rate at which the world is addressing emissions reduction is frustrating given that it is 20 years since the first major study of the impact of climate change (Flannery, 2005). In terms of cutting emissions, this target was pretty soft and its implementation painstaking. The agreement didn't come into force until Russia ratified the pact in February 2005, some 13 years after the first multigovernment commitment to address climate change.[27]

At the Earth Summit in Rio de Janeiro in 1992, 155 nations agreed to reduce emissions to 1990 levels by the year 2000. The fact that target was missed did not set a healthy precedent for government cooperation. Pat Coady, the US representative to the World Bank at the Rio Summit, said there was a lot of expectation, but there was so much detail to discuss that it is no surprise that a final protocol agreement took so long to conclude. Coady, who has a long career in investment banking and is co-founder of Coady Diemar Partners, was appointed US director to the World Bank by the first Bush government in 1989. At this time the US was under pressure to withhold its funding of the World Bank until environmental reforms were in place.

One multigovernment agreement made during Coady's tenure was the creation of the bank's green financing arm, the Global Environment Facility, GEF, which has helped raise $20 billion towards projects with environmental benefits.[28] 'It was the brainchild of the French, German and British who were keen to head off the creation of a new environment institution as they saw that it would be another bureaucracy,' said Coady, whose interest in the environment stems from his love of large open spaces, where he goes fishing and hiking.

He has founded a non-profit land trust to preserve nature in a pocket of land in northern Virginia.

The 2007 Bali meeting was the latest in talks, conferences, agreements, promises and treaties that have been negotiated and debated by government ministers, delegates and advisors around the world for the past 20 years. None of these discussions has resulted in any meaningful cuts to the rate of greenhouse gas emissions. Bali was the start of a new two-year period of discussion that aims, by the end of 2009, to formulate a successor to the Kyoto Protocol, which expires in 2012. Indications are that the next agreement will have more market-based mechanisms, and that existing emissions trading schemes will have been modified following some early mistakes. The first phase of the EU emissions trading scheme resulted in too many permits being issued to the polluters. And, even though the large European power utilities did not have to pay for them, they charged customers for the value of the carbon. In total, European utilities received permits worth more than € 40 billion at their market peak. They were virtually worthless following the first audit of emissions in April 2006 when it was discovered that there was an overallocation of permits. The aim of reducing emissions was made a mockery of because it was cheaper for utilities to burn coal than gas. While Britain imported a record amount of coal, former Prime Minister, Tony Blair, was talking up the need for the world to reduce emissions. It inevitably led to the charge that Kyoto was more about hot air than clean air. The EU episode was put down to experience. The European Union has promised it will get tougher and intends to auction two-thirds of pollution permits in the post-2012 scheme.

Towards a Mandatory US Emissions Market

Although the US is the only developed country that has not signed the Kyoto Protocol (nor does it have a national mandatory carbon trading market), it is widely accepted that the biggest polluter in the developed world will have a national carbon market after President Bush leaves office in January 2009.

Democrat candidates have been even more vocal about a mandatory scheme in the lead up to the 2008 election. On her presidential campaign website, Hillary Clinton said that she will 'Lead the charge to stop global warming by investing in clean energy technologies, establishing a national market-based program to reduce global warming pollution.' Barack Obama said he will 'Implement an economy-wide cap-and-trade program to reduce greenhouse gas emissions to the level recommended by top scientists to avoid calamitous impacts.'[29]

Although Al Gore was a key player in the initial discussions on the Kyoto Protocol, the United States did not sign up to the pact under his watch, and President George W. Bush refuted it soon after his election; although that said, many US states and local governments have made Kyoto-friendly commitments. California and its neighbouring states have signed up to the Western Regional Climate Initiative (WCI) with the goal of cutting emissions to 15 % below 2005 levels by 2020.[30] On the other side of the country, ten states[31] have formed the Regional Greenhouse Gas Initiative (RGGI), agreeing to cap CO_2 emissions from power plants. Ten states from the Midwest, including Canada's Manitoba, signed the Midwestern Regional Greenhouse Gas Reduction Accord in November 2007.[32]

More states and city councils outside of these regional accords are evaluating caps on greenhouse emissions. The city of Chicago – a member of the Chicago Climate Exchange – has asked its residents to take an environmental pledge, and New York City aims to cut its greenhouse emissions by 30 % by 2030.[33] Collectively, these initiatives are the building blocks to a national scheme.

While the Bush government negotiators were antagonistic in their discussions with other governments in Bali, the Democrat-controlled US Senate voted in favour of legislation that paves the way for a national cap-and-trade emissions scheme in the US with the goal to cut greenhouse gas emissions by 2050.[34] 'We have 39 states that have signed up to measuring their carbon emissions, which is the first step towards regulating carbon emission, 27 of the 39 have developed comprehensive climate action plans that would be in line with the Kyoto convention. Five have already put that into law and another 15 are going to do so in 2008, and 25 of the 27 have signed for regional greenhouse gas emissions,' said Terry Tamminen, an energy and environmental adviser to Arnold Schwarzenegger.[35] 'The US will put a price on carbon. There are 39 states out of 50 that are on their way to some form of carbon trading scheme. That is a strong mandate for any president.' I spoke to Tamminen in Los Angeles just weeks after California, along with its fellow WCI members and other regional and national carbon trading schemes, formed the International Carbon Action Partnership (ICAP) with the aim to create a global carbon market.

A mandatory US carbon market together with the emergence of other carbon markets around the world, including New Zealand in 2008, Australia in 2010 and possibly Canada and China in the foreseeable future,[36, 37] has led to predictions that carbon could become the biggest commodity market of all.

Voluntary Schemes

As mentioned, there are now voluntary carbon offset schemes, where conscientious consumers buy carbon credits. Funds are then invested in forestry schemes, which mean planting more trees or looking after existing ones. But voluntary schemes are not regulated and they can be opaque.

Consumers who want a carbon neutral lifestyle can install solar panels, put a wind turbine on the roof, sell the car and wear more clothes around the house in winter – or they can purchase carbon credits via carbon brokers such as The CarbonNeutral Company, Climate Care and co2balance.com to offset their carbon footprint. Despite some confusion in how these different schemes calculate emissions (a flight from London to Sydney, for example, can cost between £14.25 and £36 to offset), Britons spent £60 million offsetting their CO_2 emissions in 2006 and this is expected to rise to £250 million by 2009, according to the Department for the Environment, Food and Rural Affairs (Copping, 2007).

Even religious leaders want to be carbon neutral. The Vatican has created the Vatican Climate Forest in Hungary's Bükk National Park, where thousands of hectares of trees will be planted to offset the Vatican's energy usage (KlimaFa Ltd, 2007). "The Book of Genesis tells us of a beginning in which God placed man as guardian over the Earth to make it fruitful. When man forgets that he is a faithful servant of this Earth, it becomes a desert that threatens the survival of all creation," Cardinal Paul Poupard said at the time of the Vatican's announcement.

It still remains to be seen whether all of these schemes will survive as they are not independently audited and it is difficult to verify how much money from selling carbon offset credits actually goes to the designated project. They might be more effective as a way for people to buy a clean green conscience than a sustainable way to reduce greenhouse gas emissions. With any new market there is an initial proliferation of competitors before rationalization creeps in. Even the most well-intended schemes have not had uniform success. The British rock group Coldplay vowed to offset emissions from the production of their 2002 album *A Rush of Blood to the Head*. They paid for 10 000 mango trees to be planted in India. Since then 4 000 of the trees have died (Pearce, 2007).

The New Carbon Economy

An industry that hardly existed a decade ago – the new carbon economy – is now firmly established with consultants, carbon offsetters and specialist publications. It is as if those dot com companies that set up in trendy offices in the 1990s have metamorphosed into carbon consultants. Since few people went to university to study carbon emissions or global warming, they have come from all walks of life and backgrounds. There is also a proliferation of online companies selling carbon, neutral products, from offsetting to eco-kettles.

A leading figure in the establishment of a market in pollution is Richard Sandor, who was an economics professor before joining the

CBOT. In 2000 he founded the Chicago Climate Exchange, the voluntary US emissions market where some of America's largest companies have agreed to cut their emissions. It's a good example of business acting before government. Sandor's Chicago exchange is owned by the London-based Climate Exchange Plc, in which Goldman Sachs owns a stake. Sandor is the chairman of Climate Exchange, which also owns the European Climate Exchange – Europe's largest carbon futures market where emissions contracts reflect the physical price of the pollution permits regulated by the EU. The Chicago market also accepts forestry credits, whereas the European market does not.

Sandor has a pedigree in introducing new markets. He spearheaded the introduction of futures contracts on Government National Mortgage Association (Ginnie Mae) certificates (Sandor, 2004), and the 30-year Treasury bonds when he was the chief economist at the CBOT, which until then was an agriculture exchange.

Sandor is one of many advocates for market-based environmentalism. He has preached his ideas to colleagues, among them Eric Bettelheim, a corporate lawyer specializing in derivatives law. Bettelheim's transition from lawyer to market environmentalist stemmed from his involvement in the UK Countryside Alliance (which campaigned against the UK government's ban on foxhunting), where he struck up a friendship with Robin Hanbury-Tension, the explorer and conservationist. One of Hanbury-Tension's first major studies was on the people of Mulu in Sarawak, the Malaysian part of Borneo. The study was conducted with Professor Ian Swingland, a zoologist and renowned for his work as a herpetologist (among other things, he was the first to discover that the gender of reptiles and turtles depends on heat and drought conditions).

The turning point for Swingland came after a visit to the Mulu forest, where he discovered that loggers had encroached the area where the Borneo tribes live. Swingland thought there had to be some way to establish a financial incentive to maintain the rainforest because of the pivotal role it plays in the world's ecosystem.

Swingland and Hanbury-Tension talked to Bettelheim about their experience in Mulu, and the Chicago-born lawyer turned to his fellow

American, Sandor, to devise forestry carbon credits under the Kyoto Protocol. The discussions led to the launch of Sustainable Forestry Management, which includes Guy Weston – the biggest shareholder in Associated British Foods, one of Europe's largest food producers.

The importance of forests was emphasized by the Stern Review, which highlighted the need to have robust property laws: 'At a national level, establishing and enforcing clear property rights to forestland, and determining the rights and responsibilities of landowners, communities and loggers, is key to effective forest management' (Stern, 2006).

The Lungs of the Earth

The demands for carbon offsetting have heightened the need to preserve forests for their valuable role in stabilizing the climate. Prince Charles has called for the forests of the world – the lungs of the planet – to be priced for their value as a carbon sink. 'The world's forests need to be seen for what they are – giant global utilities, providing essential services to humanity on a vast scale' (HRH The Prince of Wales, 2007). 'Rainforests store carbon, which is lost to the atmosphere when they burn, increasing global warming. The life they support cleans the atmosphere of pollutants and feeds it with moisture. They help regulate our climate and sustain the lives of some of the poorest people on this Earth,' said the future monarch.

Support for a monetary value on forests has been endorsed by the World Bank, the IPCC, the Stern Review and the Pope. The World Bank said in its 2007 report *At Loggerheads*? 'Global carbon finance offers an ungrasped opportunity for mitigating climate change, supporting sustainable land use, and conserving forests. About a fifth of global CO_2 emissions come from tropical deforestation – and the costs of abating some of these emissions appear low (World Bank, 2007).

A tree that dies, is burned or chopped down, on the other hand, releases CO_2 into the atmosphere. A vast number of trees are cut down each year, primarily for expanding agricultural demands from livestock and grain production (Stern, 2006). Deforestation is driven by both wealth and poverty: poor farmers need more land to feed their families; and increasing global wealth demands that commodities are produced at the forest edge. Poor people need fuel wood, and a wealthier world demands more wood and pulp for furniture and for paper that is only partly met by plantations.

The UN Food and Agriculture Organization predicts that the growth in demand for agricultural land will slow, but it still expects croplands in the developing world to expand by a net 3.8 million hectares a year over the next three decades (Bruinsma, 2003). Global Forest Resources Assessment 2005 suggests that forest now covers less than four billion hectares, or 30 % of total land surface, compared with 50 % 8 000 years ago. It is estimated that two-thirds of the global forest area is located in just ten countries.[39] Of which five countries, Russia, Brazil, Canada, the United States and China, account for more than half of total forest area.[40] Russia alone accounts for 20 % of the world total.

This area continuously decreases, although at a slowing pace. The net loss in forest area is estimated at 7.3 million hectares, an area about the size of Sierra Leone or Panama, per year over the 2000 to 2005 period, compared with 8.9 million hectares between 1990 and 2000.[41]

Tree Hugging

The focus on forests as a carbon sink comes at a time when there are more specialist investment companies owning forests for both timber production and carbon credits. In addition, timber companies are signing up to sustainable forestry development programmes to ensure that there is not an overexploitation of forests (although this is still a small number: only 7 % of forests are under sustainable management programmes and only 3 % are under certified management).

Bettelheim and Swingland's company Sustainable Forestry Management owns and leases forest area in Africa, Brazil, Australia and the United States. New Forests has forestry assets in Australia,

New Zealand and the US to earn carbon credits. The Swiss-based Precious Woods owns and manages forests in Latin America and Gabon in Africa. Then there are timber plantation investors looking to earn carbon credits on top of their timber business, such as The Lyme Timber Company in the US and Four Winds Capital Management, which raised $500 million through its Phaunos Timber Fund in 2007. 'The only thing that has changed with the timber business today is that you can get certification of the carbon that has been sequestered and sell it and in no way has it changed the timber business,' said Kimberly Tara, Chief Executive of Four Winds. Four Winds has a venture in New Zealand (scheduled to start in 2008) to grow forests on former farmland whereby the carbon sequestered by the new trees will be certified and sold into the carbon market in New Zealand (Parker, 2007).

Forest Economics

In its Fourth Assessment Report the IPCC estimated that reducing emissions from deforestation by 50 % could save 1.6 billion tonnes of CO_2 annually at less than $20 a tonne of CO_2 equivalent, or about $10 to $15 billion per year. Far cheaper than the amount needed to develop carbon storage technology (CCS) (Stern, 2006).[42]

If a carbon price is put on forests then the farmer, logger and forest dweller have a choice. This could slow down the rate of deforestation and the expansion of agricultural land, which in turn could have a knock-on effect for global food production. In the developing world, trees are often cut down for ephemeral gains, creating croplands and pastures worth a few hundred dollars a hectare; less than their potential carbon value.

Based on the EU carbon market prices in February 2008, the value of CO_2 abatement is $20 a tonne, and each hectare of forest is able to absorb between 500 tonnes of CO_2 and 1000 tonnes per hectare. This means that farmers are destroying a $10 000 to $20 000 asset to create one worth $200.

The exact income derived from forestry carbon offsets versus farming or logging depends on land use and location. The Stern Review estimated that the income ranges from $2 per hectare for pastoral use to more than $1000 for soya and palm oil plantations, with one-off returns of $236 to $1035 for selling hardwood – far less than the potential income from forestry carbon offsets. The price of forest carbon needs to be well above the alternative income from agriculture or the timber industry to preserve forests and slow down the rate of deforestation, which in turn would have a knock-on effect for food prices.

Putting a value on forestry has helped reverse deforestation in Costa Rica, where landowners can receive up to $45 a hectare per year if they volunteer to maintain forests in the interests of carbon sequestration, biodiversity and tourism – a big foreign currency earner for Costa Rica. This measure has helped increase forest cover in the Central American country from 21 % of the land mass in 1977 to 51 % in 2005 (Stern, 2006). China, too, is offering farmers incentives and legal tenure to encourage forest growth, although this has little to do with carbon offsetting; it is driven by other environmental concerns such as soil erosion and flooding. China has added 7 million hectares of forests, a rate equal to nearly half of global deforestation over the past five years.

The issue of price on forests has caused huge consternation within the emissions world. Opponents to the inclusion of forestry offset say it is too difficult to measure carbon storage in forests.[43] Forests are prone to fires, and each tree absorbs carbon at a different rate, depending on its species, age and location.

Forests at What Price?

Forests were not included in the carbon market until the Bali UNFCCC meeting. The delay was largely due to the complexity in measuring the carbon storage in trees. In Bali, delegates agreed that credits from forestry offsets could be included in the post-Kyoto Protocol regime that begins in January 2013.[44] The agreement, known as 'Reduced emissions from deforestation and degradation' (REDD), will create a new type of carbon credit for deforestation that can be traded in the carbon markets around the world. The propulsion of deforestation onto the climate change negotiating table is a change in stance by developing nations, who now see the market as a way to value their natural resources by preserving them. This shift in opinion gained momentum in 2005 when the Coalition of Rainforest Nations of developing countries, headed by Costa Rica and Papua New Guinea, offered voluntary carbon emission reductions for the first time by conserving forests in exchange for access to international markets for emissions trading.

It is ironic that the negotiation took place in Indonesia, which in 2007 became the world's third largest greenhouse gas emitter after the US and China, largely due to deforestation for the expansion of palm oil plantations to make biodiesel for Europe.[45]

Only one forestry offset project had been accepted through the Kyoto Protocol's clean development mechanism (CDM) of a total of 765 projects approved by the CDM Executive Board, the mechanism's governing body, up to September 2007.[46]

The CDM acts as a bridge between the carbon markets in the developed world and CO_2 reduction initiatives in the developing world (that do not have their own cap-and-trade schemes). CDM approved projects earn carbon credits known as Certified Emissions Reductions (CERs) that can be traded for permits in the EU scheme, the Chicago voluntary market and other emissions markets subject to Kyoto obligations. There is also a scheme for developed countries to earn carbon credits from cleaner energy projects, known as Joint Implementation (JI). For instance, under both schemes, a company that emits 20 000 tonnes of CO_2 equivalent per year could offset its emissions by planting a certain number of trees or investing in wind farms that would absorb the 20 000 tonnes of CO_2 and earn tradable CERs.

Case of Deferred Mitigation (CDM)

The CDM is one of the main ways for polluters to offset their emissions in excess of their allowances to buy carbon credits through the

CDM that are registered and approved by the CDM board. In his report on the CDM process in 2006, Michael Wara, a lawyer, said the CDM process has its shortcomings because only a small percentage of the CERs under the programme came from renewable energy projects. Most of the carbon-offset projects were associated with reducing emissions from refrigeration factories, nylon-making facilities and capturing methane from animal manure (Wara, 2006).

Wara estimated that renewable energy projects accounted for just 18 % of the CERs. Refrigeration and air-conditioning unit production facilities, which emit chlorodifluoromethane (HCFC-22), make up 37 % of the CER supply, while projects that capture nitrous oxide (N_2O) as a by-product of nylon production account for another 11 %. Finally, 24 % come from methane (CH_4)) capture and flaring projects that are located at large landfills and intense farming businesses, where animals are kept in factory-like conditions, otherwise known as concentrated animal feeding operations.

These projects have taken up so much of the CERs because they involve more potent gases than CO_2. Methane is 21 times more powerful at warming the atmosphere than CO_2 over a 100-year period (US Environmental Protection Agency, 2006).[47] Nitrous oxide, a colourless gas with a slightly sweet odour, is about 310 times more powerful than CO_2 on a per-molecule basis and stays in the atmosphere for more than a century.

The abatement of HCFC-22 and N_2O accounts for more than half of the carbon credits transacted under the CDM between 2002 and 2006 (Capoor and Ambrosi, 2007).

Carbon Sinks

Forests are carbon sinks in the natural environment. Today, technology is being developed to strip away the carbon in fossil fuel production and store it in a way that does not release it into the atmosphere. This technology is known as carbon capture and storage (CCS), with the storage space otherwise known as a carbon sink. So far, no commercial technology has evolved that will reduce emissions. But the US and Western governments forecast commercial availability over the next decade.[48] Statoil, the Norwegian government-controlled oil and gas operator, has been a pioneer of carbon capture and storage. Since 1996, about one million tonnes of CO_2 per year have been stored using this method, a fraction of the total amount required.[49]

The concept of pushing CO_2 back under the surface is not new. Oil companies have injected large volumes of CO_2 underwater as a pressure pump to push oil upward so that it can be extracted.[50] At present any storage of CO_2 underwater without enhanced oil recovery would be illegal (Stern, 2006).

The CCS technology has political support, but the rhetoric is not backed by investment. In 2004, the IEA estimated the amount spent on R&D was more than $100 million a year, which is below the sums required to develop a commercial CCS technology.[51] The CCS process is costly because it involves three steps: the first is to capture CO_2 from the gas streams emitted during electricity production or fuel processing; secondly, the captured CO_2 has to be transported by pipeline or in tankers; and thirdly, the CO_2 has to be stored. These three processes have been around for a long time, but they have never been linked for the purpose of storing CO_2.

The cost of CCS could range from $50 to $100 per tonne of CO_2, according to the IEA (International Energy Agency, 2004). The Electric Power Research Institute (EPRI), a California-based energy research group, said in the report 'The Power to Reduce CO_2 Emissions' that adding the CO_2 capture technology to coal-fired power-stations would increase the wholesale cost of electricity by 40–50 % (Electric Power Research Institute, 2007). The cost of carbon abatement will be added to electricity bills. Consumers won't have to worry about an immediate rise in their power bills though; the EPRI does not predict wide-scale use of the technology until after 2020.[52]

Since power production is responsible for about 30 % of global CO_2 emissions, any progress on capturing carbon is dependent on regulatory and financial dynamics at electricity utilities.[53]

Farm Sinks and Manure Lagoons

The impact of global warming is forcing all industries to reconsider how they do business. Farmers may face the option of farming trees instead of using their land for grazing or planting crops. They also may not have to do anything and will still be regarded as fighting climate change. Farming is a big emitter of greenhouse gases.

Besides the problem of deforestation for agricultural expansion, existing farm practices generate a lot of greenhouse gases. Agricultural activities contribute almost two-thirds of the world's man-made non-CO_2 emissions, and 15 % of all greenhouse emissions (US Environmental Protection Agency, 2006). Some of these emissions come from those flatulent cattle written about earlier. Others come from a soil preparation process known as tillage – organic matter that would otherwise be protected by vegetative cover is exposed to the air and, in turn, decomposes and creates CO_2.

The farmers of the world are also sitting on a very valuable carbon mitigation source. The Earth's vegetation and soils contain the equivalent of about 7500 gigatonnes of CO_2, more carbon than is contained in all remaining oil stocks, and more than double the total amount of carbon accumulated in the atmosphere (Stern, 2006). With farmland both a large greenhouse gas emitter and a large carbon storage bank, farmers can play a vital role in carbon mitigation through more environmentally friendly farming practices such as reducing nitrogen fertilizer use on crops and capturing the methane from cattle in manure lagoons.

Philip Sundblad, the corn farmer and district director of Iowa Farm Bureau, said farmers in Iowa can earn additional income from generating carbon credits – mainly by not doing any tillage – which they can then sell on the Chicago Climate Exchange. The exchange also accepts credits generated from agricultural methane emissions, planting grass and carbon sequestration of the soil. None of these options is available under the EU emissions trading scheme. 'They would not be changing their farming practices and they would still be able to capture the credits, but at $2 to $4 an acre it is not making a big difference one way or the other; it is just a little extra money in the pocket, enough money to take their wife out to dinner,' said Sundblad. Independent verification experts monitor the farmers under the carbon-offsetting programme. The Iowa Farm Bureau works in close cooperation with the Chicago Climate Exchange, advising it on agricultural emission matters.

Biodiversity

Farmland is not only valued for carbon mitigation but also for its biodiversity functions, providing wildlife and native species with habitat and in some areas the potential for wetlands. This means converting farmland that was once drained in the great US agricultural expansion of the 19th and early 20th centuries, back to its original habitat.

John Ryan sits in his office in Rosemont with Chicago's O'Hare Airport as a backdrop. His office walls are maps of the Midwest, showing in great detail the various water catchment areas of the region. Ryan's job is to find land that is suitable for turning into a nature reserve, which in turn will play an important environmental role by reducing flood damage, enhancing water quality and providing open space for recreation. 'The wetlands are nature's kidneys. They move pollutants from storm water, and absorb different compounds such as phosphates. Since they are acting as kidneys, without them you are not purifying yourself and you get poisoned,' said Ryan, head of Land and Water Resources Inc., who comes from many generations of earth-moving contractors. 'Earth-moving you are digging up earth in one place and dumping it in another. Wetlands banking require a greater skill-set from permitting, financing, biology and development,'

It was not so long ago that the unrelenting spread of urbanization and expanding farmland was building over these habitats in the pursuit of economic growth. Between European settlement and 1954, almost half of the original wetland area, or more than 80 million acres (about the same size as the US corn-growing area), were drained or filled in. Most of this happened after 1885 for the purpose of farming (Hansen, 2006).

'Back in the early 1900s, two of the biggest problems in this country were malaria and population growth. There was not a lot of farmland to feed the country. So the government came up with this great idea to pay people to drain the swamps, so that way we got rid of the malaria and significantly increased the farmland. People didn't really think about the environment, they had other things on their mind,' said Ryan, who is now considered a veteran in the wetland regeneration business. 'Now, we are putting the water back that was previously drained,' said Ryan, who draws a parallel to the Dr Seuss story of the 'Sneetches' and the cycle of trend: where something that was previously popular (the Sneetches putting stars on their bellies) suddenly becomes unpopular again.

The wetland business was born following a tightening in US environmental laws with the introduction of the Clean Water Act of 1970 (Anderson and Snyder, 1997) that was ushered in following environmental campaigns of the late 1960s, when awareness of these issues increased.

The Federal Clean Water Act has halted any further net wetland loss and created a market mechanism for wetland regeneration. People like John Ryan can earn credits from creating a new wetland reserve, which he can sell to developers wishing to encroach on wetland elsewhere. This is why the industry is known as wetland banking. 'The value of the wetlands is not driven by the agricultural value (of the land), but by what these developers are prepared to pay for building permits, which exceeds the value of the land for farming purposes,' said Ryan.

The wetlands banking business has also attracted private equity; Boston-based Parthenon Capital, which once tried to buy a stake in the New York Mercantile Exchange (Nymex), bought a slice of Wildlands Inc., a wetlands bank based in California. This may signal that the industry is becoming big enough to attract professional investors.

The focus on wetlands, endangered species and biodiversity is another aspect of climate change. The Millennium Ecosystem Assessment Board, established by the UN to monitor world biodiversity loss, said: 'The current rate of biodiversity loss, in aggregate and at a global scale, gives no indication of slowing, although there have been local successes in some groups of species. The momentum of the underlying drivers of biodiversity loss, and the consequences of this loss, will extend many millennia into the future' (Millennium Ecosystem Assessment, 2005).

Adam Davis, a partner in The Sustainable Land Fund – an investor in environmental projects – said every improvement in the environment is worth money. 'It is not just the atmosphere, it is not just carbon, it is the water purification, the biological productivity of the ecosystem, the flood storage capacity of wetlands, the pollination services that are provided by ecosystems, they are incredibly valuable.' Davis set up Ecosystem Marketplace to track trades in environmental markets, including mitigation banking, water quality permits and salinity permits. 'These markets are too small to be on an exchange, but they are important to be recorded, and I wanted to create a central electronic marketplace where people could come and see prices and trades, just like a normal exchange,' said Davis, who also has his own environmental consultancy, Solano Partners.

Investing in biodiversity does not always guarantee a return. John Wamsley, an outspoken Australian conservationist, was renowned for wearing a hat made of dead cats because of his dislike of the feral cats he blamed for damaging Australia's native wildlife. His towering frame and long white beard made him instantly recognizable, as I discovered when I interviewed him in the mid-1990s while working for Reuters. Wamsley was forthright about how the environment should be protected; there should be an economic value put on it. He backed his view with money and at one stage became the largest private owner of conservation land in Australia. The former mathematics professor listed his company Earth Sanctuaries on the Australian Stock Exchange in 2000, but within two years Wamsley was forced to sell many of his properties because of financial difficulties.

Water – The Irreplaceable Commodity

'When the wells run dry, we know the worth of water,'
attributed to Benjamin Franklin

Population growth and climate change have led to forecasts of water demand outpacing water supply. The World Water Council estimates that $180 billion needs to be invested each year to achieve the goal of adequate drinking water and water waste treatment for a world population expected to reach 8 billion by 2030 (Cosgrove and Rijsberman, 2000). The council said this will put more strain on a global system that is already under stress due to the tripling of the population during the 20th century and the use of water multiplying six-fold. People are using more water than ever before because they are eating, drinking and washing themselves and their clothes more often.[54] Having said that, the water needed to feed a person for a year has, in fact, halved in the last 40 years, from 6 to 3 cubic metres a year. But a lot of water is needed to grow food. The Water Council estimates that it requires 1900 litres of water to produce 1 kilogram of rice, and 15 000 litres to produce 1 kilogram of beef.

The World Bank, the Organization for Economic Cooperation and Development (OECD), the European Union and the chief executives of the world's food and beverage organizations are calling for more efficient use of water. The US is ranked as the most inefficient user of water by the Marseilles-based World Water Council. William Reilly, president of Aqua International Partners, said America's inefficiency was due to the fact that they paid less than other countries for water, a similar pattern to gasoline. 'The Germans pay $1.78 for a cubic metre of water, the French $1.08, the British $1.23. What do you suppose we pay? Fifty-four cents,' said Reilly. 'If that cost were buried in the monthly bill for cable TV . . . a lot of consumers might not even notice it, since basic cable costs $45 a month or more; for an average American family of four, a water bill is about $14 or $15,' said Reilly (2004). 'The need to price water more realistically will come with greater recognition of the value of water trading,' he said.

Household usage is far smaller than that of industry and agriculture. Farming accounts for between two-thirds and three-quarters of global water usage due to the invention of irrigation systems. This watering process has enabled farming to push the frontiers of crop and grazing land. 'There is no agricultural commodity that can grow without water, it does not matter what it is, whether it is a plant or an animal, it needs water,' said Kimberly Tara from Four Winds, the commodity investment fund. 'The usage of water is very much tied to agriculture,' she said.

About 250 million hectares are irrigated worldwide, nearly five times more than at the beginning of the 20th century. Irrigation has boosted agricultural yields and production, which has helped stabilize food prices for most of the past 50 years. Most of the irrigated water is coming from rivers, reservoirs, underground aquifers and the hundreds of new dams that were built around the world to supply new irrigated systems. However, the aquifers are not replenished as quickly as their water has been taken. Further expansion of irrigated water will be required to meet the increase in future food demand. The World Bank said the opportunities to harness new resources are fewer and more expensive, so the focus will be on improving the productivity of existing water use and reusing water. 'Today, irrigated agriculture supplies about 40 % of the world's food, though occupying only 17 % of the cultivated land' (World Bank, 2005). The Food and Agriculture Organization (FAO) estimates that half of the increase in food demand projected to 2030 will come from irrigated agriculture (World Bank, 2005).

The OECD warns about potential water supply and demand problems, saying that it is expected to be the major constraint on sustainable development in some countries in the 21st century, and cautions that the agricultural industry will have to start paying a fairer price. The OECD has said that water pricing shows that for many of its member countries, industrial and household water users pay more than 100 times as much per cubic metre of water as agricultural users (OECD, 1999).

Both the World Bank and the OECD say most countries would take water from agriculture, allocate it to other sectors and rely on increased food imports to meet their domestic needs. To reallocate this water, market-based water prices will need to be adopted, according to the World Bank, where water pricing is the most commonly promoted incentive of its projects.[55]

The European Union is also looking at putting a price on water. Water scarcity has affected 17 % of the EU population and 11 % of its territory (DG Environment, 2007). 'At the heart of such policy options is the need to put the right price on water with the "user pays" principle becoming the rule regardless of where water is taken,' an EU report said. 'Water saving and water use in a more efficient way is very important. The combination of the two could save us 40 % of our consumption,' Stavros Dimas, Commissioner for Environment for the European Union told me. Dimas said to lower water usage, more investment has to be made in water-saving efficiency technologies rather than on new water infrastructure. 'Having the right water-pricing system will lead to lower prices,' said Dimas. 'This is one of the most important issues for the European Union and, together with climate change, it is a very big challenge,' said the Greek-born politician.

The increase in water demand and the move to the user pays principle would see a rise in water prices, as governments reduce the subsidies for water users – the main reason for today's low water prices.[57] In the other commodity markets we have seen so far, the increased demand for raw materials comes at a time when supply is constrained. Water is another example, but it is not priced like other commodities and has largely been regarded as free. This is starting to change. 'You can find all sorts of alternative energies to oil, but so far they have found no alternative to water. That is one of the basic truths out there,' John Ryan, the US wetlands expert, told me.

To balance this perceived mismatch in water supply and demand, the marketplace is seen as part of the solution, through the allocation of water rights or permits. If the price is high, consumers will conserve water and if the holder does not need all of their allocation, they can sell it. Alternatively, if prices are low, major users of water can choose to enter the market and buy more water. The adoption of water trading around the world is likely to be slow. While most countries have formal water codes, very few recognize that water rights can be traded, with the exception of Australia, the United States, Chile and Spain (Calatrava and Garrido, 2006).[58]

Market-based water pricing could also stimulate more supplies. The world is not short of water, just freshwater – that is the water that we drink, wash, grow food with and use to make things. Freshwater makes up only 2 % of the world's water – the remaining 98 % is salt water. Almost three-quarters of the world's freshwater is frozen in icecaps and most of the remainder is present as soil moisture. Turning the abundance of sea water into water that is suitable for our needs has taken on greater emphasis. Desalination plants are popping up all over the world, the downside being that they are energy intensive and costly – although this is falling. The water industry is already a big user of energy, accounting for about 3 % of US power consumption (NRDC, 2004).[59]

With agriculture being the biggest user of water, volume is of course important. Quality is vital too, and there are markets for water quality. The US has developed markets to combat water pollution with water quality permits that can be traded.[60]

Water, Water Everywhere, But Not a Drop to Trade

In his novel *East of Eden*, set in the Salinas Valley in the 1920s, John Steinbeck describes the essential nature of water in California before the development of reliable water supplies.

> 'I have spoken of the rich years when rainfall was plentiful. But there were dry years too, and they put a terror on the valley. There would be five or six wet and wonderful years when there might be nineteen or twenty-five inches of rain, and the land would shout with grass. Then would come six or seven pretty good years of twelve or sixteen inches of rain. And then the dry years would come. The land cracked and the springs dried up and the cattle listlessly nibbled dry twigs. Then the farmers and ranchers filled with disgust for the Salinas Valley. Some families would sell out for next to nothing and move away. And it never failed that during the dry years the people forgot about the rich years, and during the wet years they lost all memory of the dry years. It was always that way.'

Californian farmers and their neighbours have overcome the vagaries of the weather that affected Steinbeck's farmers of the Salinas Valley through irrigation. Water comes from rivers, reservoirs and underground aquifers and can be turned on and off like a tap, just like urban dwellers are used to when they have a shower, wash the dishes or fill the kettle to make a cup of tea. The amount of water they use is determined by water rights. The price of these varies depending on jurisdiction; permits are issued by local governments, often under complex laws.

The obscure world of water rights was a sub-plot in the 1970s Hollywood film *Chinatown*. It stars Jack Nicholson as a detective who uncovers a water rights scandal, based on the real-life story of William Mulholland, a Los Angeles water engineer, who organized the purchase of the water rights and the piping of water from the Owens Valley 250 miles north-east in the California mountains to the dry San Fernando Valley. The incident became known as the '1908 Owens Valley Rape'. The result was not only that the farmers of the Owens Valley lost their water; they also became wary of trading their water rights to the state's expanding cities.

A century on, people are still battling over water rights, which are increasing in value as the demand from both the urban and rural populations rises.

Many of the ranchers that owned water in the west got very rich, by abandoning their farming activities, declaring the water excess and selling it to towns that needed it to expand their population base. The western US states of Arizona, Colorado and California are host to some of America's fastest-growing cities, as people from the east look for more space. However, these areas are also a lot drier than in the east, making access to water a very important issue for developers, residents and local governments.

The evolution of the western US water markets has been sporadic, with no uniform law in the dry western states. Terry Lee Anderson and Pamela Snyder in their book *Water Markets, Priming the Invisible Pump* said that when the early settlers arrived in the Great Plains ahead of the legal machinery of state and federal governments, they found it necessary to generate their own rules. These were voluntary agreements, often involving cattlemen, miners and towns. Anderson and Snyder wrote that if settlers found a stream that was already taken, they moved to another stream – their access to the water was essentially determined by their location.

When the water rights were then written into state laws in the late 19th and early 20th centuries, there was no contemplation that they would be leased or transferred. As a result, water rights holders were historically reluctant to lease water out, for fear of losing their right to it in the longer term. Permanent transfers and leases have recently become easier, as state laws have changed to facilitate market transactions (Howitt and Hansen, 2005).

California followed the riparian water rights rule, whereby water permits were allocated to those who live near the water source. It's a rule that California continues to follow. In contrast, Colorado has a more active water market where water is traded each year through private, voluntary transactions. The profits of the trade go to those who conserve water and sell it, with farmers and the city councils of Denver, Fort Collins and Colorado Springs among the buyers (Landry and Anderson, 1999).

The US Bureau of Reclamation, the Federal bureau that manages water resources in the western US states, recognizes the need for a market-based approach. 'Water supply-related crisis will affect economies and resources of national and international importance,' Gale Norton, Secretary of the Interior warned when the bureau released its programme 'Water 2025, Preventing Crisis and Conflict in the West' (US Bureau of Reclamation, 2005).

Nevertheless there are prohibitive barriers for interstate water trading in the United States, which make it challenging to develop a regional water market. States in the southeast affected by last year's drought are currently suing their neighbours over water (Byrnes, 2007).

This is the Way in Amarillo

T. Boone Pickens, the Texas oilman, has cast his attention on the Texas water business through his company Mesa Water, which includes other landowners in the Panhandle region. This is the most northern part of the Lone Star state that looks like a square block on the map, jutting into the western part of neighbouring Oklahoma. The Panhandle takes its water from the man-made Lake Meredith and from the Ogallala aquifer. Mesa owners believe that there is more water than the sparsely populated Panhandle region needs; they claim only 4 % of its 2.5 million acres of land is used for farming, and therefore they want to sell the water to the booming cities of Dallas and San Antonio. By February 2008, Mesa's plan was awaiting a decision by the Texas authorities.

Pickens and his Mesa colleagues have spent $30 million acquiring water rights in the Panhandle, and, as with all of Pickens's other investments, he is looking for a decent financial return. 'I believe groundwater must be freely marketable so that market pricing will eliminate the incentives for wasteful use. Assigning a value to water will provide strong incentives for conservation of water in the Ogallala. When water is priced at $500 or so an acre-foot, you rapidly eliminate a lot of wasteful practices,' Pickens said to a Senate Committee on Water Policy in March 2004.[61]

Another owner of water resources is the University of Texas, which has 2.1 million acres of land. Much of this land is leased out for oil and gas exploration and the university also earns income from selling the water that is in the aquifers below the ground. The combined income from the sales and leases has accrued billions for the university's endowment funds.[62]

Most US water trades are done between a holder (often a farmer) and a potential user (either another farmer or a city council). There is no formal exchange, although there have been several attempts, including by Enron. In 1998, Enron formed Azurix, which was headed by Rebecca Marks, who once declared that the 'world was running out of water' (McLean and Elkind, 2003). Enron never realized their water trading ambition for Azurix through Water2water.com, an electronic marketplace to replicate the online markets that it had created in energy and metals.'Water2Water.com will provide value to customers by allowing buyers to leverage purchasing power across the industry's fragmented buying base in addition to giving customers the ability to more efficiently engage in the transfer and physical delivery of water and related services,' Rebecca Marks, chairman of Azurix, said at the time of the launch. The creation of Water2Water.com occurred in the midst of the dot com boom, and saw imitators such as iAqua, but neither made any success. The bursting of the internet bubble and the implosion of Enron sealed their fate.

Down-under Drought

Enron's water company Azurix did not manage to obtain success from its online water trading exchange, but a small Australian company is trying to achieve what Enron's famed market boffins could not.

Brian Peadon formed Waterexchange in 1994 to provide irrigation services; four years later it became an online exchange for farmers and irrigators to trade their water rights. Now, Waterexchange is selling forward water rural rights contracts with other users. Peadon said it is trading inter-valley, inter-state, but the water trading has to take place around the same water system. The Murray Darling in eastern Australia is one water system and the Swan River system in Western Australia is another.

Peadon sold the business in 2007 to the National Stock Exchange of Australia for a significant stake in the enlarged company, which has the regulatory authority to sell water-based futures contracts to investors. Now that Peadon has the necessary licences, the water futures will be based on water indices that have been created to measure the level of water availability in many regional Australian water markets.[63] Peadon plans to set up water trading markets whereby householders will trade their water allocations with each other. The world's largest futures market, the CME Group, has also hinted that water futures could be a possibility due to changes in the supply and demand fundamentals (Lewis and Smith, 2007).

The water trading market has been based on the Murray Darling Basin (which lies in the east of the country); the food bowl of Australia, and the region under most stress from drought. Rice farmers in the Murray Darling Basin are among the most intensive water users. In 2007 Australia's planted rice area fell to its lowest level in more than 50 years, with production expected to be less than 5 % of what it was in the late 1990s, putting the future of the industry in question.[64]

Although Australia is a relatively small rice producer on a global scale, its fall in production came during a period when global rice prices doubled because production is not keeping pace with demand. The drop in Australian rice production is one of the contributing factors along with rice exporters hoarding stocks in fear of domestic food shortages that led to violent food protests in Egypt, Haiti, Indonesia and Yemen in 2008. Since white settlement, Australia has been a big agricultural exporter, but its ability to grow crops, graze animals and produce food products is dependent on water availability. The lack of it caused an estimated 60 % reduction in the size of the area of Australian summer crop plantings, which include wheat, rice, cottonseed, maize, sunflowers and sorghum, compared with the start of this decade (Australian Bureau of Agricultural and Resource Economics, 2007).

Cotton was also affected, with the smallest irrigated cotton area planted in 30 years in 2007 (Australian Bureau of Agricultural and Resource Economics, 2007). Australia's cotton industry consumes almost a tenth of irrigated water and had become the world's fourth largest exporter by the end of the 1990s. The majority of Australian rice and cotton is exported, but the existence of these industries is almost entirely reliant on subsidized irrigated water.

'For Australia it defies economic sense to sell our water overseas when the country is facing its worst drought in more than 100 years,' said Richard Lourey, managing director of MFS Aqua Managers, the manager of the MFS Water Fund based in Melbourne. Lourey said the export of Australian food is, in effect, exporting water that is subsidized by taxpayers and not reflected in the price. This trade of water in food is known as *virtual water*. Many countries depend on importing food because they don't have sufficient water to grow their own food. UNESCO said in a recent report that international water dependency accounted for about 16 % of the global water use, and four-fifths of this is agricultural trade. 'With increasing globalization of trade, global water interdependencies are likely to increase,' it said.[65]

With water priced according to the value of the end produce, it will always flow to those that can sell their products for a higher value. Vegetable growers earned eight times more than rice producers from a gigalitre of water.[66]

Connoisseurs of Australian wine may also have to pay a higher price for their glass of Cabernet Sauvignon as vineyards pass on higher water charges. In order for a market to work there have to be rules to prevent water going entirely to one industry over another, such as mining over agriculture where the former can normally afford to pay more than the latter.

The user pay model has forced farmers to switch to other crops or go out of business.[67] The Australian government has set aside A\$3 billion to buy back water entitlements (Australian Government, 2007). The aim is to reduce the overallocation of water rights, which may lead to more farmers leaving the land.

Australia has known many long, persistent and costly droughts, and like California, Australia has its own history of water battles between farmers (Fullerton, 2001). This decade the droughts have been the worst experienced in recorded history. Australian politicians, farmers and environmentalists are connecting it with climate change. This has led to a reform in the management of water resources, which has opened the door to more market-based mechanisms for allocating water. Placing an economic value on water has seen Australia separate water access entitlements from land titles, making them more tradable, creating a viable trading market in water entitlement rights (Heaney et al., 2005).

Keith Walker, a professor at the University of Adelaide who has written about Australia's water problems for 30 years, said part of the issue is cultural. 'Most of the white settlers came from Britain, and so they want to replicate that by having a nice green lawn and plenty of plants and flowers in their garden. To have a nice green garden you need plenty of water, so people often water their garden every day, even though they are living in the driest city of the driest state in the driest continent,' said Walker, who originally came to Australia by boat from Scotland as a '£5 pom.'[68] 'I think it is hard for people to change their habits,' said Walker.

There is also the schism between rural and urban Australia. The big wide open country and its reputation as a major food exporter has created the impression that Australia's rural community is large, when in fact 'Down Under' is the most urbanized nation on Earth, with most of the population located on a strip along the east coast of the country.

The Australian government highlighted the water wastage in agriculture when it unveiled a plan to tackle the problem in January 2007. It estimated that up to 30 % of the water diverted from rivers into irrigation systems is lost before it reaches the farm gate, and of the water that reaches the farm gate, a further 20 % is lost in distribution. Once it reaches the plants between 10 and 15 % of water is lost through overwatering (Australian Government, 2007). Another factor is the intense Australian summer heat that causes evaporation of water. The reservoirs and channels where water is stored and transported are open channels and substantial volumes of water are lost to evaporation (Business Council of Australia, 2006).

Lourey admits he is not an environmentalist, but he recognizes the classic supply and demand imbalance for the water industry. Supply is constrained because of drier climate in some countries and the demand is increasing because of a higher population and global economic growth. Lourey said water will behave like other commodity markets whereby the value of water will rise to a point where it is necessary to invest in infrastructure and technology to save it, clean it, measure, transport and store it and bring on new supply through desalination plants. The city of Perth in Western Australia built Australia's first desalination plant earlier this decade and plans to build a second plant; Adelaide and Sydney are also intending to build desalination plants.

Securing the Future

Fears about global warming and water shortages have become a security issue too, warns a group of retired American generals and admirals. 'We will pay for this one way or another,' said General

Anthony 'Tony' Zinni, former commander-in-chief of US central command (CENTCOM), which is responsible for US military operations in the Middle East and the Horn of Africa (CNNNA Corporation, 2007). 'We will pay to reduce greenhouse gas emissions today, and we'll have to take an economic hit of some kind. Or we will pay the price later in military terms. And that will involve human lives. There will be a human toll. There is no way out of this that does not have real costs attached to it. That has to hit home,' said Zinni.

Climate change is one of the biggest challenges facing mankind, and it requires many solutions. Economic tools include taxes and the creation of a market price for pollution, and polluters will have to pay for the environmental impact of the emission of greenhouse gases. All the signs point to the fact that environmental markets will become more pervasive. The UNFCCC meeting in Bali in December 2007 paved the way for more market-based mechanisms from forestry sequestration projects to an expanded CDM board that will increase the capacity to approve clean energy projects.

With the expansion of CO_2 markets around the world and greater government commitment to CO_2 reductions, carbon pricing may become as common as oil or gold. A price on carbon will be an additional cost to the price of oil, gas and coal, meaning consumers will pay more for consuming fossil fuels. A successful global carbon trading market will, in turn, encourage the development of other environmental markets such as water and biodiversity. Hopefully this will provoke a deeper understanding of the economics of the environment and the effect our lifestyle has on it.

Notes

1. Bali conference by numbers, *The Daily Telegraph*: http://www.telegraph. co.uk/earth/main.jhtml?xml=/earth/2007/12/03/eabali203.xml.
2. There is the conference of parties (Cop) for the UNFCCC and the member of parties (Mop) for the Kyoto Protocol. The reason for this is that the Mop delegates are from the countries that have ratified the Kyoto Protocol, which does not include the United States. The US delegates only participate in the Cop discussions.

3. The Intergovernmental Panel on Climate Change (IPCC) released its fourth assessment on climate change throughout 2007 through draft and final reports on the various issues associated with global warming from the scientific basis to adaptation and mitigation. The IPCC was constantly in the news and added to the expectation that the Bali meeting would conclude with strong action on combating climate change.

4. The Marketing Association of the English Wine Industry – http://www. englishwineproducers.com/history.htm

5. The reference to Evelyn was taken from the Museum of London website – http://www.museumoflondon.org.uk/archive/exhibits/changing_faces/ change/change1.htm. Henson (2006) said that the Thames Frost Fairs were rarely held outside the mid-16th century as the Thames froze once every 20 to 30 years from 1400 until 1814.

6. http://www.environment.newscientist.com/channel/earth/climate-change/dn11644)

7. The GISS report on surface temperature analysis (see http://www. data.giss.nasa.gov/gistemp/) said that results showed that global cooling after 1940 was small, and there was net global warming of about 0.4 °C between the 1880s and 1970s.

8. According to the Institute of the Environment (2006), the film and television industry in California accounts for about 8.4 million metric tonnes of CO_2 equivalents, this compares with 33.4 million for the petroleum refining industry, which is a lot bigger. 'It may be surprising that the GHG emissions are even of the same order of magnitude as in the other sectors.'

9. A report by Intertanko, the International Association of Independent Tanker Owners, said the quantity of carbon dioxide pumped into the atmosphere by tankers and container ships is 50 % more than was previously estimated, and almost double, about 1.2 billion tonnes of CO_2 the amount of emissions from aviation. Shipping accounts for 90 % of the world's goods that are traded around the world.

10. A short ton (2000 pounds) of coal when it is fully burnt emits almost three times as much weight in carbon dioxide (CO_2). Carbon dioxide is formed during coal combustion; the atomic weight of carbon is 12 and that of oxygen is 16, the atomic weight of carbon dioxide is 44. Based on that ratio, and assuming complete combustion, 1 pound of carbon combines with 2.667 pounds of oxygen to produce 3.667 pounds of

carbon dioxide. For example, coal with a carbon content of 78 % and a heating value of 14 000 Btu per pound emits about 204.3 pounds of carbon dioxide per million Btu when completely burnt. Complete combustion of 1 short ton (2000 pounds) of this coal will generate about 5720 pounds (2.86 short tons) of carbon dioxide (Energy Information Administration, 1994).

11. The average emissions rates in the United States from natural gas-fired generation are: 1135 lbs/MWh of carbon dioxide, 0.1 lbs/MWh of sulphur dioxide and 1.7 lbs/MWh of nitrogen oxides. Compared to the average air emissions from coal-fired generation, natural gas produces half as much carbon dioxide, less than a third as much nitrogen oxides and 1 % as much sulphur oxides at the power plant.

12. The Stern Review said that human activities are changing the composition of the atmosphere and its properties. Since pre-industrial times (around 1750), carbon dioxide concentrations have increased by just over one third from 280 parts per million (ppm) to 380 ppm, predominantly as a result of burning fossil fuels, deforestation and other changes in land use. This has been accompanied by rising concentrations of other greenhouse gases, particularly methane and nitrous oxide.

13. According to IPCC's fourth assessment 'Climate Change 2007, The Physical Science Basis', 11 of the last 12 years (1995 to 2006) rank among the 12 warmest years since 1850.

14. Other statistics include Oklahoma having its fourth wettest summer.

15. India has two monsoons, one in the south and one in the north.

16. John Howard not only lost the election, but his parliamentary seat as well - partly due to his head in the sand approach to climate change. His successor Kevin Rudd signed the Kyoto Protocol as his first act as the new Australian Prime Minister.

17. According to Mills *et al.* (2005), a study commissioned by Ceres – a group of companies and environmentalists concerned about climate change, including banks, airlines and car companies. For a list of members, see http://www.ceres.org/coalitionandcompanies/company_list.php

18. Externalities in production or consumption mean that their costs or benefits are not reflected in the market price. They are consequences of an economic activity that are experienced by unrelated third parties. An externality can be either positive or negative, in regards to the impact of economic activity on the environment.

19. An estimated \$5 billion to \$12 billion was saved over the life of the programme (Hahn and Hester, 1989).

20. The lead credits worked in such a way that if refiners produced gasoline with a lower lead content than was required, they earned lead credits. EPA terminated the programme at the end of 1987, when the lead phase-down was completed. EPA estimated savings from the programme of about 20 % over alternative programmes that did not provide for lead banking, a cost saving of about \$250 million per year.

21. The act established an allowance trading programme to cut SO_2 emissions by ten million tonnes from 1980 levels, a 50 % reduction, and nitrous oxide by two million tonnes from 1980 levels. The first phase of sulphur dioxide emissions reductions was achieved by 1995, with a second phase of reduction to be accomplished by the year 2000. By 2000, the NO_X programme had encouraged the installation of advanced NO_X combustion controls, such as low-NO_X burners, and the development of new power plant designs with lower NO_X emission rates. In 2006, about 980 coal-fired electricity-generating units were affected by the NO_X programme. Economists estimated the compliance costs to achieve such reductions were up to 40 % lower than would have been the case under the existing command-and control requirements.

22. 'In most areas of the northeastern and Midwestern US wet sulphate deposition, a major component of acid rain, declined by 25 to 40 % from 1990 levels. The reductions in wet sulphate deposition contributed to improvements in the ability of many lakes and streams, including very sensitive regions like the Adirondacks, to buffer acid deposition. These improvements are an important signal that recovery from decades of acid rain has begun' (Napolitano *et al.*, 2007).

23. The EPA introduced other cap-and-trade systems, including the Ozone Transport Commission's NOx Budget Program in 1999 to reduce NOx emissions from power plants in the eastern US. The EPA added the NOx Budget Trading Program under the NOx State Implementation Plan (SIP) Call in 2003 and 2004 respectively. These programmes were aimed at cutting NOx emissions from regional transport during the summer season. The Clean Air Interstate Rule (CAIR) provides states with a solution to the problem of power plant pollution that drifts from one state to another. CAIR covers 28 eastern states and the District of Columbia. The rule uses a cap-and-trade system

to reduce the target pollutants – sulphur dioxide and nitrogen oxides by 70 %.

24. The European Commission presented a green paper in 2000 that proposed the use of emissions trading. It showed that a comprehensive trading scheme could reduce the compliance costs of meeting Kyoto by a third, compared to a scenario with no trading instrument. The 2000 green paper estimated the cost of meeting Kyoto at € 9 billion without trading, € 7.2 billion with trading amongst energy producers only, € 6.9 billion with trading among energy producers and energy intensive industry and € 6 billion with trading among all sectors (Stern, 2006, p. 327).

25. The signatories to the Kyoto Protocol emitted 3.87 gigatonnes of carbon, the rest of the world emitted 2.22 gigatonnes. Therefore the protocol requires the reduction of 0.2 gigatonnes a year over the five years to 2012 (Swingland, 2003).

26. The IEA (2005) estimated that economies in transition would be in a position to sell 1190 tonnes of carbon dioxide equivalent in the year 2010, greater than the 840 million tonnes of CO_2 required by the EU-25, which excludes Romania and Bulgaria.

27. The ratification by Russia brought the number of ratifying countries to 55 and the proportion of world emissions above 55 %.

28. The facility, which is a collaboration between the World Bank, the United Nations Environment Programme and non-government organizations' Global Initiatives and Artists' Project Earth, has become the prominent financing vehicle for addressing climate change. Its use was widened at the UNFCCC meeting in Bali to fund the cost of sea defences and other climate adaptation measures, together with the financing of technology transfer of low carbon technology projects from developed countries to developing countries.

29. http://www.barackobama.com/issues/energy/

30. Arizona, New Mexico, Oregon, Washington, Utah and Manitoba again joined California in the Western Climate Initiative.

31. The ten states are Connecticut, Delaware, Maine, Maryland, Massachusetts, New Hampshire, New Jersey, New York, Rhode Island and Vermont.

32. The states that signed the pact, on November 16,2007, are Wisconsin, Minnesota, Illinois, Indiana, Iowa, Michigan, Kansas, Ohio,

South Dakota and Canada's Manitoba. The state governors plan this year (2008) to establish regional targets for greenhouse gas emission reductions and complete development of a proposed cap-and-trade system. See http://www.midwesterngovernors.org/govenergynov.htm.

33. By May 2007, about 500 city mayors in the US had signed the US conference of mayors' climate protection agreement. See http://www.usmayors.org/climateprotection/agreement.htm.

34. The US Senate Committee on Environment and Public Works backed the Lieberman-Warner Climate Security Act by 11 votes to 8.

35. The Climate Change Registry is a collaboration between states, provinces and tribes aimed at developing and managing a common greenhouse gas emissions reporting system. See http://www.theclimateregistry.org.

36. A Canadian-government-commissioned report 'Getting to 2050: Canada's transition to a low-emissions future', published in January 2008 and written by former politicians, businessmen, economists and academics under the name National Round Table on the Environment and the Economy, recommended that Canada either introduce a carbon tax or establish a carbon price as quickly as possible to achieve its target of a 65 % reduction in GHGs by 2050. 'The most effective and efficient policy that would result in deep GHG emission reductions is a market-based policy, such as an emissions tax, a cap-and-trade system, or a combination of the two. This core policy then needs to be complemented by other regulatory policies to force emission reductions from parts of the economy that do not respond to a price policy' (p. iii).

37. On January 7, 2008, the Chinese-controlled territory of Hong Kong introduced new tariff controls on the island's utilities, which penalized excessive pollution emissions and set up a fund for energy efficiency and renewable energy. This is seen as a test bed for other major Chinese urban areas.

38. Bruinsma (2003) says the factors driving deforestation will not disappear in the coming decades, with the world's population predicted to rise by another 50 % by 2050.

39. According to a report by the Food and Agriculture Organization (FAO), seven countries – the Falkland Islands, Gibraltar, the Holy See, Monaco, Nauru, South Georgia and South Sandwich Islands and Tokelau have no areas that qualify as forests using the FRA 2005 definition, and an additional 57 have forest on less than 10 % of their total land area.

40. 53 % equates to 2097 million hectares. The remaining 34 % is spread among 212 countries and areas.

41. South America suffered the largest net loss of forests from 2000 to 2005 – about 4.3 million hectares per year – followed by Africa, which lost 4.0 million hectares annually. North and Central America and Oceania each had a net loss of about 350 000 ha, while Asia, which had a net loss of some 800 000 ha per year in the 1990s, reported a net gain of 1 million hectares per year from 2000 to 2005, primarily as a result of large-scale afforestation reported by China.

42. United Nations Framework Convention on Climate Change, Subsidiary Body for Scientific and Technological Advice. Twenty – seventh session, Bali, 3–11 December 2007, item 5 of the provisional agenda 'Reducing emissions from deforestation in developing countries: approaches to stimulate action.'

43. About 104 million hectares of forest are reported to be significantly affected each year by fire, pests (insects and disease) or climatic events such as drought, wind, snow, ice and floods. As those trees burn and rot, they release CO_2 to the atmosphere – an estimated 500 tonnes of CO_2 per hectare.

44. The grouping proposed that a country establishes a national baseline rate of deforestation (converted into carbon emissions) and negotiates a voluntary commitment (over a fixed commitment period) for reducing emissions below the baseline. Any reductions that are achieved below the baseline could then be sold under Kyoto or other carbon markets. No trading would be allowed if emissions were above the baseline in a commitment period. The proposal has focused attention on how deforestation might be included, either as part of future commitments under the protocol or under the Climate Change Convention itself.

45. According to a report entitled 'Indonesia and Climate Change: Current Status and Policies', 'Historically, oil-palm production in Indonesia has been a major driver of deforestation.' The report said that demand for (Indonesian) biodiesel is expected to increase in 2025, when it reaches 4700 million litres, or 5 % of total diesel consumption. This will need 1.4 million hectares of oil palm plantations – about 2.5 times the area of Bali.

46. The Marrakesh accords rejected the inclusion of deforestation within CDM projects during the first commitment period, primarily because of

concern about the risk that protecting forest in one project area would simply displace deforestation, which would take place elsewhere. The CDM could only accept afforestation and reforestation projects.

47. According to the US Environmental Protection Agency (2006), Methane is more abundant in the Earth's atmosphere now than at any time during the past 400 000 years. Since 1750, global average atmospheric concentrations of CH_4 have increased by 150 %, from approximately 700 to 1745 parts per billion by volume (ppbv). Although CH_4 concentrations have continued to increase, the overall rate of CH_4 growth during the past decade has slowed. In the late 1970s, the growth rate was approximately 20 ppbv per year. In the 1980s, growth slowed to 9 to 13 ppbv per year. From 1990 to 1998, CH_4 saw variable growth between 0 and 13 ppbv per year.

48. The IEA forecast in its 2004 report that a large-scale uptake of capture and storage technologies is probably ten years off and that without a major increase in research and development investment, 'The technology will not be in place to realize its full potential as an emissions mitigation tool from 2030 onwards.'

49. According to the International Energy Agency (2004), Statoil traps about 2800 tonnes a day at its Sleipner oil field in the North Sea, at a cost of about $125 000.

50. Press statement to announce the launch of The Carbon Capture and Storage Association, October 5, 2005. Since 1996 over seven million tonnes of CO_2 has been stored in the central North Sea. CO_2 has been injected into oil fields, mainly in the United States, to enhance oil recovery. Its behaviour is well understood and predictable, with currently more than 25 million tonnes injected annually.

51. The IEA said in its World Energy Outlook that carbon capture and storage is assumed not to be deployed before 2030 because of doubts about whether technical and cost challenges can be overcome.

52. The report states that the greatest reductions in future US electric sector CO_2 emissions are likely to come from applying carbon capture and storage (CCS) technologies to nearly all new coal-based power plants coming online after 2020.

53. The Intergovernmental Panel on Climate Change's 'Carbon Dioxide Capture and Storage – Summary for policymakers and technical summary' gives a breakdown of the volume of emissions from each sector.

54. In 1900 the global annual water use per capita was 350 cubic metres. In 2000, that number had grown to 642 cubic metres, said John Dickerson in his speech 'The Economic Paradox That Spawned A Compelling Investment Theme', at the Case for Water Investing conference in 2007.

55. The World Bank says that Water rights create incentives to efficient use and can underpin water markets that increase agricultural efficiency. Water rights may be a share or a fixed quantum. Assignment of transparent and stable rights, together with a measure of accountability and transferability, requires a workable property regime, the right ecological characteristics and clear definition of the resource, which is particularly hard with groundwater.

56. A report compiled by DE Environment (2007) said the overall area affected by water scarcity can be estimated at $418\,600$ km^2 and the overall population at 76.37 million, or at least 11 % of the EU territory and 17 % of the EU population.

57. The Water Council has said that mispricing is largely due to government subsidies, which distort the market price.

58. In Chile, water permit holders can sell water rights, but this is very opaque as there is no national registry. Sales of water rights are registered in the local municipality at the office of Bienes Raices, which is a private sector entity and is not part of the government. Trading records eventually filter back to the Director General of Water. There is no transparent state mechanism for trading water permits and trades are private contracts between parties.

59. A report by the NRDC (2004) says the energy for the US water industry, including the activity of heating and cooling water, is equivalent to the release of about 30 million tonnes of carbon dioxide – the equivalent of more than four million cars.

60. The United States Environmental Protection Agency (EPA) has supported the concept and implementation of water quality trading for several years, including financial support for water quality markets. Most of these markets are focused on either phosphorus or nitrogen-based trading, though increasing interest has emerged for trading sediment run-off, biological oxygen demand and temperature.

61. See reference to Pickens's speech on the Mesa Water website – http://www.mesawater.com/ReferenceResources/Speeches_detail.asp?id=8

62. See http://www.utlands.utsystem.edu/aboutus.asp#history

63. The process for developing water markets was formalized through the 1994 COAG water reform framework, in which the state and territory governments agreed to introduce arrangements for water trading. The various jurisdictional governments subsequently developed separate *water entitlements* that were, for the most part, perpetual, separate from land titles and provided guaranteed access to a share of the consumptive water pool. In general, the entitlements were allocated on a 'grandfathering' arrangement on the basis of existing licences and irrigation activities.

64. Abare forecast Australian production to amount to 50 000 tonnes of rice this season. In the late 1990s this was 1.3 million tonnes.

65. The global volume of virtual water flows related to the international trade in commodities is 1625 giga m³/yr. About 80 % of this relates to the trade in agricultural products, while the remainder is related to industrial product trade.

66. In 1996–97, it was estimated that there was $200 000 (gross value) of rice produced per gigalitre of water used, while at the other end of the scale there was around $1.6 million of vegetables produced per gigalitre of water used.

67. After three years of deregulation, 2242 farmers had left the industry, a decline of 17 %. The average annual exit rate was 225 farms during the previous five years, according to the CSIRO.

68. Pom is Australian vernacular for a prisoner of mother England, which English people are commonly referred to in Australia.

4

Metals

'Then, I said, let us begin and create in idea a State; and yet the true creator is necessity, who is the mother of our invention.'

The Republic of Plato, by Plato.

Copper and Robber

A Mercedes truck and a Daihatsu four-wheel drive with black tinted windows pull up at Perry Green; a quaint little hamlet in the Hertfordshire countryside complete with traditional red telephone box and 16th century cottages. The postcard village is a welcome contrast to bustling London, less than an hour's drive away, and is home to city financiers and British celebrities such as members of the 1980s band Pet Shop Boys and the Cockney singing duo Chas and Dave, whose greatest contribution to music was a song called *Gertcha*.

The Mercedes-borne visitors are not sightseeing. They are paying a nocturnal visit to the estate of the village's most famous former resident, Henry Moore, known worldwide for his modernist sculptures of the female form in marble and bronze. It's a mild December night, only ten days before Christmas Eve and around 10 pm – outside the visiting hours of the 70-acre Henry Moore Foundation centre, home to one of the best collections of sculptures, sketches and paintings by one of Britain's finest artists of the 20th century. The visitors' centre is hidden from the road by a clutch of trees, and Moore's 26 sculptures are displayed on plinths in the fields on the other side of the road, far from the view of passing traffic.

It was too dark on that night for the grainy footage from the CCTV cameras to identify the hooded intruders. The men's entry into the yard triggered the light sensors, but the glare of the lights did not make any of them flinch. Two men got out of the green Mercedes and one out of the black Daihatsu, in full view of CCTV cameras, and went straight for a large object in front of the storage shed. It weighed a little over two tonnes; the equivalent of a Volkswagen Golf. The men wrapped webbing straps around the chunky, curved shape, and then the Mercedes flatbed truck came by with a mounted crane, stolen from a local farmer. The Foundation regularly moves the sculptures around, dictated by the requests from art galleries around the world to exhibit Moore's sculptures.

On that December night in 2005 the stolen Mercedes truck had come for one sculpture only – the 'Reclining Figure,' which had been sitting in the yard for a number of weeks awaiting repositioning. The sculpture, which Moore had designed and worked on throughout 1969, was swiftly lifted and placed onto the truck. It took the thieves eight minutes to enter and leave with a £3 million cargo of art on their truck. They then sped through the quiet narrow winding roads of the Hertfordshire countryside with the sculpture – three and a half metres long and two metres wide – sitting on the back of the truck exposed for everyone to see.

Only two witnesses reported seeing the truck. The theft was widely publicized, which would have made any potential art buyer nervous about purchasing the bronze treasure. Police and staff at the Henry Moore Foundation have resigned themselves to the fact that it was most probably stolen for its scrap metal value. The tragic thing is that even based on the high metal prices at the time, the thieves could have only expected to get about £4000 at most; about double the scrap value of 12 months earlier. 'It probably suffered irreparable damage within an hour of it being taken, and was probably broken up,' said Jon Humphries, Detective Inspector and senior investigating officer for the Hertfordshire Constabulary.

Most bronze sculptures are not solid metal all the way through and can be shattered by a large impact. The thickness of the metal was no more than a few inches, wide enough for it to be able to be cut by an angle grinder; a hand-held power tool. Although nobody has been charged with the crime and the evidence is still inconclusive, it is probable that the 'Reclining Figure' was cut into small pieces not too far from the Foundation before being taken to the scrap yard. 'It was probably melted down, shipped off to China where it was turned into wiring for computers, digital cameras and televisions and imported back here,' said Charles Joint, the administrator of the Foundation. There were no more leads, despite the £100 000 reward – a sum far greater than the scrap value of bronze work – put up by the Henry Moore Foundation for the return of the sculpture. Both vehicles used in the theft were found abandoned two weeks after the crime, but no finger marks were found; the thieves wore gloves. Local travellers (more colourfully known as gypsies), some of which reside in their own communities in the Harlow area, were interviewed after the theft but no arrests or charges were ever made.

For the Foundation, the impact has been far greater than the loss of one of Moore's more famous pieces of work. Security has increased, and more lights and CCTV have been installed. There are also now automatic parking bollards, and microchip tracking devices have been attached to the sculptures. Mr Joint from the Foundation, who has been at Perry Green for 11 years, is still shaken by the event more than 15 months later; disturbed that this work of art that Moore spent so much time designing, that was admired around the world and exhibited in Lisbon for 16 years until 1999 before returning to England via São Paulo and Rio de Janeiro, could come to such a brutal end. But the theft was just one of thousands that have occurred in recent years. It's a response to the fact that copper has risen in price to its highest since modern records began more than 100 years ago. Britain has 15 000 sites with bronze, marble and stone statues in public places, as well as cemeteries and churchyards; and the trend in copper theft has been concerning.

Copper in Demand

It is not just the sculptures of Britain that have attracted metal thieves. It's part of a global crime that has seen power lines, manhole covers, sewer plates, aluminium light poles, parking meters and motorway signs all disappear as thieves cash in on the rise in global metal prices. An estimated 1% of global copper supplies, or about 175 000 tonnes, with a market value of more than $1 billion (at early 2008 prices) comes from stolen copper. The British Transport Police (BTP), the national police force for Britain's railways said that 'after terrorism, (copper) cable theft is one of BTP's biggest challenges.'[1] The problem is so serious that the BTP have established a nationwide taskforce to tackle metal theft in conjunction with other British police forces and Railpol, the international network of police forces responsible for rail crime. A Google news search will come up with hundreds of stories of copper thefts across the world; often with deadly results – ambitious thieves trying to steal live power lines have been electrocuted through their endeavour. Building merchants have installed high security fences and construction sites put up signs saying 'no copper on site', reminiscent of the signs shop owners display to put off potential thieves looking for cash.

Copper can be melted down and its shape altered from a thick chunk of metal to a wire thinner than a human hair, so thieves can easily dispose of metal loot. Other precious metals – such as gold, silver or platinum – are malleable, but they are a lot more expensive than copper. While Moore liked to build sculptures from copper, modern industry has found other applications for one of man's oldest metals.[2] The red metal is one of the most essential materials used for creating today's sophisticated technology including mobile phones, iPods, laptops, high-speed internet access and Blackberries. No decent cook would use anything but copper-bottomed cookware, and even a glass of beer would not be possible without it: the vats for brewing beer are made of copper and the fridges that keep it cold have copper wiring.

Quite simply, copper made the electronic age possible. Without it, we would not be able to switch on a light, make a telephone call, search the internet, watch television, refrigerate food and drinks or listen to an MP3 player. Copper is also responsible for some of the music you listen to. Whether it is Miles Davis playing the trumpet or John Coltrane on the saxophone, both those instruments are made from brass, which contains copper. The rapid urbanization of China and other developing countries in the past 15 years has led to large scale electrification and the wiring of billions of copper cables across the globe, transmitting electrical power from the power station to the kitchen and living room to feed a multitude of power hungry electronic goods.

The world's copper supplies mostly come from large mines in re-mote parts of the Americas, Africa and Asia. The rest comes from sources closer to home – in many cases from inside the home, from discarded televisions, stereos and microwaves. These redundant elec-tronic goods are stripped of their thin copper wires by scrap metal merchants who are the conduit for the recycling of metals from motor vehicles, homes, buildings or industrial sites. Recycled copper is an important part of the supply picture, but the more important issue is mine production. Only 2.5 % of the 400 million tonnes of copper produced during the past millennia was mined and smelted before 1900 (Gibson-Jarvie, 1976).

Metals have the potential for infinite recovery and reuse. By and large they do not perish – unlike oil which is mainly burned in engines and power stations (becoming carbon emissions) or used to make plastic products, which can be recycled. Agriculture produce is also almost entirely consumed, though ultimately converted into manure that can be used for fertilizer to enhance the soil and grow more food.

The level of recycling depends on price and availability of the met-als. 'As affluence has increased, there has been a tendency for the quantities of waste to increase. We are living in a complex society where it is very difficult to recognize materials as such. We see products, buy services, and only in times of stress is it recognized that materials are the building blocks of things we use and energy we need.' These words pretty much sum up the contemporary situation, but they were actually written in 1974 (Blum, 1974). Recycling is a commodity. 'It is less expensive to extract copper and aluminium from scrap than it is to dig out of the ground,' says Kimberley Tara, chief executive at Four Winds Capital, the Swiss-based investment company.

Copper recycling has been around since copper was discovered 10 000 years ago. More than a third of the world's annual copper usage came from recycling in 2005. In Europe it was 41%, according to the International Copper Study Group, an intergovernmental body. Recycling of the red metal has been important throughout history and it is estimated that 80 % of the copper used since antiquity is still in circulation (European Copper Institute, 2007).[3] Weapons used in ancient battles are probably now reused for playing war games on computer consoles.

There are limits though. The processing of metal from the ground into a finished metal plus corrosion and wear creates waste, and some ends up in landfill. Also, some end-of-life products are not recycled. It is estimated that one-third of global steel production is recycled, along with 25–30 % of aluminium, 25 % of nickel, 45–50 % of lead, 15–20 % of tin and 20–25 % of zinc (Lomborg, 1998).

The use of scrap copper is important, because the discovery of new copper has not kept pace with the rate at which the metal is extracted and consumed. Most of the increase (around five-sixths to be exact) in the world's copper reserves in the past 80 years is from the re-evaluation of existing copper deposits (Gordon et al., 2006).[6] At the same time demand for copper continues to rise; strong global economic growth this decade along with new applications for the metal, such as in wind turbines and hybrid cars, have all boosted demand. In their 2006 report, Gordon, Bertram and Graedel suggest that the world will have to rely on recycled metal to meet future copper demand. To provide for the projected world population by the turn of the next century, the copper per capita of North America (170 kg) would require an additional 1700 million tonnes, it says. This is more than the world's total copper resource of 1600 million tonnes (Gordon *et al.*, 2006).

Consumers and corporations have jumped on the recycling band-wagon and many recycle unwanted electrical items. Governments are also on the case, trying to ensure that mountains of unwanted electrical equipment do not pile up. The European Union has laws governing what manufacturers can put in their computers, mobile phones and televisions, so that no toxic or hazardous materials are used in their production. There are also laws on collecting and recycling unwanted equipment.[5] The lifespan of consumer electronics is fast diminishing as new designs replace the old, so waste is a real issue. The EU introduced the Waste Electrical and Electronic Equipment (WEEE) in July 2007[6] and most US states have similar legislation whereby manufacturers are responsible for collecting and recycling electronic waste. Mobile phones are one of the biggest culprits; about 20% of the weight of a handset is copper (European Copper Institute, 2007). Car owners will also have to think about recycling their cars. Accredited professionals (scrap yards, scrap metal merchants and demolition contractors) clean up and then grind the bodies of automobiles at the end of their lives in order to extract the recyclable materials, such as copper.[7]

An Old Soul

Copper is one of the oldest metals known to humankind. It is not a precious metal but, like gold and silver, it has been used as currency throughout most of its history; the first copper coins dating back to 8700 BC (European Copper Institute, 2007). The Romans also used copper for money (Smith, 1776) and medals at the Olympics have historically been made from copper and tin; or nickel, which makes bronze. The rise in the use of copper and tin led to the Bronze Age, a period historians say started as far back as 5500 years ago in Anatolia, modern-day Turkey. During the Bronze Age copper was largely produced around the southeastern part of the Mediterranean and the Persian Gulf, but the history of the metal is closely linked to Cyprus. It was on this Mediterranean island that the first open-pit copper mine was operated, enabling the Hellenic, Mycenaean and Phoenician civilizations to prosper from the trade of metal around the Mediterranean.

The words 'copper' itself is also linked to the island. The Romans called it 'aes cyprium' which means 'metal from Cyprus' and this word has evolved over time to become 'copper'. The link to the Hellenic and Roman worlds is further underlined by the fact that the symbol for copper is the mirror of Venus; a circle on top of a cross that is associated with the Roman goddess of love and beauty and the Greek god Aphrodite, both revered on Cyprus (Gibson-Jarvie, 1976). In the early days copper was used for money exchange and for making weapons and decorative dress, such as crowns for the nobility, and by the 18th century it was used on ships' hulls to protect their oak bases from rotting, and in brewing vats and for distilling. But it was not until the beginning of the electrical industry that copper's importance really came to the fore.

It's Electrifying

In the early 19th century English inventor Michael Faraday built a small generator that produced electricity. One of its first applications was telegraphy, and the first commercial telegraphy system began in England in the 1830s. In 1843 the US built its first telegraph line (Lynch, 2002) which began as a network of copper wires traversing the vast distances of America. By the 1870s the telephone was invented and in the 1900s came wireless telegraphy, which led to the development of modern electronic information technology (Hall, 1998).

In the 1870s and 1880s came further innovations in the form of high-voltage electrical power for lighting and the electric light bulb, invented by Thomas Edison in 1878. This led to the construction of the electricity network, which of course meant that more copper wires needed to be laid. By the turn of the century, two-thirds of global copper production was devoted to electric wiring (Lynch, 2002). The start of the electricity industry gave birth to the commercial aluminium sector, a metal later used as a substitute for some copper applications.

Robo-Copper

Today, copper is embedded in our everyday lives. It's inside television sets, computers, cars, behind the light switch and inside the electrical socket; and in the underground power cables that connect our homes, offices and factories to the power network. In fact it's contained within pretty much anything to do with electricity.

Copper is vital for communications; found inside all mobile phones, telephone lines and high-speed internet cables. The expansion of the communications and information technology industries has revolutionized the way we live, work and communicate, and it has been one of the key drivers for economic growth in the latter stages of the 20th century. Copper has played a major role, making it as important a commodity as other raw materials such as oil, steel and agricultural produce.

Copper serves more basic functions too, such as turning on the hot water tap, and it's a good conductor of heat, that's why chefs prefer copper panware. It's also good for cooling; refrigerators in the home and supermarket all contain copper, as do air-conditioning systems in offices and industrial complexes. Copper can be found in other services we take for granted too, such as gas pipes and time control systems for lighting and heating.

The global economy is enduring one of its strongest periods since the 1960s and sales of electronic gadgets are rising, partly due to greater urbanization and wealthier consumers. In 2007 more of the world's population lived in cities than in rural areas. This movement of people reflects the industrialization of China, which has become the 'workshop of the world', churning out electronic goods and cars.

All these new homes, flats and apartments are connected to the rapidly expanding Chinese power grid, which added 70 gigawatts of electricity in 2006. In layman's terms it's the equivalent of adding the entire power network of Britain in one year. This requires an awful lot of copper and aluminium. 'The urbanization process involves staggering numbers of people. In the 30 years from 1994 to 2024, China's urban population is likely to rise from 350 million to 750 million. This represents a net addition to the urban population of over 13 million people a year, larger than the current population of Greece every year,' (Garner, 2005). The addition of this number of people is equivalent to the urbanization of Europe, Japan and the US after the Second World War.

The electrification of China has been a key reason for the increase in copper demand; metal used for wiring the country accounting for about half China's copper usage in the mid-2000s, which represented more than a tenth of global demand at the time. China's power network construction is expected to slow after 2010, by which time the country's power grid will have increased seven-fold from the late 1980s. The power grid is central to China's economic growth. It has invested heavily in power-intensive industries such as steel making, aluminium and copper smelting, along with manufacturing activities from car making to electrical appliances.

Once a building is connected to the power grid, dwellers can plug in their electronic consumer goods. The 1920s marked the start of the consumer durable boom; refrigerators, freezers and washing machines became commonplace in American homes, and radios were also invented. A similar boom did not happen in Europe until the 1950s, and the 1960s for Japan; the 1970s was when the telephone became prevalent in homes in Europe. When I was a child growing up in Islington in the 1970s, we shared the phone connection in our house with a Turkish Cypriot family down the road. I could always tell when they were on the line because I couldn't understand a word they were saying.

The 1970s ushered in the colour television (black and white TV was invented in the 1930s) and video recorders. Then, in the 1980s the CD player was introduced – 1982 to be exact – and the brick-sized and very expensive mobile phones, which became synonymous with the rich young professionals – or 'yuppies' – of the era. The 1990s brought more slimline mobile phones to a wider audience along with personal computers, digital cameras, DVDs, TV set-top boxes for satellite and cable TV, games consoles and – for the elderly – pacemakers. The 2000s is the era of MP3 players, the iPod, plasma TV, digital TV and digital radio.

Innovative design or planned obsolescence means that computers are being updated every couple of years. A teenager's bedroom in the developed world is full of many more electronic gadgets than the stereo I boasted about having when I was a teenager. Now the average teenager has a personal computer and a laptop, an MP3 player, CD player and television. Mobile phones are updated annually among some groups, and even the largest copper-using items, such as cars, are traded in after five years. Together these items have created a mass media culture where people around the world can watch, listen to and read the same films, sports, music and news, all brought about through technology dependent on metals such as copper.

More than 6 million televisions including plasma screens, were sold in 2006 in the US, along with 10.8 million video recorders. Americans are no longer the biggest owners of consumer electrical goods though. China already had the largest number of TVs in the world, overtaking the US, back in 1991. It has nearly twice the number of sets in the US (Garner, 2005). In 2001 China also surpassed the US with the world's highest mobile phone handset ownership. It has the largest number of fixed-line phones in the world as well, but lags behind the US when it comes to personal computers. 'PC ownership can be taken as a reasonable proxy for demand for other larger ticket electrical good items,' (Garner, 2005).

Our modern lifestyles are becoming more and more electronically enabled. About 40 billion computers are expected to be embedded within devices in cars, home appliances and office machines by the year 2020, all of which will increase the need for copper (Cohen, 2007). Other applications for the future include the use of timer switches and controls to reduce power consumption, popular because of their potential to cut greenhouse gas emissions. Copper is used in these electronic items because it is a good conductor of electricity and, although it's not as good as silver, it is a more economical alternative. It makes copper all the more sought after in an energy-efficient world. Good conductivity means that less electricity is lost carrying electrons over the wire, and improved electricity efficiency reduces carbon emissions because less electricity is lost through transmission. Copper is also in transformers, which are a key part of the power supply network, designed to raise or lower the voltage to meet specific electrical needs.

Demand for copper is on the rise, and for much of the first decade of the 21st century has outpaced mine supplies. In 2005 global copper stockpiles were reduced to their lowest level in decades and, as a consequence, copper prices went beyond the wildest dreams of those people who in bygone days tried to corner the market.

Aluminium is an alternative but it is two-thirds as efficient as copper for conducting electricity. Aluminium cables therefore need to be 65% bigger than their copper equivalents in order to be as energy efficient. This is appropriate for overhead power cables, where there are no restrictions on space, but in more confined spaces (like in electrical wiring in houses and underground where they need to be insulated), thinner copper cables are preferred. In addition, copper has a higher resistance to corrosion than aluminium and a higher level of fire resistance. It also has a better thermal capacity than aluminium, meaning less space needs to be dedicated to ventilation. In 2008, in another ironic twist the demand for power exceeded supply in many places including China and South Africa, which led to rationing by users, which led to intensive power users such as aluminium producers cutting their output and in turn pushing metal prices higher.

Motor Copper

A major use of copper is in motor vehicles, trucks, buses and other transportation such as railway, marine, aircraft and aerospace equipment.

In 1900 the United States had 8000 cars and Japan only had sixty-two in 1909 (Pointing, 2007). A century on, annual global car sales were an estimated 53 million in 2007, with China and India accounting for 11 % of new sales, compared with around 1.6% throughout the 1990s (Gomes, 2007). There are now 800 million motor vehicles in the world, and sales are increasing. This means there is a larger pool of potential recycled copper available as the lifespan of a car diminishes, with consumers trading in their cars for newer ones much more often than they previously did.

The modern car has become more electronic, with power steering, brakes, heating, central locking, Global Positioning Systems (GPS) and on-board computers with internet access. Users can now consult traffic or weather information online while on the road, and even receive faxes and emails. The quantity of copper in passenger cars ranges from 20 kg in small cars to 45 kg in luxury models and new hybrid vehicles. With concern about oil supplies, more efficient cars are a priority. The electric vehicle – which goes beyond a hybrid as it does not have a conventional internal combustion engine – requires even more copper parts.

General Motors spent billions of dollars developing the electric vehicle – known as EV1 – to comply with tighter clean air regulations in California, but by the end of the 1990s the world's largest car maker recalled the few hundred EVs that it had made and they were crushed due to a legal case brought by car makers against the California state government. This was shown in the documentary 'Who Killed the Electric Car?' A decade later it has a new electric vehicle – the Concept Chevy Volt, which can run on electricity, petrol, ethanol or biodiesel. This is the spearhead of General Motors' campaign to catch up with Toyota Motor Company, the maker of the hybrid pioneering car, the Prius. Launched in Japan in 1997, the Prius is a hit in Europe and the US.

With 'green technology' the new economy of the 21st century, entrepreneurs see an opportunity for electric vehicles including Telsa Motors, founded by internet mogul Elon Musk, as do university research departments at points around the US, the UK, Europe and Japan; all of which will require more copper.

Motor vehicles are big polluters; combined with air travel, transport as a whole accounts for 14% of global emissions each year. It has been the fastest growing source of emissions because of continued increases in car transport and the rapid expansion of air travel (Stern, 2006).

Metals also play a key role in the reduction of pollution though. The catalytic converter (a device put in the car exhaust to reduce car emissions) is made from platinum and is responsible for dramatically lowering car emissions.[8]

Platinum has the potential for cutting emissions even further. Millions of dollars have been spent on research to test platinum as a catalyst for fuel cells, a device that can convert hydrogen into electricity. Fuel cell technology can be traced back to the 1830s (Hall, 1998). Fuel cells gained a new impetus with the oil crisis of the 1970s as budgets increased for research into alternative energies.

The US government had already done a lot of work on fuel cells in the previous decade; its space agency – the National Aeronautics and Space Administration (NASA) – had been looking for technologies to power manned space flights. Fuel cells were seen as a lighter solution to batteries, cheaper than solar energy and less risky than nuclear. And fuel cells with platinum-made catalysts have since been used on the Apollo missions and space shuttle flights.

In his State of the Union speech in January 2003 President George W. Bush brought fuel cells to the world's attention when he unveiled a $1.2 billion research grant to fund the development of hydrogen-powered motor vehicles. 'A single chemical reaction between hydrogen and oxygen generates energy, which can be used to power a car – producing only water, not exhaust fumes. With a new national commitment, our scientists and engineers will overcome obstacles to taking these cars from laboratory to showroom, so that the first car driven by a child born today could be powered by hydrogen, and pollution-free.' He concluded by saying 'Join me in this important innovation to make our air significantly cleaner, and our country much less dependent on foreign sources of energy.' But the US has to import 95% of its platinum needs; hardly a strategy for resource independence (US Geological Survey, 2007).

To date there has been scant tangible evidence of a technological breakthrough, despite the launch of the first fuel cell car in 1993 by

Ballard, the Canadian fuel cell development company. Estimates back in the 1990s of a fuel cell car market worth billions by the middle of this decade, as part of the new 'hydrogen economy', have so far fallen well short of the mark. This may be due to fuel cells getting caught up in the technology hype of the 1990s. The availability of platinum has meant that fuel cells remain a key part of research for the car industry, though other fuel cells have also been introduced this decade to replace batteries in mobile devices such as laptops and lawnmowers.

Companies have been very guarded about their research pro-grammes. One factor that could be holding back commercial success is the cost of platinum – it's about double the price of gold and far rarer. More than three-quarters of the world's platinum reserves lie in one country – South Africa. The current technology uses about 60 grams of platinum for each fuel cell, and if the world's 800 million cars were all equipped with a fuel cell, this would equate to 48 000 tonnes. There's one problem: the world's reserves of platinum and its sister metals palladium, rhodium and iridium, which are normally found together in the same deposits, only amount to about 43 351 tonnes.[9]

General Motors has planned a production-viable fuel cell vehicle by 2010 and Toyota, the second largest car manufacturer, wants to lower its production cost of more than $1 million per car to $50 000 by 2015, when it plans to begin sales (Mackintosh and Morrison, 2005). At around $1700 a troy ounce in January 2008, platinum cost per fuel cell is more than $3280. A 100-page research report commis-sioned by the US Department of Energy in 2003 estimated that mined platinum demand could rise between three and six times the levels seen between 1960 and 2000 if fuel cell vehicles are commercially viable (US Department of Energy, 2003). An increase in demand at this rate would cause prices to rise, which in turn could affect the economics of mass deployment of fuel cell technology. The report acknowledged that there might not be enough platinum resources to achieve a high penetration of fuel cells in cars.

The world may still wait for the first commercial platinum fuel cell, but the metal will be used in more and more motorized items by the end of the decade; catalytic converters will be found in everything from lawnmowers to oil tankers as part of a new wave of international legislation for cleaner air.

Emission Copper

Copper plays a significant part in reducing greenhouse gas emissions. Professor Ronald Belmans of the University of Louvain estimates that each tonne of copper used in improving the yield from energy systems leads to a saving of 200 tonnes of CO_2 (European Copper Institute, 2004). Both Europe and the United States have established high-efficiency motor standards to boost electric motor efficiency, and reducing CO_2 emissions is now recognized to be the responsibility of both consumers and industry. A 15-minute shower, cooking with gas for 20 minutes, driving a car for 4 km: each of these activities produces 1 kg of CO_2.[10]

Electricity generation is also set to become more copper intensive as many more wind turbines are projected to be installed. The blades on windmills are normally copper tipped and underground copper wire cables connect the wind farm to the electricity grid. A one megawatt wind turbine contains about three tonnes of copper and each one saves about 1000 tonnes of carbon emissions each year.[6] Because of this carbon saving the International Energy Agency predicted that global wind power would achieve the biggest increase in power generation among renewable sources by 2030 (International Energy Agency, 2006). The European Union forecasts that by 2010 wind energy will save around 140 million tonnes annually, or the equivalent of more than 30% of the EU's Kyoto Protocol obligation.

Copper is also found in the silicon film of solar panels[11] and in the control system components of solar technology.

Focusing attention on carbon emission reduction, energy efficiency, hybrid cars and wind farms has provoked another wave of demand for copper, on top of its core demand areas in power generation, consumer electronics and telecommunications. At a time when the world's population and the global economy are expanding at the fastest rate in four decades, demand for copper is greater than ever. Car makers source copper from fabricators who buy the metal from the producers. The consumer rarely gets involved in the extraction of the material, and the miner rarely gets involved downstream, the exception possibly being the aluminium industry, a big supplier to the motor vehicle and aircraft industries. But in the early days of the motor vehicle industry it was different.

Henry Ford was keen on other commodities – particularly those that helped make cars. After rolling out the first black Model T in 1908, Ford's empire had, by the late 1920s, extended from a rubber plantation – called Fordlandia – in Brazil's Amazonian forest for his tyres, to coal mines in Kentucky, West Virginia and Pennsylvania to feed a secure power source for his sprawling River Rouge plant in Michigan, which employed 100 000 people (Dempsey, 1994).

The company also had iron ore mines in northern Michigan, Minnesota and Wisconsin to turn into steel for the frames and bodies of the cars, plus thousands of acres of forests in Michigan,[13] the wood was used to make panels for the interior of the cars (Iacocca, 1998). Few companies in the free-market societies ever matched Ford's vertical integration plan. The business fashion today is still scale, but specialization is also a focus: return on capital is key. Ford's concept was disbanded after he died in 1947.

The car industry and industrial consumers pay close attention to the supply of copper, where it comes from and the security of supply.

Red Hot Chile Copper

Global copper production quadrupled from the 1880s to 500 000 tonnes in 1900, much of the increase coming from new mines in Montana and Nevada. This was to meet the early demand from the newly created electricity industry. This new source of supply brought with it technical breakthroughs in deep mining and by 1883 the US had overtaken Chile as the world's leading mine producer of copper, a position it maintained until the late 1970s. Chile itself had only recently surpassed Great Britain, Cornwall and Devon having been the world's main area of production for around 100 years until 1857 (Schmitz, 1986).

Depletion of the resource led many Cornish miners to look farther afield for new resources, so they went to Chile. British ships brought the mineral back to process in the smelters in Swansea, which had already been processing Cornish copper (Mayo, 2001). The copper trade link between Britain and Chile helped influence the trading structure within the London Metal Exchange, the key centre for metals trading; in fact one of the benchmark contracts is the 'three-month copper contract', which is based on the time it would take ships to travel from Chile to the UK ports of Swansea, Bristol and Liverpool (Lynch, 2002).

Chile's reign as the world's top copper producer was to be relatively short-lived though, as it was soon surpassed by the US. Chile had been the world's leading copper producer in the 1870s, accounting for as much as 43% of global output, but in subsequent decades the industry stagnated. After the turn of the 20th century, the nation's share of the world market fell to less than 5%.

Although Chile had the resources, it was the ownership structure of the industry that held back expansion. For most of the 19th century copper mines were owned by wealthy and politically powerful Chilean families, creating inertia in the industry. The industry also failed to adopt many of the new techniques used in the US for mining at deeper levels. It could have done with these; much of the country's near-surface copper deposits were approaching exhaustion. Chilean mines were not even using the steam power that had been adopted in US mines; relying instead on manual labour and mules (Young, 1983; Volk, 1993). From 1892–1929 the US dominated global copper mining, accounting for between 50 and 65% of world output. It was a major supplier to the rest of the world; domestic US consumption accounted for up to 45% of total global demand (Schmitz, 1986).

The fading force of the Chilean copper industry resulted in a government turnaround that allowed foreign companies to operate copper mines almost tax-free (Volk, 1993). The friendly corporate tax rate particularly attracted US investors and by the end of World War I, more than 87% of Chilean copper production was in the hands of American shareholders (Volk, 1993). At the forefront were the Guggenheim brothers. The Guggenheims are better known today as patrons of art, with their network of impressive galleries around the world from the Basque town of Bilbao in northern Spain, to Venice, Berlin, Manhattan and Las Vegas, but they made much of their early fortune from mining, in particular from copper.

The Guggenheims developed the Chilean copper deposits El Teniente and Chuquicamata, which was later to become the largest copper mine in the world. To develop the large copper deposit, the family formed the Chile Copper Company, which was to be nationalized by the Chilean government in the 1970s (O'Brien, 1989). The Guggenheims also had mining interests in Mexico; they were among the biggest US investors in Latin America, which accounted for almost half of all US direct foreign investment before the outbreak of World War I.[14] One of the first big steps for the Guggenheims came in 1901 when they took control of ASARCO, the American Smelting and Refining Company set up by Henry H. Rogers, one of the senior executives of John D. Rockefeller's Standard Oil (Yergin, 1991, p. 102).

The Guggenheims sold out of their interest in Chuquicamata in 1923[15] and reinvested the proceeds in Chile's other major industry, the nitrate deposits of the Atacama Desert, which were highly sought after to fertilize the corn and wheat crops in the United States as well as the manufacture of explosives. In hindsight it was not such a good trade for the family; Anaconda found more copper reserves at Chuquicamata and the Chilean nitrate sector was entering the twilight of its economic prowess. When the Guggenheims entered the Chilean copper sector at the start of the century, the nitrate industry was Chile's principal source of export revenues and government income.[16] By the end of the 1920s the natural nitrate industry was facing intense competition from synthetic nitrate producers, with the costs of natural nitrates 30% more, and Chile's share of the world market in nitrate had fallen from a prewar 58 % to 24%. With the natural nitrate industry on the verge of collapse, the Guggenheims and the Chilean government combined their interests (O'Brien, 1989).

The rich deposits of nitrates and guano – the nutrient-rich waste of sea birds (otherwise known as bird droppings) – were a key factor behind the War of the Pacific (1879–83) between Chile and its neighbours, Bolivia and Peru. The three countries shared the Atacama Desert; Peru had the northern ports of Iquique and Bolivia had Antofagasta. The ramifications of the war still linger in Andean politics, weighing down the Chilean copper industry even today.

The origin of the War of the Pacific is still open to much debate, but there was a lot of tension between the three countries ahead of the war. Chile's share of global copper production had peaked and output from the emerging US was quickly taking market share. Copper prices had declined sharply[17] due to the world depression, triggered early in the decade when the collapse of America's leading banker Jay Cooke – a financier to the US railway expansion – led to the New York Stock Exchange closing for the first time in its history.[18] The contagion spread to Europe where markets crashed as well (Gray et al., 2007). The United States entered a period of depression that lasted until 1879, which many consider second only in gravity to the 'Crash' of 1929 (Sater, 1979).

Chile's seizure of Peru and Bolivia's nitrate regions during the War of the Pacific opened a new era of prosperity for the Chilean economy (O'Brien, 1989). The nitrate industry was to be dominated by the British who had 69% of the nitrate industry by the end of the 19th century (O'Brien, 1979). The British had large investments in Chilean railways, banking and property, but not in mining (Centner, 1942),[19] still wary after the 'bubble-mania' of 1824–1825 in Latin America when the new found optimism of British investors towards the newly independent countries of central and south America did not reap rewards, as Latin American mines produced meagre results.[20]

Much of the British investment in nitrates came through British shipping and merchants. John Thomas North, a Yorkshireman, was referred to as the 'nitrate king.' North established a base in Iquique in the early 1870s when it was still part of Peru, but there were British merchants all along the Pacific coast of South America. The merchants bought the minerals and arranged the shipping and the sales to the industrial buyers in Europe and North America (Monteón, 2003) (a similar role is fulfilled by the large commodity traders of today, such as Glencore, Vitol, Trafigura and Noble Group). North was also one of the early resource entrepreneurs on the London Stock Exchange, a financial species that exists to this day. Michael Monteón, in his paper on John North, wrote that the (London) Stock Exchange Year-Book listed a total of 23 companies linked to nitrate production on the London stock market in 1890, of which North appeared as a major stockholder or founder of 15.[12] Although there is nobody that can boast as many listed companies as this today, there are a number of mining entrepreneurs that have almost as many outfits, such as the Scottish-born Harry Dobson, Australian Andrew Forrest, Canadian Robert Friedland and the French-speaking Jean-Raymond Boulle.

Chile was very much at the centre of foreign investment in minerals in Latin America. The country's nitrate and copper output had exceeded the mineral production of all the other countries of South America combined until 1927, when the production of petroleum in Venezuela became more established (Whitbeck, 1929).[22]

The four large US copper producers: Anaconda, ASARCO, Kennecott Copper and Phelps Dodge had increased their share of global production by the end of the 1920s to more than half, from around a third in the 1880s (Schmitz, 1986). It was during this period that mining developed from the rudimentary enterprise of the early 19th century into a technologically sophisticated industry. This was also the 'Gilded Age' when powerful businessmen built their fortunes, many based on raw materials (as has happened again in the 21st century, many of Russia's billionaires building their empires on the country's natural resources: Roman Abramovich from oil, Oleg Deripaska and Viktor Vekselberg from aluminium and Vladimir Potanin from nickel and palladium).[23]

But there is a contrast between today and the period of the late 19th century and early 20th century in regards to the way the copper market and copper prices function. The proposed merger between fellow Anglo – Australian miners BHP Billiton and Rio Tinto has raised the spectre of a dominant player in the global supply of iron ore, which is used for steelmaking, aluminium, coal, uranium and copper. Out of all the metals, copper has been the subject of the most attempts to control supplies to the market.

The rise in copper price this decade has been accompanied by accusations of manipulation. They remain allegations, whereas more than a century ago there were concerted efforts to control the copper market. In the autumn of 1887 The Secretan Syndicate, which was conceived by Pierre Secretan, manager of French company Le Societé des Metaux started buying copper, causing Chilean copper prices to more than double. The aim was to corner the market but the higher prices brought more scrap to the market and Secretan had to spend more money to maintain his grip. This ultimately led to more production and consumers were put off paying the higher prices. Global copper stockpiles trebled during 1888, which forced the undoing of Secretan's scheme (Gibson-Jarvie, 1976). Producers were led by Amalgamated Copper Company, backed by Henry Rogers of Standard Oil and William Goodsell Rockefeller, nephew of John D. Rockefeller. Amalgamated floated in 1889, bought fellow copper producer Anaconda (Schmitz, 1986), and in the same year attempted to corner the copper market by holding back shipments to Europe. This pushed prices higher, which stimulated supplies from other sources. Amalgamated was left holding very large stocks at a time of rapidly plunging prices (Gibson-Jarvie, 1976).

The Rothschild bank – which had historically been involved in the gold trade, and which was a financier to the oil rush in the Caspian Sea in the late 19th century, and the diamond trade through its interests in De Beers – was also interested in copper during this period; it was financier to the Secretan scheme at a time when it was a key shareholder in Rio Tinto, and also to Anaconda. This combined interest gave the Rothschilds 'real power' in the world copper market in the late 19th century (Ferguson, 1998).[24]

A second copper producer scheme was set up – the Copper Producers' Association – which attempted to peg price and limit production when market demand weakened. The association's efforts were defunct due to the increased requirements of industry for World War I (Mingst, 1976). Once the war finished, yet another producer-led group formed – the Copper Export Association – founded in the United States in 1918. The Association purchased copper from members to dispose of excess stocks and determined both the price paid to members and the export price. In 1923 excess capacity in the copper industry had been substantially reduced and the association sold its last stock. But members suffered financial losses, confronted with price competition from a new non-member producer – the Belgian Congo (Mingst, 1976).

Only a few years had passed before copper producers were once again trying to control the market – American producers together with Rio Tinto, the London-based miner, Katanga of Congo and German interests formed Copper Exporters Incorporated (Gibson-Jarvie, 1976) in 1926 (Walters, 1944)[25]. By 1929 and into 1930 the cartel, which held about 95% of global copper production, had tried to hold the price at nearly 18 cents a pound of copper in the face of world depression (Schmitz, 1986). This led to a collapse in price and excess capacity and the cartel was dissolved in 1932 (Walters, 1944). The group was formed under an American law, the Webb–Pomerene Act, which allowed US companies to do abroad what antitrust laws forbade them to do at home (Yergin, 1991). Again, the higher price prompted more supplies, this time from the Northern Rhodesian (Zambian) copper belt, as well as substitution by aluminium, which was cheaper than copper (Schmitz, 1986).

Despite the lack of success, yet another attempt was made to control copper prices. The International Copper Cartel was formed in 1935, members agreeing to restrict output to three-quarters of their capacity (Gibson-Jarvie, 1976). This cartel also appeared to have the blessing of Western governments and the US called for an international agreement to coordinate production and marketing of copper (Walters, 1944). But even government agreements lost their meaning upon the outbreak of the Second World War, which terminated the cartel. The 1930s saw the emergence of copper supplies from more countries. The American grip on the copper market loosened, and African copper production started to take hold.

Out of Africa

From 1870 to 1939 global copper production rose twenty-fold, far greater than the increases in lead, tin and zinc (Fetter, 1999), with the higher output coming from Chile, Canada, Northern Rhodesia and Belgian Congo.

Just as in the battles of antiquity, copper was again used in warfare, but on a bigger scale during the Second World War: 'Copper played a fundamental part in the slaughter that took place during the war with hundreds of thousands of pounds worth devoured by the assembly lines that made brass cartridges and cannon shells. Thousands of miles of copper wiring were required for the complex electrical systems in aircraft, tanks and warships' (Dumett, 1985).

Africa's natural resources were used further for the war; uranium from Katanga led to the development of the atomic bomb during World War II. Union Miniere, the Belgian mining company that held the mining rights in the Congo, sent its entire uranium supplies to New York. It was all the US had to work with, and it was with this supply that the atomic bomb was developed. [26] The war saw America emerge as a military power in its own right and the looming Cold War with the Soviet Union prompted the US to set up its stockpile of strategic materials (Heivilin, 1992).[27] Much of this was metals; the US imported its entire needs for platinum, tin, chromium and tungsten, and the materials were used for military and space research purposes. Following the collapse of the Berlin Wall, the US government started selling down its stockpile, raising billions of dollars.[28]

The post-war reconstruction in Europe and Japan and the economic boom in the United States led to a huge boost in copper demand, and by the 1960s a wave of independence was spreading throughout colonial Africa. Northern Rhodesia became Zambia, Congo became Zaire, and then was renamed Congo again in the 1990s. Independence was followed by the nationalization of their respective copper industries; the locals felt that they had not been given a sufficient share from the wealth of their natural resources. Zambia started its nationalization programme in the late 1960s (Mupimpila and van der Grijp, 1998), followed by Zaire and later spreading to Chile. At the end of the 1960s, Chilean copper mines were mainly owned by US producers, such as Anaconda and Kennecott. This was about to change. In 1971, the Chilean congress voted to nationalize the mines owned by the US producers, and in 1976 the military government created Codelco to operate the nationalized copper mines such as Chuquicamata, giving the government an 85% share of the country's copper output.

The air of liberation and nationalization gave developing countries more power. Chile, Peru, Zaire (Congo) and Zambia set up the Intergovernmental Council of Copper Exporting Countries (CIPEC) in 1967; the copper equivalent of Opec (Gibson-Jarvie, 1976). The grouping accounted for 40% of global copper production, but more importantly it was responsible for 80% of world copper exports (Mingst, 1976).[29]

During the early years CIPEC lacked a coherent strategy. It was not until Opec had success with higher prices following the Arab oil embargo that the grouping decided to take some action. In 1974 copper production was cut by 10%, the motivation being Opec's new-found fortune that had caused deterioration in copper market conditions as the quadrupling in oil price had triggered inflation leading to an economic slowdown (Mingst, 1976).

The success of Opec in the 1970s brought a wave of producer cartels across many commodities, in particular metals, which had the International Bauxite Association (IBA) and the International Tin Council. Opec succeeded where other producer groupings, for many reasons, did not. The oil reserves in Opec were fairly concentrated, whereas reserves of metallic minerals are more widespread, and substitution of metals is more readily available than is oil for transportation. The lack of success of these groupings displaced the initial fears of consuming countries that the cartels would distort the price of the metals.

The unity of the copper grouping was tested in April 1975 when CIPEC gave the go-ahead for a further 15% increase in production, but as the membership widened, with Australia, Indonesia and Papua New Guinea joining the grouping, members failed to abide by the quotas. CIPEC failed to become an effective force in the world copper market and was disbanded in 1992. Of all the commodity producer groupings only Opec has remained in operation, and there has been no attempt to form another copper producer grouping – although there has been at least one known attempt (the Sumitomo scandal – see Chapter 5) to corner the copper market in the past 40 years. Aside from this incident, copper prices have been determined by the market.

Although Chile had nationalized its copper industry, the Santiago government did not close the door on foreign investment or to the London Metal Exchange (LME) to hedge its copper production. It provided low tax incentives for outside investors, which led to a surge in Chilean copper production and, by 1996, foreign investors again accounted for the majority of Chile's copper production. It was during this period that Chile overtook the United States again and resumed its mantle as the world's largest copper producer (Spilimbergo, 1999). The two countries combined hold almost half of the world's copper reserves.[30]

This increase in copper production meant that Chile was now largely responsible for meeting the increase in the world's copper consumption. Since the turn of the 20th century, global copper production has doubled every 30 years: in 1900 copper output was 495 000 tonnes and by 1912 it had doubled to 1 million; it had doubled again by 1937 and reached 4 million by 1961, exceeding 16 million tonnes in 2006. On this trajectory, by 2037 there will be a 32 million tonne production output. This increase in demand will be met by mines that are in the planning and development stages now. [31]

Copper Country

The world has relied on Chile to meet increased copper consumption for the best part of the last 20 years and political stability has returned, with the re-establishment of civilian rule following the December 1989 election, when Chileans were able to demonstrate their democratic rights again for the first time in 19 years.

I remember the election well. I had just endured a backbreaking bus journey from the Bolivian capital of La Paz to the coastal town of Arica in northern Chile when I arrived at dawn to hordes of men out celebrating; they had been out all night long. There were no women among them. One man held court in the café where I was trying to wake up with several cups of coffee. For the benefit of the assorted tourists who had gotten off the bus he was saying, 'Pinochet gone, kaput' and then pointing his thumb to the floor, repeating this line and gesture several times. Then I got the picture: democracy had returned to Chile. With it came a flood of new investment in copper.[32]

Now, though, Chile is facing constraints on further mine supply growth due to water and power issues, as well as some existing mines that are striking arsenic in their ore bodies. Many of Chile's large copper mines were developed around the expansion boom period of the 1990s, so they are now simultaneously digging in the part of the rock ore where arsenic is present. Arsenic occurs at varying levels in some copper ore bodies and is a significant environmental hazard in the copper smelting process, when emissions are released into the atmosphere. The arsenic in the ore is contained in copper–arsenic sulphide minerals, such as enargite and tanzanite. It is not a subject the industry wants to talk about publicly, but it is an issue they all acknowledge and is of great concern because it strikes at the heart of the world's copper body.

Flying over the Andes in northern Chile in the red-purple light of dawn, I remember looking down on the giant mountains below and seeing the dark reddish tone of the rock, which gave the impression that I was flying over mountains of copper. More than a quarter of global copper output is produced in one of the driest places on the planet, the Atacama Desert in northern Chile, where miners are battling with local villagers and environmentalists for access to the meagre water supplies. The owners of the world's largest copper mine, led by BHP Billiton – an Anglo–Australian resources group – spent $200 million on a desalination plant to pump nearby 9.9 million gallons of water a day along a 124 mile (170 kilometres) pipeline from Antofagasta to the Escondida mine 3000 metres above sea-level, high in the Andes of Chile. But the desalinated water is only a tenth of the mine's total daily water requirements of about 2.35 million barrels, which equates to about half of Latin America's entire daily oil consumption.

Mining copper is a thirsty process. To produce one tonne of copper, 100 tonnes of earth and rock has to be removed; a process that uses between 100 and 300 tonnes of water, and the scarcity of water has put restrictions on many mine operations. The Collahuasi mine, in Chile's most northern region of Tarapaca, was ordered in 2006 to cut its daily water usage by a quarter; other mines have also complained that restrictions impede their growth plans. Information on water is conspicuous by its absence. The most recent report by the Director General of Water was published in 1999 and the few private studies on Chile's aquifers make for worrying reading. US consulting firm Golder and Associates concluded that the River Copiapó basin, which is in the heart of Chile's copper region, had enough water for just four years. This forecast was made in 2006 (Harris, 2007).

The Atacama is a very dry place. It was a very unusual place to play a tennis match on a grass court as I did when I visited there almost 20 years ago, on a court fed by water from a borehole. It was at a villa high on the pampas up from Iquique, the northern port that gained much of its early wealth from nitrate exports and borax, with which it is very well endowed. The road from Iquique zigzags up about 2000 feet. Chile is one of the few countries in the world that issues water permits that allow the holder to consume a defined amount of water, a system it has adopted in an attempt to better manage its constrained water reserves, but it has not gone smoothly, with critics claiming that too many permits have been issued. One of the main problems is that there have never been any studies done to estimate how much water Chile actually has and therefore what is a sustainable amount of water to be used by the permit holders; as a result there was no restriction on the amount of permits issued. The Santiago government has stopped issuing more permits, but it is not buying any back.

The scarcity of water has pitted miners against farmers and created a major challenge for Chile in terms of expanding its copper production, compounded by the rising cost of water and the lack of domestic energy sources to generate power for the energy-intensive mining operations. Water from desalination is about five times the cost per cubic metre of water from groundwater. Given the amount of water required, this implies that the cost of production will rise, underpinning higher copper prices – prices do not fall below the cost of production for long. The need for water has also pushed up the value of permits to extract water from aquifers and kickstarted a water exploration industry – water exploration companies play a similar role to the small mineral exploration companies. Added to this, Chile is not endowed with bountiful energy resources; it imports about two-thirds of its energy requirements, compared with less than half in 1990. The importation of fuels for power generation is therefore particularly important for the copper industry (Poniachik, 2006).

In the mid-1990s Chile invested billions of dollars in new pipelines to import natural gas from its largest neighbour, Argentina. But with a rebound in the Argentine economy after its economic crisis in 2001/2, domestic natural gas demand overtook supply and the Buenos Aires government restricted gas exports to Chile. Such was Argentina's gas demand that it struck a deal with gas-rich Bolivia; the Bolivian government's condition was that Argentina would not re-export the gas to Chile. Bolivia and Chile have not had diplomatic ties with one another since 1978 – a dispute that harks back to the five-year War of the Pacific, when Bolivia lost its coastline to Chile; it has been landlocked ever since. Chile and Bolivia are not expected to resolve their differences and instead Chile has turned to a country thousands of kilometres away – Indonesia will start exporting gas to Chile in 2009.

Further copper production in Chile is dependent on secure water and power supplies. The state-owned Codelco, which has copper-plated lifts in its Santiago headquarters and accounts for about a third of Chilean production, has struggled to lift copper output since 2004.[33]

Water and power limitations have curbed the rate of increase in the production of Chilean copper, and having more than doubled in the ten years to the mid-2000s, Chile's copper supply growth is projected to slow. Despite this, Chile will still be very important and remain by far the biggest copper producer in the world. Its prominence in the industry draws hordes of executives, financiers, hedge funds and industrial consumers to Santiago each spring to make deals and discuss projects, and to renew contacts. This annual gathering for the copper club used to take place in New York, but the warmer climate and the reduction in the number of US copper producers has seen it shift south in recent years. When I was in Santiago in the spring of 2006, the main dinner for the annual copper conference was preceded by a horse race, with delegates drinking Pisco Sours.

Copper accounts for the majority of Chile's exports but the country is finding itself becoming more and more a miner of copper concentrate, the sand-like form of the metal that is obtained once its has been fully extracted from the ore in which it is found. The country now exports more copper in this powder form than the sheet metal version which fabricators can turn into pipes, electrical wire and brass furnishings. Chile exports the copper powder to China where it is turned into refined metal; China is projected to become the world's largest copper refiner by the end of the decade. Chile's production of refined copper has remained static for most of the 2000s, and it has not developed a new smelting and refining complex for the past 40 years, though it has upgraded refineries during this period. Part of the reason for not expanding is because of the increase in the energy Chile would have to import to run the plants – the process of converting concentrate to copper cathode relies on processing at extremely high temperatures to keep it in its liquid state (Morrison, 2006).

Another factor is that copper-importing countries such as Japan, South Korea and China have all benefited from government subsidies to build their own copper smelters, which has led to over-capacity and a drop in smelter margins. Chile, on the other hand, does not provide subsidies for smelters.

The presence of copper is not the issue – Chile has the copper it needs, it just doesn't have the tools to extract it, and this has forced companies to look elsewhere. Antofagasta, named after the Chilean port town (no prize for guessing where its corporate roots are) has broadened its search outside of Chile for the first time in 100 years of operations and is now looking for copper in Pakistan, a country not renowned for its metal production or political stability. Explorers are searching the Earth and its oceans for copper; though no longer with a pick and a shovel – they now have sophisticated rock-drilling machines. They're looking in Mongolia, Kazakhstan, Congo, Zambia, Peru, Brazil and Mexico, and there is also a renewed copper rush in the United States and in Australia.

For much of the developing world the legacy of mining has been an unhappy one: polluted rivers, scarred lands and no sharing of the wealth extracted from the mines with the local population – far from the 'frontier thesis' that Frederick Jackson Turner proclaimed of the West: 'Not the constitution, but free land and an abundance of natural resources open to a fit people, made the democratic type of society in America... These free lands promoted individualism, economic equality, freedom to rise, democracy.'

Africa has once again become the target for foreigners looking to extract wealth from its lands. Even the Guggenheims and the nitrate king John North were attracted to the rich promise of the Congo.[34,35] China has ploughed billions into securing oil and minerals from the vast continent. When I visited mainland China for the first time in December 2006 to give a speech at a steel conference – aside from the sheer scale of the Chinese capital, the number of people, the multitude of cars and traffic, and the new apartment buildings, offices, hotels and shopping centres, all host to swarms of people – one of my first impressions was the number of images of Africa. Giant pictures of elephants, giraffes, zebras, antelopes, African tribesmen, the sunset over the African savannah and the pyramids of Egypt stretched for blocks at a time, accompanied with slogans proclaiming 'Africa, the land of myth and miracles, friendship and partnership.' Beijing even dubbed 2006 'China's year of Africa.'

This was more than a friendly gesture towards the African continent; it was about business, as underlined by another slogan, 'Developing country, solidarity and partnership' and a photograph of a black and a pale-skinned hand (which I took to be Chinese) shaking,

below the sentence 'Welcome to Beijing Summit.' The Beijing government had brought together the heads and delegates of 48 African
countries to talk about business. China's trade with the African continent had increased more than five-fold from the start of the decade,
to an estimated $55 billion in 2006. The summit was held on the 50th
anniversary of diplomatic relations between the People's Republic of
China and African countries. This time the link was politically very
different though – fifty years ago Mao's China had forged relations
with President Nassar of Egypt in what was seen to be an 'anti-West'
alliance. China's hunger for raw materials has put a new global power
in Africa, which is still dealing with the legacy of European colonialism; nowhere more so than the Congo, which is once again the focus
of international companies wanting to tap its riches.

Doing the Congo

Congo is unique in terms of colonialism. It became the private property of King Leopold II, constitutional monarch of Belgium, and the
absolute ruler of the Congo during the 1880s, but there was no legal
link between the two countries until 1908, when it was renamed the
Belgian Congo (Wauters, 1930). One of the lingering political issues
is the province of Katanga, where Congo's share of the African copper
belt lies.[36,37] It is the area Cecil Rhodes intended to grab when the
British-born founder of the De Beers diamond company was coloniz-
ing southern Africa (Lynch, 2002).[38]

Since independence Katanga has had a number of secessionist attempts, but the current Congo leader Joseph Kabila has a support
base in the eastern part of the country, where Katanga lies beside the
Zambian border. Katanga is also host to most of the country's mineral wealth. Besides copper the region has the world's largest reserves
of cobalt and columbium (niobium)-tantalum (known as coltan), diamond, tin, gold, zinc and uranium. 'The mineral riches of an under-
developed country like the Congo will always be the root of both the
happiness and misfortune of its people. As we all know, the history of

the Congo, with all its intrigues after independence, is mainly the ruthless determination by the foreign investors to retain economic control of the key provinces such as Katanga, Kasai and Bas-Congo. Much will depend on the conditions in these wealthy regions whether the whole of the Congo will enjoy peace or face permanent confusion.' These words are as applicable today as they were 40 years ago when they were written by T. R. Kanza (Kanza, 1968).

Congo is projected to produce six times more copper by the end of the next decade, though the amount of copper it mined in 2007 has barely changed from the past 14 years (Smith, 2006). It is unlikely, however, to meet the peak in copper production it had in the 1960s, whereas by 2009 neighbouring Zambia is estimated to exceed its record output of four decades ago. This illustrates the difference between the two countries, which have similar deposits of copper; the border dividing the regions running right through the African copper belt. Both countries were populated by the same ethnic groups and Congo's troubled history has prompted a United Nations effort to bring stability through a large military presence and investment programme. The Democratic Republic of Congo borders so many countries that it is considered to be the heart of Africa; to find stability on the African continent, it has to be found first in the Congo.

Copper Pennies

The world is spending more and more money on searching for copper. Much of this money is raised in London, which has become home to several of the world's largest mining companies. These include BHP Billiton, which started life in the Australian outback and on a Dutch-ruled Indonesian island;[39] Rio Tinto, once owned by the Spanish government before British investors bought it in the late 19th century;[40] Anglo American, once the biggest company in the South African apartheid era; and Xstrata, which has Glencore, the world's largest metals trader as a major shareholder. Established mining companies from emerging markets such as India and Kazakhstan also look to London for funding from investors and the British capital is the favoured second home for Russian oligarchs, not only to buy football clubs but also to list some of Russia's largest resource companies. Foreign-born billionaires that have made their fortunes from resources and who live in London include Roman Abramovich, Laskma Mittal and Anil Agarwal.

But it's not just the large overseas companies that are attracted to London – mining explorers with little more than a piece of paper granting a right to dig for minerals in a far-flung corner of the planet also come to the city. London has become the mining finance capital of the world this decade, nudging aside regional mining centres in Australia and Canada, which have seen most of their largest mining companies taken over. The bigger companies have been using profit from higher metal prices this decade to buy other miners and together they control large swathes of the world's iron ore, coal, copper, nickel, alumina and bauxite. There are also more mining companies listed in the leading UK company index, the FTSE 100, which accounted for more than 10% of the total value. Resources companies (which include oil and gas companies) account for more than a quarter of the value of the biggest stock market in Europe; a bigger share even than the technology companies had during the dot com heyday. Miners not only list their shares in London, but they also look to the city to hedge the metals that they mine; the London Metal Exchange is where metal price risk across the world is managed. China may dominate demand for metals, which are produced in remote places around the world, but they turn to London to set prices. Metals are the one commodity grouping that London dominates. New York has oil (although London is the world's second largest oil-trading market) and Chicago grains, but London is the leader for base metals, copper, aluminium, lead, zinc, nickel and tin, as well as being the world's largest physical gold bullion market. It is also home to the world's premier global marketplace for the shipping industry: the Baltic Exchange.

Metals are produced in one country, refined in another and end up as a finished good somewhere. Going between each location requires ships, so shipping is an integral part of metals and commodities trading. Both the Baltic Exchange and London Metal Exchange have their origins at the Jerusalem Coffee House near Corn Hill in central London (Gibson-Jarvie, 1976). London is also home to one of the world's biggest carbon emissions trading markets, which together with metals and energy make London the largest commodity trading centre in the world.

The London Metal Exchange may be small when it comes to global derivatives and equity exchanges, but it is big in the clubby world of metal merchants, producers and industrial consumers. Relationships are key in metals; as they are in all commodity markets. Tradition is also important to the LME, which has eschewed the trend to float on the stock exchange and is the only commodity exchange where open outcry trading still takes place. The LME withstood the pressure to fully embrace electronic trading when Enron attempted to grab the lion's share of the metals market. Through its Enron Online, it built up substantial market share. The LME did then launch an electronic trading system, but the need to pursue online trading eased following the collapse of Enron in 2001.[41]

The LME has also managed to fend off competition from New York, which set up a metal trading exchange around the same time as the LME. Its metals exchange – Comex – has only managed a less than 10% share of the world's metals exchange dealings,[42] despite the fact that at the time of its founding the US was the biggest consumer of copper and that American miners controlled a vast amount of global supplies. Those companies preferred to set their own price for copper rather than having it set in a trading exchange. For much of the early period the British pound was the currency of international trade, so the LME's contracts, together with the imposition of tariffs were more suitable for global trading and London was therefore able to remain the centre of global copper trading. Copper trade on the LME really took off after the nationalization of Codelco, which preferred to sell its copper at a price set by the market rather than a producer price mechanism. The other main competitor to the LME is the Shanghai Futures Exchange.

Copper Rush

Even the US is having a new copper rush, just as it did in the late 19th century. In some ways things have not changed; there was an 80% increase in the number of active mining claims on public lands to more than 370 000 in the four and a half years to July 2007, mainly in the western US states, though some are near iconic American sites like the Grand Canyon and Yosemite National Park.

The issue of mining claims has become a political one. Miners of hard rock minerals, which include copper, gold, silver, nickel and uranium, do not have to pay royalties, unlike the coal, oil and natural gas producers who pay royalties of 8% or more on sales from production. Environmentalists, hunters, recreational fishermen and Democrats argue that proceeds from the imposition of a mining royalty would help clean up the waste left behind by old mines – the copper mines that were opened in Montana more than 100 years ago are still being cleaned up today.[43]

These groups are looking to revise the Mining Law of 1872, signed by President Ulysses S. Grant to promote the development and settlement of publicly owned lands in the western United States.[44] The cost of finding new copper reserves is rising due to higher energy costs, water, equipment and the infrastructure required to take the copper to the refinery or the port for export; but the world is not running out of copper. In January 2007 the United States Geological Survey, an arm of the US government, raised the global copper resources land-based estimate to three billion tonnes, compared with the previous estimate of 1.6 billion tonnes. The US copper resources estimate rose by 60% to 550 million tonnes, which means they account for about a fifth of global resources, though the number of copper nodules under the seabed remained at 700 million. This increased estimate of the world's copper resources lies in stark contrast to the early 1970s, when the publication of *The Limits to Growth* claimed that the world would run out of most resources; gold by 1981, silver by 1985 and zinc in 1990 (Meadows *et al.*, 1972). There were even concerns about resource depletion at the beginning of the last century.

In 1908 the steel magnate Andrew Carnegie issued warnings about resource depletion, as did another industrialist of the time, James Jerome Hill – the railway millionaire. 'The most favourable view of the situation forces the conclusion that iron and coal will not be available for common use on anything like the present terms before the end of this century; and our industrial, social and political life must be readjusted to meet the strains imposed by new conditions.'[45]

Resources are determined by geology and money. Copper reserves deemed uneconomic in the 1990s when the copper price slumped to $1200 a tonne after the Sumitomo scandal looked much more profitable when copper prices rose to $8000 a tonne in 2007. Price will determine supply and demand for copper and all commodities. In the late 1950s Orris Herfindahl, a US economist, did a historic study of copper prices, in order to answer questions about the long-term cost and depletion of nonrenewable resources. Herfindahl concluded that with a few exceptions, copper prices could be taken as a proxy for costs, arguing that since 1913 the copper industry has been dominated by a secular downturn in deflated prices (Herfindahl, 1959).[46]

If metal prices remain above their average price for the rest of the century, it will turn upside down the conventional academic view on commodity prices; that commodity prices fall over the long term. The view being that because technology innovations boost efficiency, their direct share of the global economy will fall, meaning that they have less importance.

The metal price rise of this decade has been fuelled by China's industrialization. The industrialization of the United States and Germany in the early 20th century, the post-war reconstruction of Europe and the industrialization of Japan in the 1950s and 1960s, on the other hand, coincided with a fall or flattening of commodity prices, as increased demand was met with technological innovation leading to lower costs of production of raw materials.[47]

So far the rise in metal prices has not filtered through to higher costs for consumers, as manufactured goods, such as home electronics, made from metals are produced in low-cost manufacturing countries such as China. The country's large workforce works longer hours for lower wages than in other countries and this keeps the cost of consumables down. But the cost of large infrastructure projects such as electricity power network construction goes up.

Such is the low cost of consumer electronics that they have become almost a throwaway item. People no longer try to fix a toaster if it goes wrong; they just buy a new one, which could cost less than £10 at a budget UK retailer – less than it would cost to repair. This is the case with many other electronic consumer goods too. "I was at my parents-in-law's house and I wanted to buy a DVD for my kids to watch. My wife said they didn't have a player but I thought they may have some cheap DVD players in Tesco. There, the DVD was £14 and the Chinese-made DVD player was £17. It was just astonishing,' said one London-based hedge fund manager. 'At £17 a lot more people, billions of people, can afford to have a DVD and the raw material impact of all those consumers being able to buy all those sorts of goods is very great,' he said.

China's manufacturing prowess is partly why its influence on metals is far greater than on either energy or agriculture. It is the largest or near largest global consumer of all metals from copper, aluminium, lead, zinc and steel. For example, China's global share of copper usage has risen from 9.4% in 1995 to 21.8% in 2006; aluminium has also increased from 9.4% to 22.5%; zinc from 10 to 28.6 % and steel from 12 % to more than a third over the same period according to The Australian Bureau of Agricultural and Resource Economics (ABARE).

Rising prices cannot continue forever though and new sources of supply will become economic. In the 1990s the advancement in mining technology changed the dynamics of copper mining when the leach-solvent extraction-electrowinning process, or SX/EW Process, was widely adopted, paving the way for new mines in Chile and Latin America. About 40% of Latin American copper mine production comes from this process, and ore bodies previously considered uneconomic are now able to be brought online. Further innovation could change the structure of the industry even more.

Under the Sea

Mining the world's sea beds has resurfaced, so to speak. Some of the world's biggest miners are backing ventures that are seeking their fortunes below sea level, just as the big miners did in the 1970s. Back then though, interest in undersea mining abated when metal prices fell later in the decade.[48] A study of sub-sea rock in the Pacific in the late 1950s had indicated potential economic value.[49]

How much of this would be economically viable to recover has yet to be determined. Extraction of copper from the sea bed faces opposition from environmentalists, as well as concerns about the untried technology on a commercial scale of removing rock from the sea bed and processing the metal content.

A Nickel for a Dollar

The meteoric rise in nickel prices best illustrates the boom in metals this decade, with the subsequent effect of making nickel deposits more economic. The World Bank wrote in its report on May 29, 2007 'Nickel prices are not projected to ease because no significant new supply is expected in the immediate term.' Within three months of this statement the nickel price had halved because of new supplies that none of the experts had anticipated.[50]

Global nickel demand is driven by stainless steel, which is used in the construction of office buildings, power generation facilities, petroleum and petrochemical plants, or facilities where it is vital that the pipes do not corrode.[51] It is also an important part of the kitchen; sinks and taps are made from stainless steel because of its hygiene when it comes to food. Nickel is also a key material for batteries, particularly long life batteries for hybrid cars.

The rise in price of more than 1000% over five years changed the economics of mining for nickel. As we saw with higher oil prices, which have brought on new oil supplies such as the oil sands in Canada, the rise in the price of nickel triggered the production of low-grade nickel resources – known as nickel pig iron – in China, Indonesia and the Philippines in 2007.[52] 'Ten years ago, if someone would have asked me "have you heard of oil sands" I would have said "I don't know why you are asking me, because it is high cost science. You need oil to be $30 or $40 a barrel or don't even think about it", said Paul Touradji, head of Touradji Capital. 'It was the same with nickel pig iron; it is a high cost production. You need nickel at $25000. Nickel was a $4000 to $10000 commodity, don't even worry about it. It is a science experiment. All of a sudden we have seen a boom and you have these new technologies of supply,' said Touradji. The Chinese were able to bring on nickel pig iron production, he said, because they were desperate for new sources of supply to feed the boom in the stainless steel sector. From almost nothing, global nickel pig iron rose to almost a tenth of global output and cut nickel prices in half within a few months.

China is well endowed with resources but it also has a fifth of the world's population. The Chinese have traditionally been ambivalent about miners. 'In China the miner was considered to be almost necessarily a robber and a bad character. The Chinese farmer occupied an honourable position, but the miner was ranked with common thieves and soldiers' (Frey, 1930). But today, such is the demand for new resources that new mines, both legal and illegal, are popping up all over China.

With China's urbanization and industrialization still far from the desired level by Beijing, as well as the economic growth in other large developing nations such as India and Brazil, demand for metals remains firm. The latest rush in exploration for resource riches may result in the same pattern that has followed previous metal price booms in the 1960s, 1970s and 1980s when supply outstripped demand, as was experienced with nickel in 2007.

Striking Metal

The search for metals is like the search for oil; explorers are looking for riches. It is an expensive business, with drills, rigs, generators, sensor equipment and the cost of living in remote places of developing

countries for long periods at a time. This adds political risk to resource project development and supply. Not only do governments
change their policies, ministers, officials and sometimes their leaders, but a new government might have a totally different set of
rules. There is also the issue of foreign investment and national resources. This is a sensitive subject at the best of times, and it all
adds up to political risk for a money lender to oil, gas and minerals
explorers.

The worst case scenario would be that the political risk could lead
to all of the investment being lost in a single venture. It could mean
going to court, as happened to Roddy Fleming, scion of one of Britain's
famous banking families. Through his family company, Highland Star,
he had a lease to explore for nickel in Cuba, host to rich deposits of the
metal, with the consent of President Castro. That is until the veteran
leader of the socialist island state decided to issue the exploration
lease to the People's Republic of China following a visit by Chinese
President Hu Jintao in November 2004. The case has since gone to an
international court.

Once the explorer has found a deposit of oil, gas or a metal, the
investment risk continues. Saudi Arabia, for instance, has forbidden
foreigners from exploring for oil in its Kingdom, but it has allowed
foreign companies to scour its desert land for gold and other metals.
Tertiary Minerals, the Yorkshire-based miner, was looking (successfully as it turned out) for tantalum, which is used in electronics, when
it came across a great big lump of uranium. This triggered a sensitive
issue for the Saudis who desire to create their own nuclear industry –
so the Riyadh government removed Territory Minerals' right to take
the uranium, but allowed them to develop the less sensitive mineral,
tantalum.[53]

A Finite Boom?

New technologies, the development of new materials and an even
greater emphasis on recycling (preferably not by theft) will continue
to alter the dynamics of the mining and metals sector. For consumers
though, the biggest impact from the current metals price boom might

be a cancelled train service because the copper wiring used in the overhead power supply has been stolen.

Just as with the energy and agricultural industries, there are constraints on supply due to depleted resource bases, political risks, water availability and substitution from new mineral sources. The dynamics in energy and agriculture on the demand side are also the same for metals, particularly copper, which is creating huge problems in terms of security due to rising levels of theft of the metal.

The focus on emissions and global warming will create a big boom for technological solutions, which involve the use of metals and stimulate new sources of demand. The adoption of these technologies – from hybrid cars to wind farms and photovoltaic panels – using copper, should all outweigh the cost of sourcing the metal from more and more remote parts of the planet. Meanwhile the search for new reserves will go on . . .

Notes

1. British Transport Police (BTP) annual report. The report said that the northeast of England is a particularly active area for metal theft, which is the single biggest cause of train delays in the area.
2. Copper Development Association website – http://www.copper.org/education/c-facts/c-general.html.
3. Total worldwide copper use is 22.45 million tonnes (2004 figure), broken down as follows: 66% of refined primary copper, 9% of refined secondary copper (recycling of end-of-life products), 25% of scrap melted directly–recycling of 'new' process scrap.
4. Since 1925, the rate of increase of discovered new copper stock in the lithosphere has been 0.63 % per year, significantly less than the rate of increase of the reserve base (3.9 % per year) and of the stock in use (3.3 % per year). Thus, although the increase in the reserve base has kept pace with the rate of extraction, only about a sixth of this increase has resulted from the discovery of new sources of copper (Gordon *et al.*, 2006).
5. The European Chemicals regulation (REACH) came into force on June 1, 2007. REACH stands for Registration, Evaluation, Authorization

and Restriction of Chemicals. Companies that manufacture or import more than one tonne of a chemical substance per year will be required to register it in a central database administered by the new EU Chemicals Agency. See the European Commission website – http://ec.europa.eu/ enterprise/reach/index_en.htm

6. European Commission website – http://ec.europa.eu/environment/waste/ weee/legis_en.htm. The directive stipulates, for each EU member country, an average recovery objective of 4 kg/inhabitant/year.

7. European Commission website – http://ec.europa.eu/environment/ waste/elv_index.htm

8. In 1960 a car would typically pump out more than 100 grams of carbon monoxide, hydrocarbon and oxides of nitrogen for every mile. A new car bought in the US, Japan or Europe would emit 2 grams of these pollutants per mile (Johnson Matthey, 2004).

9. The United States Geological Survey estimated in January 2007 that the world's reserves of platinum group metals (PGMs) in mineral concentrations that can be mined economically are estimated to total more than 100 million kilograms. The largest reserves are in the Bushveld Complex in South Africa.

10. Figures are taken from Leonardo Energy (www.leonardo-energy.org), which is an Initiative managed by the European Copper Institute, dedicated to building information centres about electrical energy.

11. Copper is used in making copper indium diselenide film for photovoltaic (PV) systems. Copper has long been used in solar heating/hot water systems, where it is commonly used in heat exchangers. See the website of the Copper Development Association – http://www.copper.org/ innovations/2007/05/solar_energy.html

12. Dempsey (1994) wrote that Ford bought 2.5 million acres of the Amazon rainforest near the Tapajos River in 1927. The plantation never produced as much rubber as Ford expected and it never made any money, and was sold back to Brazil in 1945 for $250 000.

13. Details on locations of mines and plantations were taken from the Henry Ford Museum website http://www.thehenryford.org/rouge/history.asp.

14. O'Brien (1989) referenced this information on the Guggenheims to Wilkins (1974) and Rippy (1958). The Guggenheims' empire came to include smelters, mines and refineries for lead, silver, copper, nitrates and tin in the continental United States, Alaska, British Columbia, Mexico,

Peru, Chile, the Belgian Congo and southeast Asia, as well as diamond and rubber interests in the Congo. By 1923 their far-flung interests had already created a family fortune that was conservatively estimated at $200 million (Hoyt, 1967; O'Connor, 1976).

15. Guggenheims sold it to fellow US miner Anaconda. The sale caused bitter conflict among the Guggenheim family. Proponents of the sale included Daniel, who thought the 25 % premium to the share price as well as a retaining interest in the mine was a sufficient offer. Daniel's son Harry opposed the sale. He had been instrumental in the development of Chuquicamata and believed it foolhardy to surrender control of what was now the lowest cost copper mine in the world, with ore reserves that could carry into the next century.

16. Chile's nitrate era coincided with an explosive episode of world capitalism as Britain and other advanced nations increased investments in peripheral areas in order to develop new markets and extract raw materials. This was the era of Latin America's 'export-led' growth, when such exports did not include manufacture. This appears to be similar to the current era (Mentéon, 2003).

17. The price of copper in London fell from £91 10s. per ton at the beginning of 1873 to £58 15s. by January 1879 (O'Brien, 1979).

18. Cooke (1821–1905) is thought to be America's first investment banker. Between 1865 and 1887, Jay Cooke was instrumental in doubling the size of the rail system in America, adding some 30 000 miles of track at a cost of nearly $1.5 billion.

19. Britain was also a big investor in Latin America; it had invested more than $766 million, of which 44 % was invested in railway, 38 % in government bonds and 2 % in banks and shipping companies.

20. Stone (1968) wrote that the bubble-mania was burst in January 1826 when the first default of the Latin American issues occurred, when Colombia, which included Ecuador and Venezuela at the time, defaulted on interest payments. This was followed by defaults by Mexico, Chile, Buenos Aires and Guatemala. Of the original group of states which borrowed in London between 1822 and 1825, only Brazil, with a brief interruption, continued to meet its obligations for any length of time. The defaulting states remained in arrears for periods ranging from seven to forty-seven years.

21. Monteón cites the paper by Rippy (1948).

22. Although at this time, the value of all the minerals annually produced in South America was less than half that of Pennsylvania alone.

23. Gilded Age is a term used by Mark Twain and Charles Dudley Warner in their book *The Gilded Age: A Tale of Today* that covers the excesses from the fortunes made in the late 19th century. A time when John D. Rockefeller and Andrew Carnegie built their empires on oil and steel respectively. Although Carnegie gave most of his wealth to philanthropy, a trend that become prominent again over the past decade with Bill Gates and Warren Buffett, who have committed most of their fortunes to charity.

24. The Rothschild link to Rio Tinto has been maintained for more than 140 years as the bank was an advisor to the miner in its takeover defence against BHP Billiton in 2008.

25. In a report by the subcommittee of the Monetary and Economic Conference, the following statement appears: 'The delegation of the United States of America calls attention to the desirability of considering plans for the coordination by the international agreement of the production and marketing of copper... Accordingly, it is proposed that the Governments of the copper producing countries submit to the Secretary-General of the Monetary and Economic Conference, before September 15, 1933, their views and proposals concerning the organization of the production of copper and of the international trade in this product, with a view to the summoning of a suitable meeting to examine whether it is possible and expedient to conclude an agreement.'

26. Dumett (1985) wrote that in October 1940, the Union Miniere company director, Edgar Sengier, reacted to Nazi confiscation of mineral supplies in Belgium by deciding to ship all uranium ore stockpiled in Katanga to New York. These 1200 tonnes of high quality Congo ore plus small quantities of ore from Canada and the US were practically all that the US atomic scientists had to work with on the Manhattan project up to 1944. Thus, African uranium was essential for the experiments that led directly to the atomic bomb.

27. In 1946, Congress enacted the Strategic and Critical Materials Stock Piling Act. The act enabled the creation and management of materials needed to supply the military, industrial and essential civilian needs of the United States during a national emergency.

28. In the early 1990s, the Department of Defense determined that over 99 % of the inventory was excess to the Department's needs and Congress authorized its disposal. From 1995 through 2005, it raised $5.1 billion from sales.

29. According to Mingst (1976), CIPEC members were highly dependent on copper for their foreign trade revenue: Chile earned 80 % of foreign exchange from copper; Zambia, 80 %; Zaire 50 %; and Peru, 30 %.

30. According to data from the International Copper Study Group, world copper mine production rose by 34 % during the ten-year period, rising from 11.1 million metric tonnes in 1996 to 14.9 million in 2005. During this period Chile's copper production rose by 71 % or 2.2 million metric tonnes of copper, and in the United States output fell by 41 %. Also notable was the revival of production in Zambia and Congo; the entry of Argentina and Laos as copper-mine producing countries; and the significant growth of production from expansions and new projects in Australia, Brazil, China, Indonesia, Kazakhstan, Myanmar, Peru and Russia, that together added more than 2 million metric tonnes to world mine production. Besides the United States, significant decreases in mine production during this period occurred in Canada, the Philippines and South Africa.

31. According to copper statistics from the US Geological Survey, May 5, 2006, US consumption was 166 500 tonnes in 1900, doubled to 320 000 by 1907, and doubled again to 641 000 by 1915, US consumption was 2.55 million in 2004, down from its peak of 3.13 million in 1999, and compares with 2.43 million in 1979. 1996 and 1997 were the peak production years, with more than 2 million tonnes.

32. My trip to South America in late 1989 and early 1990 was a busy time for democracy in the region. Carlos Menen posters were all around Buenos Aires with his distinguishable sideburns and holding a glass of champagne celebrating his first of ten Christmases as president following his election in May 1989. And in Peru, posters and television adverts of author Mario Vargas Llosa were all over Lima. Llosa lost to Alberto Fujimoro.

33. Production figures taken from Codelco website – http://www.codelco.com/english/la_corporacion/fr_cifras.html.

34. Michael Monteón (2003) wrote that North acted as a front man for a company for King Leopold's rubber empire in the Belgian Congo.

35. O'Brien (1989) wrote that the Guggenheims' empire came to include smelters, mines and refineries for lead, silver, copper, nitrates and tin in the US, British Columbia, Mexico, Peru, Chile, the Belgian Congo and southeast Asia, as well as diamond and rubber interests in the Congo.

36. The copper belt comprises an area of about 14 000 square miles that straddles northern Zambia and crosses into the Democratic Republic of Congo by trending north-westward within the border.

37. The earliest report of copper in Katanga was made by a Portuguese governor of a Mozambique district in the year 1798. David Livingstone noted, 'By smelting malachite, a copper ore, the natives of Katanga obtain large ingots in the shape of a capital I'. Belgian exploration of Central Africa commenced from 1876 onwards. In 1891, the Compagnie du Katanga was formed to organize all activities in Katanga. In the same year, this new company was granted large concessions by the Congo Free State (later the Belgian Congo). In 1900, the Congo Free State and the Compagnie du Katanga formed the Comité Special du Katanga and vested their interests in Katanga in this new body in the proportions: Congo Free State 2/3; Compagnie du Katanga 1/3 (Birchard, 1940).

38. Lynch (2002) writes how parties related to King Leopold and Rhodes negotiated with Chief M'siri, who ruled over the Katanga area. Leopold won out.

39. BHP is the acronym for Broken Hill Proprietary company, which found lead and zinc in the outback town of the same name. BHP merged with Billiton in 2001.

40. In Spain, the Rio Tinto mines in Huelva near where Christopher Columbus sailed for the new world were purchased in 1873 by a consortium of British and German investors for £3.85 million. The consortium included the Rothschilds banking family and Hugh Matheson, one of the founders of the trading group Jardine Matheson. The Rio Tinto mines, which were a national treasure to the Spanish government at the time, were originally mined in Roman times.

41. Enron Online tried to recreate the LME network of registered warehouses where metals are stored when Enron bought the metals trader

MG plc, which also owned Henry Bath, one of the biggest owners of warehouses. After the purchase, metals trading volumes on Enron Online rose, but it was not sustainable.

42. Comex can trace its origins back to the New York Iron and Metal Exchange, and Iron and Metal Limited were formed in 1882, five years after the LME was formed. These two New York exchanges merged to form the New York Metal Exchange, which became the National Metal Exchange, before it was renamed the Commodity Exchange, (Comex) (Reitler, 1931).

43. BP's affiliate company, Atlantic Richfield, has been working for more than 20 years to clean up surface water, groundwater and soils in Montana's Upper Clark Fork Basin, which were impacted by more than a century of mining activity. BP is responsible for the clean up through its past acquisition of Atlantic Richfield, which had bought Anaconda Copper in 1977.

44. The Mining Law of 1872 states 'All valuable mineral deposits in lands belonging to the United States, both surveyed and unsurveyed, are hereby declared to be free and open to exploration and purchase, and the lands in which they are found to occupation and purchase, by citizens of the United States and those who have declared their intention to become such.' These are the words of the original law, which are still relevant today.

45. Andrew Carnegie was talking at a conference of governors in the White House, Washington DC that was held between 13–15, May, 1908. James Jerome

46. Herfindahl is also known for his eponymous index to measure market concentration in different industries.

47. The Reserve Bank of Australia (2007) said that after falling sharply in the first two decades of the century, metal prices fluctuated within a fairly tight range between 1920 and 1980, and these prices declined for two decades thereafter, broadly in line with food and non-food agricultural prices.

48. Payne (1978) wrote that 'nodules were dredged from the Pacific in 1957–58 by the Institute of Marine Resources of the University of California. That study indicated that manganese nodules could be economically exploited. With rising prices for raw materials, political uncertainties and

nationalizations, they began to attract the attention of mineral companies.'

49. Payne (1978) wrote that mining consortiums in ocean mining included Kennecott Copper, Noranda Mines, Rio Tinto, Gold Fields and Mitsubishi Corporation, which allocated at least $50 million to develop the necessary mining ships, dredging devices, and other equipment. Another consortium included Tenneco, which formed Deepsea Ventures in 1968 solely to explore and exploit manganese nodules. This consortirm has linked up with Nichimen, C. Itoh and Kanematsu-Gosho, Union Miniere and United States Steel. Sumitomo and Metalgesellschaft also invested in deep-sea mining ventures. Nautilus Minerals holds licences and exploration applications in the territorial waters of Papua New Guinea, Fiji, Tonga, the Solomon Islands and New Zealand and its shareholders include Barrick Gold, Anglo–American and Teck Cominco. The Nautilus information comes from its website – http://www.nautilusminerals.com/s/Home.asp.

50. Nickel closed at $48 000 a tonne on May 29; it was already sliding from its record high of $51 800 on May 9, and sunk to $25800 by August 10.

51. The estimated annual cost of corrosion in the USA. alone is $300 billion, equivalent to 4 % of gross national product. Far and away the largest use of nickel alloys is in the area of corrosion prevention.

52. Nickel pig iron is a ferronickel pig iron containing 3–5 % nickel. It contains much less nickel than conventional ferronickel (25–40 %) and has higher concentrations of sulphur and phosphorous. China is currently producing nickel pig iron from low-grade laterite ores imported primarily from the Philippines.

53. Tertiary Minerals – press releases April 19, 2006, January 10, 2007 and July 9, 2007 – http://www.tertiaryminerals.com/news.htm

5

Traders

'If orgies of speculation are permitted to spread too far . . . the ultimate
collapse is certain not only to affect the speculators themselves, but also
to bring about a general depression involving the entire country.'

Paul M. Warburg (1929)

Traders, Trading and Prices

The clock ticks down to 9.30 am. The noise levels increase, idle chat-
ter turns to serious talk and agitation begins to creep in. A sea of
coloured jackets gravitates towards the centre of the spacious room.
The assembled crowd waits for the sound of a bell, whereupon chaotic
scenes of shouting, arm waving and frantic hand signalling ensue. It
makes great theatre; but at the same time it is somewhat confusing
for the uninitiated.

In the room, situated in a tall building in the heart of Chicago,
hundreds of people are betting on what price wheat, corn, soya beans,
oats and rice will be at a given point in the future. The pits, as they
are better known, have been the place for establishing futures prices

of US grains for more than 150 years. Today, the prices set here are global.

Particularly frantic are the corn and soya bean pits as traders assess the impact that some heavy overnight rain in the Midwest might have on their corn and soya bean crops. Flooding in Europe and China was causing similar unrest in the wheat pits. Weather is omnipresent in determining the price and supply of crops. Mother Nature dealt wheat more than its fair share of unfavourable weather in 2007, from an Easter freeze in the Midwest to monsoon-type rains in Kansas; the heart of the US wheat belt. Heavy rains in northern Europe and China around harvest affected wheat crops at a time when global wheat stockpiles were at their lowest level in three decades. For the bakers and food manufacturers who rely on wheat crops to make flour, pasta, biscuits and breakfast cereals, this sort of weather is not welcome.

'Every 30 years, the wheat market makes a statement and it is making one now,' Thomas Shuff, a Chicago grains trader told me. Shuff should know about long cycles in grain trading; he was around the last time there was such a major stir in the intriguing world of soya bean, wheat and corn trading as well.

Shuff, who looks younger than his 66 years, keeps trim by going to the gym each day and became a father again in his sixties, says the futures markets are going through a change as dramatic as the one of the early 1970s. 'Changes in agriculture are subtle but seminal: we're seeing a major change in India and China, the two most populous nations on Earth. They're consuming more food.'

Chicago's role as the global price barometer for grains and oilseeds came to prominence in the early 1970s when, following severe crop shortages, the Soviet Union called on the United States for grains to meet the demands of Russia and its allies. 'We were a sleepy domestic grain market, pricing our domestic needs for our cattle operation, our hog operation, our broiler operation and we gifted food to various nations.' Shuff first started plying his trade on the CBOT floor in 1969. A few years later, there were rumours that the Russians were buying US grains, but it had been a source of speculation for years so traders were wary of any new reports. 'I happened to be down on the floor when it all exploded ... we became a thriving global grain exchange and the world began to realize that they could come to Chicago and purchase food on a futures basis,' said Shuff, who has a son who is also a trader on the CBOT floor.

And so the 'Great Grain Robbery' ensued. The Soviets bought a quarter of US grain crops, sending prices to their highest levels since 1917. It triggered a massive escalation of domestic food prices, forcing President Nixon to impose strict food price controls. The purchase by Russia also reflected a structural change in global grains trade, which had risen five-fold from its pre-World War II level by the mid-1970s (Tamarkin, 1985).

Around about the same time, a change in the Humboldt current along the South American Pacific coast provoked a shortage of Peruvian anchovies. Anchovies were a major source of protein for animal feed, and the shortage stimulated huge demand for a replacement; the soya bean. Soya bean prices per bushel rose from $4 to a record high of $12.90 in 1973. Floor speculators made fortunes from the soaring prices in 1973 amidst the Russian grain buying and the search for protein that boosted demand for soya beans. Among them were Eugene Cashman, an ex-Chicago policeman, the O'Connor brothers, Edmund and William, and Thomas Dittar, who went on to establish Refco, a commodity brokerage that collapsed in 2005. 'We thought we were the big guys, but we're just spectators now,' says Thomas Cashman, a nephew of Eugene.

Late 2007 and early 2008 were looking like the early 1970s all over again. Soya bean prices moved above their 1973 records in January 2008, the same month that corn prices rose to more than $5 a bushel for the first time ever; a signal to farmers to plant even more corn to fuel the growing demand for US corn-based ethanol. Wheat also moved above $10 a bushel for the first time in December 2007, almost doubling in six months. Palm oil prices reached record highs in this period and the rapid rise in grain and oilseed prices has triggered fears of food price inflation for the first time in three decades.

Other factors behind agricultural price rises include the world's growing affluent population, the demands from biofuels, water constraints and a sequence of unusual climatic events such as floods, droughts and frosts. The first four chapters of this book dealt with the supply and demand factors in commodities; this chapter deals with the important role of trading commodities – the part of the process that enables goods to be moved from producer to consumer.

The Electronic Age

The rise in prices has attracted more investors, farmers and merchants than ever to trade agricultural futures, but they are not doing it on the Chicago trading floor.

After the first fifteen frantic minutes of trading in the agricultural pits of the CBOT, the pandemonium becomes more sporadic, as traders step back from the pits and return to their booths to talk to their clients on the phone, or to chat with their colleagues. Trading activity is always the busiest at the open and the close of trading, as the prices set at these times become the reference prices used by producers and consumers in any supply contract. Within half an hour, some of the runners – those taking the orders from the phone clerk to the trader on the floor – are no longer running; they can be found reading the sports pages of the *Chicago Tribune*. The younger ones read comics. 'A year ago, these guys would have had a sweat on, we would be lost screaming and running, phones off the hooks,' said John Mackintosh, a veteran oilseed and grain trader at CBOT.

The change in pace at the exchange is down to the extension in the hours of computer trading on the CBOT, which took effect in August 2006. Investors can now trade on the screen even when the pits are open. Volumes from the once heaving pits of the CBOT have nearly halved, while overall volume in agricultural futures trading is up more than two-thirds of the volume traded when it was floor only: electronically matched contracts now account for the lion's share of trade.[1]

The electronic age has inspired record volumes on the Chicago Board of Trade (CBOT), which merged with its cross-town rival The CME Group to become the world's largest futures exchange in 2007.

Both parts of the enlarged group were built on a history of agricultural futures.

The CBOT was the first commodities exchange in the Western world. It started its life as a place for merchants in the Midwest to buy and sell grains and offered its first futures contracts in 1865, following the example of the world's first futures exchange (widely acknowledged to be the Dojima Rice Market in Osaka, which started in 1670). 'It sounds really noisy in here, but most of the volume is on the screen, and its never going to come back to the pit,' said Shuff, who managed to buy and sell a number of corn contracts while he spoke to me from the sidelines of the corn pit.

Shuff explained that when he started as a trader, there were large boxes of soya beans, corn, oats, rye, barley and wheat on desks near the trading pits, belonging to the merchants. The merchants sold this grain to the large users at the time; who were Pillsbury, Corn Products and Archer Daniel Midlands (ADM). Each of these buyers had their own desks near the trading floor representing the cash market – which linked back to the early days of the CBOT, when business was mainly between the merchant and the food companies and it was done face to face, without any middlemen. The boxes of grain and the physical presence of food companies are gone from the exchange; financial betting on grain prices rather than physical trade has taken over as its main activity.

'The electronic trade has really changed the market,' said Cashman, who is in his 60s. He adds that the volumes traded in the soaring markets of the early 1970s were only a fraction of today's markets as there are more players in the game. 'There were only a small number of commercial firms that used us, but they of course were international; there were no hedge funds, or managed funds or fund allocation people. Now you have a whole myriad of different people who want to invest in commodities,' says Cashman, who, like many traders at the CBOT, was introduced to trading through family links.

The amount of the money in the commodity markets has changed the tactical way of trading too. 'You used to buy (soya) beans on the first day of October, because it was the peak of the harvest and the peak supply from the harvest would sap the price and it gave you a better chance of a rally. And you'd sell (soya) beans on the fourth of July if the market was on a big rally because there was a big weather premium in the market,' said Cashman. Adages such as, 'Sell in May and go away' for equities and, 'Buy Rosh Hashanah, Sell Yom Kippur' were the watchwords of these old timers.

Adjoining the grain pits is a room the size of an aircraft hangar. This is CBOT's financial futures trading floor, which once held thousands of traders, but the individuals in the room look like the stragglers left at the end of a large party. There is very little noise and fewer signs of any trade. The remaining traders are monitoring the screens for the price of the US treasury contracts, a market that has almost entirely shifted to the computer terminal.[2]

The consequence of the shift in trading to electronic screens has meant the days of open outcry trading are numbered. The Chicago grain futures market has evolved into a global financial market; for managers of hedge funds, managed futures funds and pension funds, who have absolutely no interest in taking delivery of a tonne of wheat.

It is the speculators in the pits who have found this transition the most painful. Once they earned their money from trading against the big players in the grains markets such as Cargill, Bunge and ADM. Now they are pushed to the side by speculators with deeper pockets trading via computer in the very markets they have spent their lives screaming, shouting, sweating, hitting and kicking in. 'If you wanted to buy 2000 corn (contracts for a total of ten million corn bushels), you would just have to look at four or five guys and it would be done. Those guys aren't going to stand there and take the market on now because they don't want to stand in the way of a double-decker bus,' said Mackintosh. Where they'd have once been shouting 'sell, sell, sell!' or 'buy, buy, buy!' all day, risking damage to the nodules in their throats, today's major speculators can trade with the mere click of a button from their office in New York, London, Chicago, Gibraltar, Hong Kong and Sydney – from wherever they want really. There's no need to have a contract with traders on the floor.

Many still do though; the floor is still an effective way to exchange information and swap trading ideas, which are then fed onto outside investors.

The final obituary of the grain floor speculator has therefore yet to be written. This species of trader was born in the late 19th century when they would act to balance the natural supply and demand of the market. They fulfilled a role of providing liquidity in a marketplace that was not fully harmonious, as farmers would have the wheat or corn to sell at a time when the flour millers or food processors did not want to buy and vice versa. In both cases the natural buyer or seller would be able to trade with the speculator. However, the fact that no physical grain ever passed through the hands of the speculator occasionally led to accusations of 'fictitious dealings' that were illegitimate.[3]

The futures grain

Futures contracts were devised with the farmer in mind, as they were created to provide a hedging instrument for grain growers to sell their crop after it was harvested, so that they could start planting their seeds knowing that they had 'locked in' a selling price for their wheat, corn or barley. The alternative was to do nothing and hope that prices rise well above the cost of production, so that a profit is made. With a futures contract the farmer had the security of knowing he had fixed a price, and that it did not matter whether the price changed over the intervening period. However, if the price of corn or wheat roses above the selling price in the futures contract, the farmer would make as much profit as he would if left to the open market. This is why farmers don't hedge all of their production; another factor for this decision is that they don't want to run the risk if they have a crop failure due to adverse weather of being left with less grain that they have been contracted to sell.

While a speculator places a bet on which way the prices fluctuate to make a profit, farmers and buyers of farm produce (and any other producer or consumer wanting to protect themselves against unfavourable price movements) use futures to limit any potential losses from price fluctuation. Speculators become the buyer or seller for the company or person that wants to hedge. Many of these natural hedgers in the CBOT can be found within the network of grain elevators, the companies that assess the quality of grain, clean it, store it and market it; and they are often owned by farming co-operatives. The elevator buys the grain from the farmer.

The Bigger Speculators

The centre of gravity in commodity trading has shifted to the hedge funds, whose numbers have mushroomed from a few thousand in the late 1990s to almost 10 000 at the end of 2007. Although of these, the number of hedge funds participating in commodities number in the hundreds and the total focusing on commodities is even fewer.

Paul Touradji heads one of the more prominent commodity-focused hedge funds. During the 2007 summer, in order to escape the heat and humidity of Manhattan, Paul and four colleagues work from a small rented office in the Hamptons, the Long Island enclave of the wealthy. The room is equipped with several screens where the prices of commodities, equities and currencies are displayed. In front of the screens sit a handful of traders, some in Bermuda shorts and sandals, fitting in perfectly with the holiday atmosphere in the Hamptons. The traders sit with headphones wrapped around their heads all talking to brokers, colleagues, industry contacts and clients to gather intelligence about the markets.

Paul first entered commodities when he joined Julian Robertson's Tiger Fund in the early 1990s, a time when it was unfashionable to be investing in commodities. 'I remember people calling me and saying "Paul are you serious about this commodities business, you're going to trade corn and copper?" They really thought I was throwing my career away, they thought – who goes to commodities? It's such a backwater,' said Touradji, who heads the eponymous Touradji Capital Management. 'I quickly discovered . . . this *was* a backwater; there was nobody here; (but) this was good; there were opportunities here . . . there have been opportunities for more than a decade.' He adds that commodities are no longer a backwater; they've become mainstream. The prices of energy, metals and agricultural commodities have soared this decade, and the price boom has attracted a surge in activity from investors, including the pension and mutual funds. These conservative players have never previously been seen in commodities, except via equities, and their acceptance of the investment diversification provided by commodities has changed the face of the markets.

Despite being an 'investment backwater', the commodity markets already had some big players involved. Many of these got started in the boom days of the 70s. Richard Dennis – once dubbed 'Prince of the Pits' – made his first large fortune in the Chicago pits trading soya beans in the early 70s. Other people wanted the same success so he started managing money for outside investors. He quickly found that he could do this more effectively sitting at a desk looking at a computer screen that had the prices of commodities and currencies flickering across, than standing in the pits (Schwager, 1993).

Another commodities trader turned money manager is Paul Tudor Jones, who started out as a cotton trader on the New York Cotton Exchange in 1980. Jones – who was inspired to go into trading by an article written by Dennis – got his break in the cotton market through his uncle Billy Dunavant, who was head of the world's largest privately owned cotton merchandiser (Schwager, 1993).[4] By 1984, Jones had set up his own managed fund, Tudor Capital. Jones moved from the pits to the screen, where he expanded into equities, government bonds, currencies and financial derivatives and created one of the largest hedge funds in the world. In fact, many of the founders of today's large hedge funds got their start in commodities, among them Bruce Kovner of Caxton Associates, Louis Bacon of Moore Capital and Willem Kooyker of Blenheim Capital Management.

Managed commodity funds can be traced back to 1948 when Futures Inc. was set up by Richard Donchian. Donchian is credited with creating a marketing trading tactic known as 'trend following,' which is essentially based on the assumption that commodity prices move in long, sustained patterns. It's a strategy adopted by pro-grammed managed futures funds, otherwise known as Commodity Trading Advisors (CTAs), of which there are now thousands. The CTA is a misnomer; they do not now necessarily invest in commodities but in all classes of futures, including currencies, fixed interest and stock indices. The term harks back to the era prior to the launch of financial futures in the 1970s, and to the period when the only futures were commodities. CTAs also do little advising; they are mainly funds based on programmed trading designed by mathematical boffins. As Thomas Shuff points out, 'The markets have become very technically orientated – it's a function of money. I have always believed that trading starts with fundamental analysis; you fine tune it, you have the technical analysis.'

The move to managed funds reflected a shift by individual investors, who in the 1980s were starting to put their money into managed and mutual funds rather than investing directly themselves (US General Accounting Office, 1988). Kovner, Jones, Bacon and Kooyker grew their funds by diversifying into other financial markets. This trend un-derlined two things about commodities: firstly, the commodity mar-kets alone are too small for fund managers who want to grow their funds to tens of billions of dollars; and secondly, the trading skills learnt in commodity trading are a solid grounding for trading in other financial markets.

Jones, Kovner and Kooyker all worked at various stages of their ca-reers with the same organization, Commodities Corporation, which at the time was a privately owned commodity fund set up by Paul Samuelson, the Nobel laureate. Samuelson, who is in his 90s and is still active at the Massachusetts Institute of Technology where he is Emeritus Professor of Economics, told me how Commodities Corpo-ration was started with one of his former students Helmut Weymar,[5] who was the chief cocoa buyer for Nabisco, the US biscuit and snack maker. Weymar was tired of the commute from his home in Princeton, New Jersey to Nabisco's office in New York, and suggested to his employers that he could continue doing their cocoa buying if he set up a trading company, which Nabisco agreed to do. Among the original investors in the 1969 start-up were Samuelson and Weymar and the United Fruit Company, which is now Chiquita Brands International. 'It was more like the present day hedge funds, as it went long and short and in the beginning it was focused on commodities futures as it was before interest rate or financial futures were launched,' said Samuelson, who is credited with the famous quip 'The stock market has predicted nine out of the last five recessions.'

Commodities Corporation was, in effect, one of the first commodity-focused hedge funds. Its successes were underlined further when another of its traders – Ed Seykota – developed one of the first computerized trading systems for managing clients' money in futures markets (Schwager, 1993).

The success of the company was to spot a good trader who could manage 'leverage'; i.e. the amount of money a fund can borrow to fund its trade. The difference between then and now, adds Samuelson, is that there are a lot more smart people today. 'I would say 30 years ago, there were not many very smart kids on the block, now there are quite a lot. And that makes it a dangerous situation . . . all the trades today have relatively very small returns, but they look good when you leverage them up eighty-fold, so it becomes an issue of how much risk is someone ready to take on to improve their performance'.

Collectively, hedge funds have been blamed for increasing commodity prices, but each have their own strategy and sub-market niche, whether it is US cattle futures or cocoa futures in London. And even if they are in the same market they often have the opposing position to another hedge fund. However, the increase in credit lending to investors around the world has undoubtedly helped push up asset prices from copper in London to stock prices in Shenzhen this decade.

'These days if there are 8000 or 9000 hedge funds, it seems that most of them are dabbling in commodities. It has become the new hot thing over the last couple of years. It's like trading tech stocks in 1999 and 2000 when everyone was dabbling in tech stocks, regardless of what their speciality should have been,' said Touradji, who has a team of analysts looking for trading opportunities based on the supply and demand of the commodities as well as the effect that the influx of financial funds is creating in the market. 'A lot of time we see opportunity caused by the hedge funds as opposed to ten years ago when that was not the case.'

Commodity Indices

Hedge funds manage money for a variety of investors, including pension funds – the retirement wealth of millions of workers is therefore partly dependent upon their success. However, pension funds have also put sizeable sums into more passively managed commodity indices, which have been around since 1934 when the US Department of Treasury requested that a daily spot commodity price index be published. The first one to be based on commodity futures prices started in 1957, and is now called the Reuters-CRB Index. While the CRB index (in its various guises over the decades) has provided a good historical tracking record of a broad basket of commodity prices, it wasn't until 1986 that a futures contract for the CRB index was launched on the New York Board of Trade. This was joined in 1991 by the Goldman Sachs Commodity Index, launched by the New York-based investment bank. The commencement of these commodity indices followed the launch of the successful S&P 500 stock index futures in 1982. It opened up another avenue of investment for equity fund managers, as it meant they could track the share performances of the largest companies in America without actually buying the shares in the companies themselves.

Investments in the major commodity indices have grown more than ten-fold, from a combined total of less than $10 billion in investments in 2000 to an estimated $175 billion by the end of 2007 (Barclays Capital, 2008).[6] The GSCI (or the S&P GSCI, as it is now known; the rating agency Standard and Poor's, bought in 2007, has become the flagship for the sector). The second most prominent index is the Dow Jones-AIG Commodity Index, which was launched in 1998.

In the mid-2000s, more than a dozen new commodity indices were created by separate institutions – many of them investment banks, including Lehman Brothers and Merrill Lynch. These institutions were in fact making a return to the commodities investment sector after abandoning the market around the turn of the century (a time when banks were either scaling back their operations due to massive losses in other parts of their business after the bursting of the dot com bubble, or took the view that the outlook for resources was weak and wanted to redeploy their focus on other businesses).

These days investors are faced with a plethora of indices – they've become like a 'pick n mix' sweet counter in a Woolworths store. Investors can have a heavily-flavoured energy index, or if oil is not to their taste they can pick a more digestible agricultural laden index, or a metals only one, or a mix of all three. Indices are formatted and designed in different ways, but combine common elements to reflect the global production and consumption of the underlying commodity, along with the volume of daily buying and selling of the specific commodity contract. The index can be as broad or as narrow as it wants or needs to, and can include any or all of the different sub-groups of commodities: energy (which in turn can be split between petroleum and natural gas); base metals; precious metals; grains; oilseeds; fibres; tropical commodities (such as sugar, coffee and cocoa); and livestock. Investors can basically pick and choose according to their personal preference. A hedge fund manager or a floor trader might be in the market for a few minutes, hours, days, months or perhaps even a year or two. Investors in indices however are normally there for the long term, tending mostly to be pension funds with a longer-term investment horizon. That being said, the nature of commodities futures means that those contracts do have a limited shelf life and will expire on the given month that the commodity is to be delivered – most indices will therefore track the most traded commodity futures, which are mainly the recently dated contracts.

Each month managers of funds tracking the GSCI index will sell the contracts of the commodities expiring that month, and buy futures contracts for the next month. This process is known as *The Roll*.

Investors have traditionally made money this way; the contract being sold is often worth more than the contract being bought – a concept known as the *yield return*. It's a different type of yield to that which equity or bond traders are used to. A holder of shares in, say, Citigroup or ExxonMobil earns a yield from the dividend cheque that is sent out once or twice a year from the companies and a bond investor receives a coupon payment, which is normally above the prevailing central bank lending rate. Since commodities don't have a natural yield there is no dividend or coupon payment; marketers of commodity indices have simply created the term 'yield' for their product.

The emergence of commodity indices and 'long only' commodity funds reflects another significant change in commodity markets, which is the acceptance of commodities as part of the portfolio for pension fund managers, who control the biggest segment of assets under management in the entire investment industry. Private investors are buying into commodities through exchange traded funds (ETFs), which are in essence tracker funds that follow the underlying commodity price without having to buy a futures contract.

Portfolios

Long before the trend for commodities to be used in portfolios began, Doctor Henry Jarecki was already considering the notion of portfolio diversification. He was wondering how he would manage the financial windfall he was about to receive from selling his interest in Mocatta Metals, part of the venerable precious metals trading company sold to Standard Chartered for $300 million in 1986.[7] 'From the mid-1970s onwards, I knew I would get at some future time more money than I knew what to do with, and that I would have to figure out some way to invest it,' said Jarecki, who set up his private investment company Gresham Investment Management after receiving the proceeds from the Mocatta sale. 'I tried to think through a diversification method of stocks and bonds, domestic stocks, values stocks and the various permutations. It became pretty clear that the more you diversified your portfolio, the safer a position you were in: much greater protection against ruin, against a big market drop than if you have just one thing that you are totally dependent on,' said Jarecki, who was a psychiatrist before going into precious metals (in fact it was while Jarecki was listening to his patients that his mind occasionally wandered off and he'd start thinking about trading and financial markets).

One of his most successful trades was to purchase a tonne of gold coins from the Austrian government in the 1960s at a time when the price of gold was fixed at $35 an ounce. He found that there was enormous demand for gold coins in the US at that time, as Americans were worried about inflation and preservation of their wealth. Subsequently, he bought another five tonnes of Austrian gold coins and made $7m from the trade. He then did a similar deal with the Mexican government on pre-revolution gold coins.

'Diversification as a concept until very recently was thought of as stocks, bonds and cash. The inclusion of commodities, which has been called by some as alternative investment, did not really appear until the late 1990s,' said Jonathan Spencer, president of Gresham Investment Management. Portfolio diversification then took great credence after the dot com bubble burst in April 2000. Fund returns had taken a nose dive after a vast number of investors had piled their money into over-valued technology companies; highly leveraged telecom and dot com companies that were running out of cash.

The academic theory of portfolio diversification has actually been around since the 1950s, when Harry Markowitz developed the modern portfolio theory, which essentially highlighted the need to build a diversified portfolio. At that time though, Markowitz was still mainly focused on bonds and equities. The theory took another step in the early 1980s when Dr John Lintner of Harvard University concluded in his study that, 'The combined portfolios of stocks, after including judicious investments in managed futures accounts, show substantially less risk, at every possible level of expected return, than portfolios of stocks (or stocks and bonds) alone' (Lintner, 1983). For portfolio managers, futures provided an enhanced ability to sell short, which meant investors could make money when the markets fell. Another bonus was that there were lower transaction costs than with equity trading.

Among the first large pension funds to become involved in commodity investments were the Dutch government pension fund ABP, and PGGM, which manages the money for Dutch healthcare workers. Most pension funds have put a small proportion of their funds into commodity indices, including local government run pensions and large corporations across Europe as well as the largest US pension fund, the California Public Employees' Retirement System (Calipers) and the Ontario Teachers' Fund.[8] Commodity investment by pension, endowment and mutual funds was part of their diversification strategy into alternative assets, which also included private equity, hedge funds and commercial property. Yale University attributes its growth from a $4.9 billion fund in 1996 to an $18 billion fund in 2006 to its strategy of diversification.[9]

The amount invested in commodities is small in relation to the total funds these pensions have under management. Commodity returns will therefore not dramatically change the overall performance of their respective funds, but their funds have had a more noticeable effect on commodity markets – especially the smaller ones.

Casinos

The widening acceptance of commodities by conservatively run pension funds marked a significant change in perception about commodities as an area for investment. Jarecki said the concept of commodities trading had, for a long time, been considered immoral in some quarters. 'In the old days producers or farmers used to think that the futures markets were like gambling with their wheat field or their gold mine. Ask them about their hedging strategies and they would say "what do you take us for, gamblers?" Today almost everyone in the physical markets uses futures markets,' he said.

Alan Greenspan, the former Federal Reserve chairman, in a speech in 1997 said that throughout the late 19th and early 20th centuries, farmers were often opposed to futures trading, particularly during periods when prices of their products were low or declining. 'They presumed that the dreaded speculators were depressing their prices,' he said (Geenspan, 1997). Commodities as an investment had suffered from a tainted image after various episodes of market manipulation stretching back to the late 19th century when Joseph Leiter tried to corner the wheat market. Leiter was broken by Philip Armour, the Chicago meat baron, who delivered as much wheat as he could possibly assemble, dragging the wheat price back down, and leaving Leiter with thousands of wheat contracts that were worth far less than what he had bought them for (Leech and Carroll, 1938).

In 1958 the US government banned onion futures trading – after nine years of trading on the Chicago Mercantile Exchange – on the grounds that it was responsible for onion price volatility. The ban remains. Options trading in agricultural commodities, one of the few areas into which electronic trading hasn't made any inroads, was prohibited under the Commodity Exchange Act of 1936. The ban was lifted in 1982 for exchange traded agricultural options, and in 1998 for off-exchange agricultural options trade (Commodities Futures Trading Commission, 1998; Weiner, 2002).

Following the onion ban was the 'Salad Oil Scandal' of the 1960s when Anthony 'Tino' De Angelis – the self-styled salad oil king – tried to corner the soya bean and cottonseed oil markets, by buying the oils and storing them at his tanks in Bayonne, New Jersey. He financed the purchases through warehouse receipts for his stored oil. The $150 million worth of receipts were held by American Express, which decided to sell on the receipts, saying that they needed an audit of the oil to complete the receipt sale. They found little oil, and De Angelis was ultimately sent to prison (Broehl, 1998).

In the early 1970s the Goldstein Samuelson gold options fraud caused $70 million in customer losses. It is credited with inspiring the US Congress to create the Commodities Futures Trading Commission in 1974 as an independent regulatory agency with jurisdiction over all futures and options trading in both physical commodity futures and financial futures (Dial, 1996). The Hunt Brothers' attempt to corner the silver market in the winter of 1979–1980, prompted thousands of people to queue to sell their silver candlesticks, cutlery, coffee pots and jewellery when silver prices vaulted to more than $50 a troy ounce (Fay, 1982).

Manipulation in commodity markets became a big concern for the Federal Bureau of Investigation. For around two years in the late 80s, FBI agents posed as floor traders on the Chicago Board of Trade and the Chicago Mercantile Exchange in an undercover sting operation. Forty-eight traders were prosecuted on charges ranging from fixing trades to fraud (Taylor, 1993). The 'sting' led to tighter trading rules such as the separation of clients' trading and personal accounts.

The Sumitomo copper scandal in the 1990s cost the Japanese trading firm about $2.6 billion in losses and led to the jailing of their top copper trader, Yasuo Hamanaka. The affair led to many of the large investment banks, including JP Morgan, Merrill Lynch, Deutsche Bank and UBS, having to pay hundreds of millions of dollars to settle claims in litigation brought by either the Japanese company or investors. Tighter trading rules were introduced at the London Metal Exchange where copper trading took place.

In recent years there have been allegations of price manipulation and excessive speculation in the crude oil, gasoline and natural gas markets, as well as ongoing litigation over Enron's distortion of electricity prices. A US Senate report in July 2007 blamed Amaranth Advisors and its head energy trader Brian Hunter for abnormally high gas prices for consumers, because they had acquired a high proportion of the US natural gas contracts traded on the IntercontinentalExchange (ICE) and Nymex. Amaranth held natural gas contracts equating to about 5 % of the amount of gas used in the US in a single year US Senate Permanent Subcommittee on Investigations and Committee on Homeland Security and Governmental Affairs (2007). The report came a year after the US Senate said financial speculators had contributed around $20 to the then-prevailing crude price of about $70 a barrel in a June 2006 report (US Senate Permanent Subcommittee in Investigations, 2006). Amaranth lost $2 billion on its natural gas positions over a two-week period to the middle of September 2006, which led to the Greenwich Connecticut-based hedge fund liquidating its entire $8 billion portfolio US Senate Permanent Subcommittee on Investigations and Committee on Homeland Security and Governmental Affairs (2007). Amaranth reported the single greatest losses ever by a hedge fund, even more than the losses of Long Term Capital Management (LTCM).

The collapse of Amaranth highlighted the vast sums that are moved in commodity markets, the fact that the US natural gas markets are notoriously volatile, the predatory nature that some funds display when they are able to borrow large amounts of money and the secretive nature in which some of the markets still operate. But, as with the Hunt brothers' attempt to corner the silver market, Amaranth (Mr Hunter) was not bigger than the market. This buying spree of natural gas contracts may have been responsible for pushing prices higher, but once it was clear that Amaranth was selling its natural gas holdings, the price of natural gas fell more than 40 % over a two-month period.

The Amaranth episode continues the pattern of attempts to corner certain commodity markets, but like all previous attempts it was short-lived and the market reverted back to the price that reflected market conditions.

The sordid perception of commodities may have put off some investors, but it has attracted others. 'One thing that I liked about trading commodities,' says Helmut Weymar, the co-founder of Commodities Corp, 'was that it was viewed as a sleazy business, so not that many people were doing it' (Lux, 2003).

Breaking New Ground

In the developing markets however, commodities trading has been viewed much more harshly. China banned futures trading in commodities in 1994, only lifting the ban in the late 1990s. By this stage it had shrunk the number of Chinese commodity exchanges from fifteen to three. A fourth exchange has since opened.[10]

India has also had a fairly fickle relationship with commodities trading. Its first commodity derivatives exchange was launched in 1875 – a decade after CBOT started grains futures (Ahuja, 2006). Unlike the US where commodities futures markets have become the biggest in the world, Indian commodities trading remains under the spectre of government intervention. There is persistent political debate about the role of speculators and whether they cause commodity prices to rise. The debate is most sensitive in agriculture, where three-quarters of the population still earns its livelihood.

The fear of speculation in agricultural futures and its effect on underlying commodity prices led to the banning of commodity options and the settling of a commodity futures trade with cash. The farmer or holder of a futures sale contract had to physically deliver the amount of beans, grains or oilseeds specified in the contract. A complete ban on commodities futures trading came about in the 1960s. It was lifted again this decade, as India's new-found economic confidence led to the re-opening of commodity exchanges. 'We had flourishing futures market until the 1960s when a ban was imposed. The primary reason for the ban was that we were not self-sufficient in agricultural commodities . . . futures trading was associated with speculation and that it had artificially pushed up the price of essential commodities. The ban on futures pushed trading underground,' said Madan Sabnavis, chief economist at NCDEX, one of three national Indian commodity exchanges. Indian investors are, however, still unable to trade in foreign commodity exchanges such as the CME, Nymex or the CBOT: India's restrictions on foreign currency prevent the movement of Indian rupees in and out of the country. Before my visit to India I was unable to buy rupees at Heathrow Airport, and was warned that any Indian currency brought into the country would be taken away from me.

The reintroduction of commodity exchanges in India was accompanied by the rule that they must be electronic and that there would be no open outcry trading (although there are 21 regional commodity exchanges that specialize in the commodities grown in the area, such as the spices in the south and pulses and grains in the northern states). The marriage of electronic trading screens and Indian farmers (among the poorest people in the country and many still use bullocks for power as they can't afford tractors) is made at the local warehouses, where their grains, pulses or spices are stored. Electronic ticker boards display the commodity prices in eight regional languages so the farmer can use them as a reference. They don't trade though; 'Most Indian farmers have yet to be educated in trading techniques and managing money to trade,' says Puranam Ravikumar, the chief executive of NCDEX.

The revival of commodity futures has not been entirely smooth. Old attitudes prevail, and the Indian futures industry is still regulated by the 1952 Forward Contracts (Regulations) Act, preventing trading in commodity options and indices. Only trading in futures contracts and physical commodities is therefore allowed. In addition, in February 2007, the Indian commodity futures trading regulator, The Forward Markets Commission (FMC), banned trading in rice and wheat – two of India's largest crops. At the time of writing, the government committee set up to study the impact on wholesale and retail prices had yet to deliver its findings.

According to Ravikumar, the Indian government is very sensitive to wheat prices because 50 million tonnes of wheat each year are distributed to the country's poor. 'The government is forgetting that the change in prices sends a signal to farmers to either grow more or less of the crop to match demand,' Ravikumar says. He spends much of his time working politicians to assure them that commodity markets are not trying to ruin the livelihood of farmers. While NCDEX waits for the full consent of the Indian government, it already has the blessing of the Lord of Beginnings in India, Ganesh; a statue of the elephant headed Hindu god sits outside the exchange's offices, which are in the same Mumbai building as the National Stock Exchange – a shareholder in NCDEX.[11] Neither China nor India allows foreign investors to trade commodity futures in their markets, although the amount of new wealth in both countries this decade has seen an explosion in commodity futures trades.

Leo Melamed, chairman emeritus of the CME Group, which owns the Chicago Mercantile Exchange and the Chicago Board of Trade, said China would have a significant global futures market in the next ten years. Melamed has some insight on China; he was made an honorary dean of the China Institute of Financial Derivatives at Peking University in 2007. The university received 100 000 applicants a year for 3000 places. 'Just think of who they are getting, they are getting the cream – that is real competition,' said Melamed. 'Within ten years, China will have a developed financial market. Compare 10 years ago with today. I could have never conceived what we have today; that they would have moved that fast,' said Melamed.

For now the foreign investment restrictions in China are in place and therefore commodity markets in the United States and Europe remain the global benchmarks for commodities prices. But developing countries are not only consuming an increasing share of global commodities, their commodity exchanges are seeing more of the world's commodity derivatives trade.[12]

Oil Flows

The most talked about commodity price of all is the oil price. It's quoted on the nightly news and even newspapers with scant business coverage are likely to print the oil price from the previous day's trade. The two most quoted oil prices are West Texas Intermediate (WTI) and Brent. The WTI presents US oil prices (and given that the cars, planes, trucks and buses of the US burn a quarter of the world's oil used each day, the US is a good indicator for global oil consumption). The Brent contract is used as a reference price for Middle Eastern and Russian oil exporters and European consumers.

These benchmarks are relatively new in the world of commodities. The WTI became the first crude oil futures contract in the modern era when it was launched in 1983 on the New York Mercantile Exchange (Nymex), more than 100 years after grain futures were launched in Chicago. The Brent contract was launched in 1987 on the International Petroleum Exchange (IPE) in London. The two contracts have become the most widely traded commodities contracts, attracting a large share of the money invested by hedge fund and commodity indices. The growth in their use mirrors the growth in the modern commodities investment market.

Until the introduction of the WTI, contract refiners, airlines and transport companies had no ability to manage their exposure to fluctuating oil prices. Prices had been through a volatile ride in the previous decade starting with the Arab oil embargo in 1974, and the Iranian revolution in 1979. Both events sent oil prices to record highs, leading to fears by consuming nations that they had little power over oil prices as Opec appeared to be calling the shots.

Prior to Opec it was the major Western-owned oil companies, known as the Seven Sisters, that set the oil price. They had controlled production in the US (which was the world's largest oil producer until 1976) (Energy Information Administration, 2006)[13] and they held long-term production concessions in Saudi Arabia, Iran, Iraq and other Gulf countries and North Africa. But as Arab nations nationalized their oil industries, the balance of power shifted. It changed again in the early 1980s, this time to a struggling futures exchange that was nearly shut down a few years before it was to take on the might of the large oil companies and Opec. This swing also gave birth to the largest component of today's global commodities market, energy trading, and this is how it happened.

Nymex had spent most of its 111-year history as an agricultural futures exchange. It started life as the Butter and Cheese Exchange of New York, having been set up in 1872 by 62 Manhattan dairy merchants (Kagan Vitiello, 1997), then expanded into eggs by the 1880s, changing its name to the Butter, Cheese, and Egg Exchange of New York (eggs and butter were the mainstay of diets at that time). It was finally renamed the New York Mercantile Exchange in 1882. When the exchange was formed, much of Manhattan was still farmland, as was New Jersey across the Hudson River. Lou Guttman – former Nymex chairman and a 30-year member of the exchange – explained that merchants would congregate together for a few hours a day to trade.

After the Second World War, restrictions constrained trading in butter and eggs so Nymex looked to diversify. Soon potatoes futures trading became the backbone of the exchange, mostly Maine potatoes which dominated trade. Idaho potatoes could also be traded, though they weren't as popular as the Maine ones. Chicago Delicious apple contracts and plywood and platinum futures were also traded. By the mid-1970s though, the volume of Maine potatoes was falling, and the worst was yet to come; there was a default with the Maine contract. 'It (Nymex) was pretty close to default. The government wanted to shut it down, because it could not make delivery on Maine potatoes,' said Michel Marks, who became chairman of Nymex in 1978 at the age of 28, four years after he started at Nymex when his father got him a job on the floor.

'He (Dad) was a speculator, he was a merchant. He never sat on the (Nymex) board. I didn't have a job when I got out of college. I didn't know anything about it (trading), and I ended up as the chairman of the exchange,' Marks said. It was a tough time for Nymex. It had no money, no resources, it had a poor relationship with the regulators, confidence with investors was at a low, and the government wanted to shut it down. It was also not allowed to launch any new contracts. Fortunately, Nymex had already traded energy futures. It had launched a gasoil futures contract to be delivered in Rotterdam in October 1974, but the oil markets were still unstable following the Arab oil embargo, and the contract was unsuccessful. At about the same time, the New York Cotton Exchange launched a crude oil contract, also with Rotterdam delivery. It, too, went nowhere (Faber, 2004).

The energy contracts lay dormant until Nymex, looking for a saviour to rescue the exchange – which by this point faced a bleak future – launched the heating oil contract in 1978. The contract, mainly for the northeastern seaboard of the US, was to start a revolution in the way oil was traded. However, it did not turn the world on its head from day one, with only 22 contracts traded the first day (Faber, 2004).

But it was enough to test the waters in the domestic energy market, which was about to undergo further changes with the election in 1980 of Ronald Reagan. One of Reagan's first official acts was to remove all remaining price controls on the US oil industry that were put in place by President Nixon following the oil price spike after the Arab oil embargo. This paved the way for Nymex to introduce the unleaded gasoline futures contract in 1981, and on 30 March 1983, the WTI contract. On the same day the CBOT launched its own crude futures, the Louisiana Light Sweet. The CBOT had got its crude futures application in first with the Commodity Futures Trading Commission, but Nymex pushed to have the approval for both contracts set on the same day. 'I thought first mover was a big advantage. (But) theirs (CBOT) only lasted one month; they had a delivery problem in their first month and that killed it,' said Marks. After enduring the experience of a default on supply with the Maine potato contract, Marks knew that security of supply was paramount in a successful market. 'The issue was not price, it was supply.'

Marks knew that if they were to launch the WTI successfully, he needed fresh blood at the exchange. The potato traders were gone, and Marks decided to double the number of seats in order to cut their price. Since they were now cheaper than the seats at its fellow New York exchange Comex and the New York Stock Exchange, new traders were attracted to the exchange. Among them were Vinnie Viola, Richard Schaeffer and Daniel Rappaport, who were all to follow Marks and become chairmen of Nymex at various times over the following 25 years. 'They were like nomads coming in together to start a market from scratch,' said Marks. He got all the traders working together to make the crude contract work. They also provided the liquidity, so when a customer wanted to make a trade, they would be prepared to go the other side of it. So, say an oil distributor wanted to take delivery of oil for the winter, which meant buying oil at a future date; the floor trader would have to sell the oil and take the risk of having to deliver the oil if he was unable to offload the futures contract to an oil supplier, or physical oil trading company.

With no domestic competition Nymex had to win over a very sceptical industry, which was not particularly ecstatic about the prospect of dealing with a former potato exchange. It had also brought back oil trading to the US (oil exchanges having first been established in western Pennsylvania in the late 19th century following the first commercial oil discoveries in 1859). The Nymex trading floor was only a few blocks from where Standard Oil had its headquarters on 26 Broadway in lower Manhattan. Standard Oil, predecessor to

ExxonMobil, founded by John D. Rockefeller, had controlled the US oil industry in the late 19th century.[14]

Local fuel distributors were among the first to start trading Nymex energy futures, Marks told me. These new customers were soon joined by oil storage companies, pipeline operators, then the refiners and finally the oil companies that had refused to deal with the exchange when it started using the WTI contract to hedge their production. But it wasn't just energy companies that started trading. The physical commodity traders such as Phibro also became customers. The large financial players also became involved, but only relatively late on. Goldman Sachs entered the commodity business in 1981 when it bought one of its clients, J. Aron & Co, a family-owned commodity-trading business (Endlich, 2000) which had been a big precious metals trader until the gold price collapsed after its peak in January 1980. Morgan Stanley was also a new customer, as was Drexel Burnham Lambert, which is better known for employing junk-bond trader Michael Milken. 'The cartel was breaking up and the trend was towards free-market oil pricing... once a commodity was established as a futures contract, it pretty much became a monopoly and a franchise... and I thought that if we could establish the franchise, it could last for ever and ever,' said Marks.

The ultimate endorsement of the WTI and Brent contracts, though, was Opec. Its ministers and their teams of advisors keep tight surveillance on these oil price benchmarks, and these days they can often be seen checking prices on their Blackberries at Opec meetings. The establishment of oil futures represented the first time that oil prices had been determined in an open marketplace rather than being set by producers that control vast supplies of oil. It also gave birth to a new financial market, a place for speculators – who knew more about taking risk than about the chemistry of oil.

The launch of WTI in 1983, and Brent four years later, gave rise to another oil trading market; the informal one between companies, banks, physical energy traders, refiners and transportation companies, known as the over-the-counter (OTC) market. It's a self-regulated market; trades are agreed between the two parties who take the risk in the other party as to trade defaults. It provides more flexibility than the standard specifications of size, time and quality of the underlying commodity. It's one where Goldman, Morgan Stanley and other investment banks are major players. However, prices negotiated in the OTC market are based on prices established in the futures markets. The two markets – futures and OTC – have helped each other to grow, and although there is no official size of the OTC market, it is estimated to be about three to five times larger than the size of the energy futures markets.

New York, New York

The success of its energy futures turned Nymex into the US's largest commodity futures exchange, far outstripping the CBOT, which had long been the largest commodities exchange. The CBOT had switched its attention to financial futures and its agricultural contracts were becoming a smaller part of its business.

New York was already the world's financial centre. The New York Stock Exchange was the biggest equity market and the headquarters of the US's largest banks were in Manhattan – they were at the centre of the world's foreign exchange and government bond markets, where trades were now mainly done over the phone and the screen. Manhattan had also become a key commodity-trading centre with five commodity exchanges in the city during the 1970s. They had little to do with each other. Guttman said the New York Cotton Exchange, formed in 1870, was dominated by 'southern gentlemen' of the cotton-growing states, and that the New York Coffee and Sugar Exchange and the New York Cocoa Exchange were largely filled with the city's Italian and Irish immigrant communities. The city's three agriculture futures exchanges combined to form the New York Board of Trade in 1998; four years after Nymex had bought its once bigger rival the Commodity Exchange Inc. (Comex), and added gold, silver and copper futures to its energy contracts.

Nybot had its trading floor decimated in the September 11, 2001 attacks on the World Trade Center. (The floor was used in *Trading Places* in one of the final scenes of the film where Louis Winthrope

III (Dan Aykroyd) and Billy Ray Valentine (Eddie Murphy) turn the financial tables on the Duke brothers, Randolph and Mortimer). After the attack it became a tenant in the Nymex building overlooking the Hudson River and Ellis Island, past which many of the Jewish, Italian and Irish ancestors of Nymex and Comex traders sailed when they came to America for the first time. The Nybot cotton, coffee, cocoa and sugar pits share the same floor as the Comex gold and silver pits. Family heritage is on display on the Nybot and Nymex floors; traders still wear green jackets with white shamrocks. The surnames of the traders also indicate a strong presence of the three communities at both exchanges.

The exchanges had become private member clubs, in that, in order to trade with the best benefits, a customer had to buy an exchange seat. This would give the owner the right to trade energy contracts on Nymex, which had 816 seats. There was a finite capacity of people that could trade on the floor and as business volumes rose, so did the value of the seats, open outcry trading being the main way to trade. During the 1980s and 1990s trading took place for no more than five hours a day; a far shorter day than at the New York Stock Exchange or for the oil traders in the pits of London's IPE. Being a trader on Nymex or Nybot was described as the best part-time job in Manhattan; traders would finish by 2.30 pm and then go and have a beer at Johnnies Fish Grill nearby.

Many of these seats were owned by Nymex board members and by traders that joined the exchange in the early 1980s. With Nymex accounting for about two-thirds of the global energy futures market (the rest being traded on London's IPE), seat values rose (as did their monthly leasing rates) to thousands of dollars a month – providing a tidy income to former traders who had by now retired to the warmer climates of Florida and California. For Nymex, too, there was little competition. Throughout the 1980s and for the first half of the 1990s there was an unwritten rule that futures exchanges did not launch new contracts that would put them in competition with an incumbent exchange. Hence, Nymex and Comex stuck to energy and metals respectively; the Chicago Mercantile Exchange stuck to foreign exchange futures, equity stock index futures, short-term interest rates and dairy and meat commodities; and the Chicago Board of Trade remained the home of grains, oilseeds and US treasuries from five- to 30-year rates.

The Enron Effect

All this was about to change. Energy merchant Enron had become a trading machine. The Houston-based company had long been a natural gas and power trader, and was looking for new markets to try to justify its sky-high share price to investors. It was Enron's presence in the OTC gas markets that led Nymex – in the spring of 1990 – to launch its natural gas futures contract, called the Henry Hub (named after the gas pipeline junction in Louisiana). It was a key reference point for gas trades (McLean and Elkind, 2003). Enron traders used Nymex and the IPE, but they had mainly traded in the OTC markets; their competitors were the trading rooms at investment banks. The company had become a market within itself, trading with different arms within its sprawling network.

In 1999, Enron announced to the world it wanted to become the market as well. An electronic marketplace – Enron Online – was the place where producers, consumers, merchants, refiners and speculators could come online and trade. What is more, Enron was prepared to do any trade that the customer wanted. Enron's chief executive, Jeffrey Skilling hailed Enron Online as part of the company's unique entrepreneurial spirit.

Enron had learnt much about online trading systems from a young start-up company that was also looking at developing its own electronic marketplace. Jeffrey Sprecher had worked with Enron when he was developing power plants in the late 1980s and the early 1990s. In October 1997 Sprecher bought Continental Power Exchange, an Atlanta-based company set up by 63 American power utilities which used it to send their power price over a high-speed network, managed by WorldCom, the failed telecommunications group. The prices reflected the amount charged to households, factories and shopping centres. The business model did not work; the CPE was at the end of the power supply chain and had less scope to increase its margins. Electricity power can be bought in blocks of months, weeks, days or hours, but by the time it got to CPE, they were dealing in minutes, which had less of a profit margin than dealing in bigger chunks of time. Despite its pitfalls, Sprecher saw that the system could be applied to other commodity markets.

Together with Charles Vice, Sprecher started talking to power companies about forming a power market that could be traded electronically. The internet boom was in full swing and every company in the world was looking to develop some sort of electronic-commerce strategy. 'Starting an exchange is really hard because you need everyone to show up on the same day with the intent of doing business and you have to orchestrate that,' Sprecher told me. 'People would say "it is an interesting idea, if you can get it going we will look at it".' Over the course of 1998 and 1999, a number of utilities became interested in the idea, including the energy merchants El Paso and Aquilla and Duke Energy, the US utility.

Then they spoke to Enron. 'They were a big player; I knew them from my business. We were showing them this platform we had built and we had got them to be part of the group,' said Sprecher. A number of meetings took place with Enron executives. 'The meetings kept on getting to a higher and higher executive level. They were flying people in from London, and we thought that they were really going to get behind this thing.' Enron credit Louise Kitchen, a London-based gas trader at the company, with creating Enron Online.

'I will never forget, in 1999 we were having a meeting where we showed them the platform. One of the technical guys asked a very specific question about streaming information through a Microsoft proxy server. Then we realized they were building something, because the questions they had started to ask us were too technical. They had been using us for information and validation and we had been telling them openly how the system works,' said Sprecher. 'So I don't know whether they had the idea or we gave them the idea, but in the late summer of 1999 Enron came out and launched Enron Online. It was an immediate success and it tapped into all the stuff that we had worked on for years. We thought it was over; we thought the whole idea was gone because they had something that we did not have and that is order flows, so they were putting up prices on the screens that we could not do yet,' said Sprecher.

Six months on, Enron Online was at the centre of the trading universe, taking market share from established exchanges and investment banks. Some people on Wall Street were becoming concerned about Enron making inroads into their business, as well as the company's strategy of moving from a bricks and mortar company – or a power station and pipeline company in Enron's case – to a trading company, and whether its balance sheet was strong enough to support this change in operation. This was in line with the internet business philosophy of the day, and a strategy that earned higher market valuations with investors who had all become enamoured with dot com companies. 'Enron was a threat. A lot of business was going though them. The thing that bothered me about them is that they became the book; they bought and sold everything and anything. How can they do that without blowing up and taking some losses?' said Lou Guttman, the former Nymex chairman.

The concern on Wall Street revived hope for Sprecher, who, one winter morning, met with Gary Cohen, global head of Goldman Sachs commodity business at the time (he became president of the bank in 2006). That afternoon he also met Neal Shear, head of Morgan Stanley's commodities business.

Unbeknown to Sprecher, Morgan Stanley and Goldman Sachs had already started talking to each other about creating an alternative electronic platform to Enron. In London, the heads of Goldman Sachs and Morgan Stanley's European commodity businesses – Isabelle Ealet and Richard (Dick) Bronks from Goldman, and Colin Bryce and Goran Trapp from Morgan Stanley – met on a December morning in 1999 on the 14th floor of Morgan Stanley's Canary Wharf building to discuss the impact of Enron and the prospect of jointly developing an electronic system for their clients. By 3 pm that same afternoon, Bronks and Ealet were back in Morgan's office with an agreement.

They met with other banks and with oil producers about the plan, to gauge the level of support and willingness in Europe to combat Enron. 'I think in the development of Enron's E-technology they were looking to control it. It was not a mutlilateral platform, but a bilateral platform where it was Enron to the market and the market to Enron,' said Bryce. 'Enron was trying to force markets down people's throats. They seemed to think that any market they could create they could dominate. That is a totally different operation and methodology from the way in which Morgan and Goldman grew up. We grew up being significant in commodity markets by responding to the needs of the incumbents in the industry; if there was a risk there that they wanted to manage, or transfer or transform, that is where we can come in and provide liquidity, rather than try and come up with the next thing to force down the throats of the corporate industrial world,' he said.

Morgan and Goldman had already been looking at investing in an alternative electronic trading platform – Altra – which was jointly owned by Prebon and Amerex, two brokers specializing in the over-the-counter market. Electronic trading platforms for power, energy, equities, foreign exchange and government bonds were popping up as fast as the click of a mouse, to challenge the incumbents – or energy and power companies – trying to get some 'internet valuations' into their share price. But, just as with the dot com mania, few survived. Royal Dutch Shell launched its coralconnect.com electronic commerce and commodity pricing system in the late 1990s, only to close it a few years later. Eventually, Goldman and Morgan Stanley decided not to invest in Altra, and to go with Sprecher and his team instead. Altra is no longer in business, but for Sprecher it was the start of bigger and better things. The relationship did not start smoothly though.

With the two biggest banks in the energy-trading world on board, Sprecher wanted to get the big utilities on board too. There were six of them; they called themselves Firewire. Sprecher hosted a meeting at his Atlanta headquarters. 'The six utilities, Morgan and Goldman all arrived in front of the building and sat in their cars because they were worried that if they got together, there would be anti-trust issues, so they wanted a confidentiality agreement. People called their lawyers, and all the lawyers said it would be an issue,' said Sprecher. 'They spent three hours in their cars, and I was running between the cars relaying the information to everyone, which was difficult because they didn't even want their identities known to each other except that they were major players in the business. It got to the point that everyone was so frustrated that they said "let's just have the damn meeting", and someone got an anti-trust lawyer to sit in the meeting,' he said. The utilities were interested in being involved in the venture, but there was a disagreement about the size of the shareholdings. At the same time, Goldman and Morgan insisted that Sprecher get the other investment banks involved in commodities on board, as well as the oil companies BP, Shell (which is now Royal Dutch Shell), Elf, (which is now part of Total), Société Générale and Deutsche Bank.

The European based oil producers were more involved in energy trading than their US counterparts. Both Exxon (which had taken over rival Mobil in 1998) and the second biggest US producer Chevron had a policy of not using the 'paper' oil market to hedge their production. Mobil, on the other hand, had been an active energy derivatives user. BP was acknowledged to be the most aggressive trader among the oil companies under the leadership of Sir John Browne, who also sat on the Goldman Sachs board and was supportive of the Sprecher plan.

The next problem for Sprecher was to divide up the shares of the company and see if he could get Nymex to join the venture. Sprecher wanted his venture, which they named IntercontinentalExchange (ICE), to become an electronic bulletin board for energy prices traded in the OTC market. It had no intention of going into the futures market, the domain of Nymex. What Sprecher wanted was for users of his exchange to have the ability to offload their risk to an entity that would cover any trade that defaulted, a concept known as a clearing house. And Nymex had its own clearing house.[15]

It was Gary Cohn (who started his career trading silver), the Goldman executive – who was also on the board of Nymex – who first made contact with Sprecher. He introduced Sprecher to the Nymex chairman Daniel Rappaport, who in turn invited Sprecher to present to the director of Nymex at a board meeting.

Sprecher had offered Nymex 10 % of ICE as well as a promise that ICE wouldn't go into the futures market. They had four days to decide on the offer. Nymex directors rejected the proposal and launched their own OTC electronic platform months later. Cohn was resoundingly voted off the Nymex board months later and Rappaport announced his resignation from the board within 12 months, after eight years as chairman. Within 18 months ICE was in the energy futures business and was to become Nymex's fiercest rival.[16,17]

In May 2000, ICE launched its electronic price bulletin board for the OTC market in power, natural gas, oil and gasoline. Shortly after the launch, Sprecher met with Dr Richard Ward, chief executive of London's IPE – the smaller rival to Nymex. IPE had rebuffed takeover offers from Nymex, and a separate one involving Enron in the previous 12 months.

Ward was also concerned about the impact electronic trading was having on the London Brent market, which was conducted in a large room opposite the Tower of London. Ward had witnessed the loss of futures trading in ten-year German government bonds – known as the Bund – from the floor of the London International Financial Futures and Options Exchange (Liffe), to the electronic screens of Eurex, the online German derivatives exchange. In 1998, 16 years after it had opened, Liffe closed its floor for financial futures trading and moved electronic. Matif, the French futures exchange, also became fully electronic the same year. Electronic trading in equities, bonds and commodities was spreading rapidly.

Over in the US though, the major stock and futures exchanges – with the exception of Nasdaq – were still hooked on trading face to face, despite the fact that the US was the epicentre of the electronic commerce revolution. It was also home to the companies that built, designed and provided the internet, from Intel (the chipmaker), Cisco Systems (the plumber to the net) and numerous software companies that dominated the computer and dot com world. But this had more to do with vested interests at the exchange than any trading culture.

Ward and Sprecher met. The IPE was interested in an electronic trading system and also a clearing house (which, as mentioned earlier, covers third party risk). The IPE was a shareholder in the London Clearing House, which cleared all the trades. By early 2001 they were in serious discussions about a merger. Nymex made another attempt to buy IPE, but by June 2001, IPE members voted to accept an all share takeover from ICE. ICE was barely 12 months old – but it was the dot com era, and it had a higher valuation because of its growth prospects from its electronic system.[18] ICE was now in the futures business, and a direct competitor to Nymex, when both exchanges had many opportunities to merge. But energy markets were about to be turned on their head with the collapse of Enron.

Enron' with concealed losses in balance sheets of companies purposely set up to enhance the company's earnings to investors and its predatory trading culture, finally ate itself in the autumn of 2001, triggering a crisis of confidence in US natural gas and power markets. It took several years before confidence and volumes returned. 'People were looking at the markets and saying "are these real markets?",' said Sprecher, adding that there were investigations into the energy markets by the US Department of Justice and the Commodity Futures Trading Commission (CFTC), the industry regulator. 'When your largest counter-party in your space goes bankrupt, it questioned whether anyone can go bankrupt,' he said. It also forced ICE to change its board members, so that none of the directors were from banks or oil companies, thus avoiding accusations of conflict of interest.

The collapse of Enron had removed the catalyst for banks to back the ICE, but the aim of creating an electronic marketplace for energy trading remained. The IPE was one of the few European derivative markets that was still open outcry, and the electronic trading volumes of financial futures exchanges were booming. In addition, the once gentlemanly agreement to not step onto another exchange's patch was being breached, as growth rather than tradition became the key. Plus, commodity exchanges were turning themselves from privately owned member clubs to for-profit organizations. The Chicago Mercantile Exchange, which started as a butter and egg exchange at the end of the 19th century, had taken this a step further; it had become a top share market performer, doubling its share price after listing its shares on the New York Stock Exchange in December 2002.

The transformation of the CME from a hog and cattle futures exchange to one of the world's largest financial futures exchanges owes much to the launch of foreign currency futures in 1972, the first of a suite of financial futures that the exchange unveiled. The introduction of financial futures also helped popularize futures, which until then were confined to commodities. Financial futures quickly overtook commodities futures and can now be found in most pension or mutual fund portfolios. This acceptance of financial futures has, in turn, helped overcome the distrust that was held by investors in the past. 'When we launched financial futures, we were launching a lot more than that, which I did not know at the time,' said Leo Melamed, who oversaw the introduction of the currency futures, earning him the title 'father of financial futures.'[19] "The CME was even on the face of the map (before the launch). When I used to go to Washington DC, they used to think I was talking about the Merchandising Mart, the big Chicago building that was once owned by Joe Kennedy.'

The increase in value on CME shares was largely attributable to the increase in electronic trading. With the CME proving a good reference for trading trends, the IPE introduced the electronic buying and selling of oil futures contracts in the autumn of 2003, but floor traders refused to budge, and electronic volumes were tepid. A year later, the IPE cut trading hours on the floor to boost electronic trading volumes, a move which prompted Nymex to start an open outcry floor in London, providing an incentive for the IPE floor traders to switch to the New York exchange.

The Final Battle Cry

The world was turning electronic, and although the major players in the London Brent crude oil market were shareholders in ICE and supportive of its move to turn electronic in London, Nymex took the view that there was long-term viability for open outcry in London. Nymex did not receive the necessary regulatory approval to set up its London exchange immediately, so it had to set up its exchange elsewhere in Europe. The beachhead for its onslaught into the European energy market was a room the size of two squash courts, in an office building in the old docks area of Dublin. The room was leased to Nymex by its neighbour, Nybot, which used the place to trade Euro currency index futures.

The room was bursting with traders with cockney and New York accents, screaming and scribbling orders into their notebooks, not an Irish accent within hearing. It was hard to believe that from this tiny room the world's oil prices were being determined. The computer, telecommunication systems and the assembling of around 50 traders had all taken a matter of weeks to put together after Nymex announced its intentions. The dealing room seemed temporary; neither the London nor the New York traders were committed to staying in Dublin. Nymex had the ultimate goal of setting up in London, to capture a large slice of a market that traded billions of dollars worth of oil a day. Dublin was a fleeting stop; it reminded me of the betting parlour of Henry Gondorff (Paul Newman) in the film *The Sting*, which he set up with fellow Chicago conman Johnny Hooker (Robert Redford) to outwit crime boss Doyle Lonnegan (Robert Shaw): once Lonnegan went out of the room, the parlour closed; once Nymex had its London approval, the Dublin floor would close.

Dublin's mark on the global energy trading was therefore brief. Volumes dried up and traders went back to London and New York, but that did not deter Nymex from doing it all again in London ten months later. By this stage the IPE had closed its pits and all trading was done on the screen. Traders who had long resisted using the computer to buy and sell oil futures were setting up electronic trading arcades in offices around central London and on the city's outskirts. The large oil producers, refiners and airlines were also using the online system.

'Open outcry is back in London,' Mitchell Steinhause, the Nymex chairman, declared as the opening bell of the new exchange was rung in September 2005. 'This is a bold statement to the financial community: if ever there is a market suited to open outcry, it is energy.' The gallant words were never matched by action; the floor, equipped with expensive computer and telecom trading systems, was idle within weeks, with no meaningful trading ever taking place on the floor. The whole venture was abandoned in months. 'The market never wanted open outcry; it was the wrong idea. We made a mistake; but we were bright enough to admit, correct it and move on,' said Richard Schaeffer, who subsequently became Nymex chairman.

The battle between man and machine in oil trading had gone the way of all previous tussles: the machine won out – and the game had now shifted for both exchanges. The commodity price boom had ignited equity markets too; shares in mines, oil producers, farm machine companies and commodity and futures exchanges were all in demand. CME shares had risen ten-fold within four years of its listing, making the owners of the exchange – many of whom were traders or former traders at the pork-bellies turned financial futures exchange – multimillionaires. Its city rival, the CBOT, listed its shares, which doubled within the first week. Traders who owned CBOT seats were also turned into millionaires. A month later ICE debuted with a 60 % increase in its share price. Commodity exchanges had arrived in the mainstream. In little more than five years the company had gone from a dot com idea to being at the forefront of global commodities trading.

With valuations of its fellow commodity exchanges rising, electronic trading winning more market share by the day and members openly criticizing the management and board, Nymex had to respond. Mark Fisher, trader, founder of the largest independent clearing house at Nymex and author, had started discussions with private equity groups Blackstone and Battery Ventures. Nymex had already rebuffed an offer from another private equity group, Parthenon Capital, in June 2004. Nymex members were wary of Blackstone and Battery, who had bought and sold a 30 % stake in Liffe within six months, triggering a takeover battle for the London derivatives exchange. Nevertheless, members were open to selling a minority stake to an outside party that could help Nymex list its shares and make millions for its owners, most of whom had retired from day to day trading.

With ICE listed, and a healthy premium in its share price, Sprecher had a new currency to spend in the form of ICE shares. He talked to Nymex about a merger – the third time the two exchanges had talked about a corporate get together in four years – but Nymex was not interested. Instead, Richard Schaeffer introduced Bill Ford from General Atlantic; a private equity company with a track record of investing in electronic trading systems and exchanges. After months of haggling, General Atlantic bought 10 % of Nymex for $170 million in March 2006, with the intention that Nymex would join the public share markets by the end of the year.

But ICE had given Nymex another problem. Nymex had failed to snatch the Brent crude market from ICE; now the Atlanta-based exchange had turned the table and launched an electronic version of the WTI contract, the cornerstone of Nymex's suite of traded commodities. The market voted with their fingers. Volumes on ICE's new contract soared and posed a major threat to Nymex. 'If we hadn't gone electronic, we would not be a factor now, we would be nothing; ICE would have killed us. We would not be out of business, but we would be worth a lot less than what we are worth now,' said Schaeffer. Nymex had various electronic trading systems; one for clearing and one for out of floor hours trading, but neither was robust enough to handle the vast volumes that went through the world's largest energy market. Instead it turned to the CME, which had the Globex electronic system. After years of telling the world that oil was best traded in the pit, it launched electronic trading alongside its pit trading hours, four months after it had been faced with competition. Within months the electronic system had the largest share of Nymex's energy contracts, and it started winning back market share; but it meant the days of pit trading were numbered. The ship had been steadied as the deadline loomed for listing its shares. But before its members could cash in, Nymex still had another long-term issue to sort out. The member seat values were soaring, boosting the implied share market value for the exchange.

The Nymex takeover of Comex for $10 million in 1994 had overlooked one thing; Comex members still owned the electronic trading rights that prevented anyone except the 772 members that owned Comex seats, from trading. Even though Comex had been part of Nymex for 13 years, it had its own board, trading rules and power structure and there was still some rivalry between the two, stretching back to when Comex tried to buy Nymex out in the late 1970s when it was having problems with Maine potatoes.

Comex members were also resentful that they were not going to benefit financially from the Nymex float, which was shaping up to be a bonanza. Nymex management knew they had to resolve the Comex issue before floating its shares, and this gave Comex management leverage in negotiations with their peers at Nymex. But they knew they could not hold out for too long. 'Comex had its own concerns,' said Jan Marks, brother of Michel Marks, the former Nymex chairman. Comex's main market, gold and silver futures trading, was being eroded by CBOT, which had launched electronic gold and silver futures trading in October 2004, grabbing 40 % of the US gold futures market. 'CBOT were gaining market share and if they had breached 50 %, that was a tipping point,' said Marks. In the end, Schaeffer and his management let Comex members have a share in the forthcoming windfall, issuing each seat with 8400 shares, which turned into $1.12 million at the end of the first day of Nymex shares trading on the New York Stock Exchange; the best debut by a US company on the big board in six years, and reminiscent of the debuts of the dot com era.

Not only had Comex's seat owners struck gold, but Nymex seat owners had become multimillionaires. Each owner of a Nymex seat held shares worth almost $12 million, compared with less than $700 000 at the start of the decade. Many former traders owned multiple seats: Michel Marks and his family owned 11; former trader

Bobby Sahn had ten; Mark Fisher and Marty Greenburg had five each; and Schaeffer had one. The value of General Atlantic's nine-month old investment had risen ten-fold, and Nymex was worth almost as much as its cross-town peer, NYSE. 'I bought my seat for $27 000 – that is the best trade I have done. I complain about some of the investments that I missed, but not this one,' said Schaeffer.

For all the money that has been made by traders, banks, producers and the logistic companies that take the commodity from the producer to the consumer, the float of Nymex had created more wealth for traders than any other event during the commodities boom of the first decade of the 21st century. But the windfall was not through any great new idea or skilled management; Nymex had just been reacting to events. It happened because it is the world's largest commodity exchange. 'There are a lot of guys around here who are worth $13m to $14m. They are rich beyond their wildest dreams. There are only half a million people worth $10m or more, and we made 800 of them here,' said Schaeffer. Coincidentally, on the day I visited the New York Stock Exchange, Blackstone made its debut on the big board in one of the most publicized first days of trading since the dot com days. Blackstone epitomized money men; its shares rose by 13 %, but within three days the shares were below their issue price, in contrast to the Nymex share performance.

In January 2008, Nymex shareholders were told that the day to cash in their chips had arrived. The CME, which handles the bulk of Nymex's daily trading volume, took the next logical step and made an $11 billion offer to buy Nymex. The combination of the two will allow investors to trade all segments of the commodities pie: agriculture, metals, energy and environment, and it will be one of the biggest exchanges in the world.

The planned purchase of Nymex came shortly after the CME–CBOT merger took place; under the gaze of Ceres, the Italian goddess of grains and agriculture, who is perched on the roof of the CBOT building where the exchanges are housed. She may symbolize the CBOT origins, but the exchanges' future is now a small part of a much bigger financial market.

The NYSE, the world's largest stock exchange, bought Euronext, the European equity and financial and agricultural futures exchange in 2007, putting the NYSE in the commodities trading world for the first time since it was set up in the late 18th century.

While Chicago traders such as Shuff, Cashman and Mackintosh may not be in the pits trading, in years to come they will retire very comfortably, having made enough money from the old way of trading; as well as making a good trade on CBOT shares in the way that Schaeffer and co at Nymex made their millions.

The merging of equity and commodity exchanges also mirrors the change in investor portfolio through diversification; having commodities as part of a broader investment strategy.[20] Commodity traders have become some of the most sought-after traders on Wall Street and in London, often commanding seven figures signed on unconditional payments. The launch of exchange-traded funds – investments that track an underlying asset – is as easy as buying and selling shares. There are ETFs in gold, silver, oil, copper and corn, and there are now more than 50 commodity-related ETFs listed in London, Europe and the US. These investments have also made commodity investing more accessible to smaller investors.

With commodities now part of mainstream investing, it raises the issue of whether the performance of commodities has become more correlated with stocks and bonds, as they form part of a pension or mutual funds portfolio that can be sold off if an investor needs to cover losses incurred in other markets. During the summer of 2007, concerns about the issue of 'sub-prime' loans to people of low income in the US engulfed financial markets, causing sharp sell-offs in global equity markets. However, commodity prices continued to break new records.

Equity and futures exchanges have combined; equities and commodities are traded and brokered by the same companies, and most investors allocate funds to both the commodities and securities markets. But whereas commodities and securities are subject to different regulations in the US, in the UK they are all under one roof.

The Price of Bread

Commodity prices are politically sensitive. When they are high, politicians blame speculators for manipulating prices; when they are low, in particular where agricultural commodities are concerned, there are calls for more assistance for farmers.

Commodity prices determine behaviour and decisions about the provision and supply of resources. But with so much of the world's resources controlled by government-owned bodies, or funded through subsidies, there are limits to a truly free and open market in commodity pricing. Governments will be ready to act if there are extreme price moves, such as those seen in the 1970s, which were followed by a wave of price controls and subsidies.

Speculators were blamed for driving down agriculture prices in the late 19th century and increasing commodity prices in the early 21st century. Neither accusation was correct; prices reflect the nature of supply and demand. With greater focus on commodities from an economic and political point, they will continue to form part of a diversified portfolio as new commodity investment products are launched in more markets. Like any market though, commodities will reach a point where prices are excessive when compared to the underlying supply and demand. A good signal of that is when there is too much attention on commodities on television, the internet and in newspapers. This concentration can lead to a bubble, as seen with the dot com experience. We're beginning to see the seeds of this, with the consumer becoming more and more aware of commodity prices and markets. But we are not there yet.

Notes

1. Based on data from the CBOT website on January 15, 2008, electronic trading in agricultural commodities accounted for three-quarters of total volume.

2. The merger of the CBOT and CME, which took place when I was writing the book, will see the floors of the unified exchange also move into the same building, the iconic CBOT building on West Jackson Boulevard.

3. The accusation of fictitious trading came from the testimony of Charles Pillsbury, the largest commercial operator in grain in the United States, before the United States House Committee on Agriculture's 1892 hearings *Fictitious Dealings in Agricultural Products* (Levy, 2006).

4. Dunavant Enterprises website – http://www.dunavant.com/Home/tabid/36/Default.aspx

5. Helmut Weymar wrote *The Dynamics of the World Cocoa Market* under the direction of Samuelson.

6. These figures are based primarily on the Goldman Sachs Commodity Index (GSCI) and Dow Jones-AIG Commodity Index (DJ-AIGCI).

7. Jarecki offered to buy Mocatta back for $20 million 12 years later, but Standard Chartered sold it to Bank of Nova Scotia for $17 million.

8. The Ontario Teachers' Fund has invested mainly through the GSCI index, but has also acquired stakes in commodity-related assets, including power stations, an interest in a UK water utility and a gas distribution network in the UK. These come under its inflation-sensitive investments.

9. According to the 2006 annual report of The Yale Endowment, in 2006, 27.8 % of the fund was in real assets, which include commodities.

10. The growth of China's futures markets has been accompanied by rampant abuse, triggering two waves of reform. Over the years the authorities slashed the number of exchanges from over 40 to four: the Shanghai Futures Exchange, the Dalian Commodity Exchange, the China Zhengzhou Commodity Exchange and the Shanghai Petroleum Exchange. The number of futures contracts was cut back further to 12 from 35, and more brokers were closed, leaving just 175 standing from the early 1990s peak of 1000 (Qin and Ronalds, 2005).

11. NCDEX also counts Goldman Sachs and the IntercontinentalExchange among its shareholders.

12. According to a report by UNCTAD (2007), 'measured by contract volumes, nine of the world's 22 major commodity futures exchanges are now located in the developing world. This includes three exchanges each

in India and China, plus others located in Malaysia, South Africa and Brazil.

13. Although the USSR was a bigger oil producer than the US in 1976, the amount in Russia was estimated to be smaller (Energy Information Administration, 2006, Table 11.5).

14. Standard Oil was broken up through government anti-trust legislation at the start of the 20th century, its offshoots forming a significant part of the Seven Sisters, which controlled global oil markets for much for the first half of the 20th century, before Opec asserted its influence.

15. ICE is in fact the second futures exchange to be known as ICE. The International Commercial Exchange was set up in the early 1970s to trade currencies, but it ran into problems with the delivery of the Japanese yen contract and never took off. Foreign currency futures trading became a success with the launch of the International Monetary Market by the CME in 1972. The International Commercial Exchange was the old New York Produce Exchange, which ran into problems from the 'Great Salad Oil' scandal.

16. In the Nymex press release of May 4, 2000, exchange Chairman Daniel Rappaport said, 'The global energy and metals community has expressed a strong need for an electronic OTC platform that provides an open, independent and neutral marketplace for trading by all participants, price transparency, counter-party credit risk management and the liquidity created by simple standardized contracts.'

17. Among the first thing visitors to Mr Cohn's office will see is a New York Mercantile Exchange trading badge proudly displayed behind his desk (White, 2006).

18. The combination of Nymex and ICE, and its London futures exchange, the IPE, remained on the table for years to come. Vinnie Viola, who replaced Rappaport as Nymex chairman, had merger talks with Sprecher in 2002 and again in 2004. The second time they had agreed on the terms to tie the knot, but the powerful Nymex members were against it, they preferred that Nymex buy ICE outright and turned hostile.

19. The Merchandise Mart, on the north bank of the Chicago River, was once known as the world's largest wholesale buying centre under one roof. The Chicago Mart, as it was also known, was owned by the family of Joseph Kennedy, the patriarch of the Kennedy clan.

20. Over the last ten years, commodities trading volumes have quintupled to 3 billion contracts per year. The number of different futures contracts and options being actively traded has increased nearly seven-fold: from 179 in 1995, to an estimated 970 in 2006, to a projected total of 1120 in 2008. Investments in commodity-related funds have quadrupled from $33 billion to $137 billion.

References

Ahuja, N.L. (2006) Commodity Derivatives Market in India: Development, Regulation and Future Prospects, *International Research Journal of Finance and Economics*, 2.

Alberta Government (2007) *Alberta Environment Report on 2006 Greenhouse Gas Emissions*.

Anderson, T.L. and Snyder, P. (1997) *Water Markets, Priming the Invisible Pump*, Cato Institute.

Asian Development Bank (2007) *2007 Update*.

Australian Bureau of Agricultural and Resource Economics (Abare) (2007) *Australian Crop Report*.

Australian Government (2007) *A National Plan for Water Security*, January 25.

Babcock, C.R. (1994) Hillary Clinton Futures Trades Detailed, *Washington Post*, May 27.

Barclays Capital (2008) *The Commodity Investor 'Going with the Flow'*, January 10.

Barsky, R.B. and Kilian, L. (2000) *A Monetary Explanation of the Great Stagflation of the 1970s*, NBER Working Paper No. W7547.

Birchard, R.E. (1940) Copper in the Katanga Region of the Belgian Congo, *Economic Geography*, 16(4), 429–436.

Blum, S.L. (1974) *Materials and Energy Conservation through Recycling*, from the proceedings of a conference held at New England College, Henniker, New Hampshire, August 11–16.

Bowers, D.E. (1981) The Setting for New Food and Agricultural Legislation, in *Agricultural Food Policy Review: Perspectives for the 1980's*, US Department of Agriculture.

BP (2007) *Statistical Review of World Energy 2007*, Omani and Indian oil production tables.

Brasher, P. (2007) Ethanol May Fuel Dead Zone, *The Des Moines Register*, July 1.

Broehl, W.G. (1998) *Cargill, Going Global*, University Press of New England, Hanover, New Hampshire.

Brown, W. (1983) H.A. Wallace and the Development of Hybrid Corn, *The Annals of Iowa*, **47**(2), 167–179.

Bruinsma, J. (Ed.) (2003) *World Agriculture: Towards 2015/2030 and FAO Perspective*, Earthscan.

Buckler, E.S. and Stevens, N.M. (2006) Maize Origins, Domestication and Selection, in *Darwin's Harvest*, T.J. Motley, N. Zerega and H. Cross (eds), Columbia University Press, New York, pp. 67–90.

Burkart, C. and Jha, M.K. (2007) Nitrate Reduction Approaches, *Choices*, 2nd quarter.

Business Council of Australia (2006) *Water Under Pressure: Australia's Manmade Water Scarcity and How to Fix it.*

Byrnes, N. (2007) The South: In Hot Water About Water, *BusinessWeek*, October 18.

Calatrava, J. and Garrido, A. (2006) Difficulties in Adopting Formal Water Trading Rules Within Users' Associations, *Journal of Economic Issues*, **40**(1), 27–44.

California Energy Commission (2007) *2007 Integrated Energy Policy Report*, December.

Capoor, K. and Ambrosi, P. (2007) *The World Bank State and Trends of the Carbon Market 2007*, World Bank.

Carrier, L. (1923) *The Beginnings of Agriculture in America*, Mc Graw Hill.

Cashin, P. and McDermott, J. (2002) The Long-Run Behaviour of Commodity Prices: Small Trends and Big Volatility, *IMF Staff Papers*, **49**(2), 175–199.

Centner, C.W. (1942) Great Britain and Chilean Mining 1830–1914, *The Economic History Review*, **12**(1/2), 76–82.

CNNNA Corporation (2007) *National Security and the Threat of Climate Change*, March.

Coase, R. (1960) The Problem of Social Cost, *Journal of Law and Economics*, October.

Cohen, D. (2007) Earth's Natural Wealth: An Audit, *New Scientist*, May 23.

Collins, K. (2007) *Prospects for the US Farm Economy*, Agricultural Outlook Forum, March 1.

Commodities Futures Trading Commission (1998) *CFTC lifts ban on agricultural trade options, announces pilot programme*, press release, April 9.

Conway, R.K. and Duncan, M.R. (2006) Bioproducts: Developing a Federal Strategy for Success, *Choices*, 1st quarter.

Copping, J. (2007) Carbon Offsetting Schemes Not So Green, *Sunday Telegraph*, August 20.

Cosgrove, W.J. and Rijsberman, F.R. (2000) *World Water Vision Making Water Everybody's Business*, Earthscan, London.

Covey, T., Green, R., Jones, C., Johnson, J., Morehart, M., Williams, R., McGath, C., Mishra, A. and Strickland, R. (2005) *Agricultural Income and Finance Outlook*, USDA-ERS AIS-83, November.

Crabb, A. R. (1947) *The Hybrid-Corn Makers: Prophets of Plenty*, Rutgers University Press, New Brunswick.

Critser, G. (2004) *Fat Land: How Americans Became the Fattest People in the World*, Mariner Books.

Crocker, T. (1966) The Structuring of Atmospheric Pollution Control Systems, in *The Economics of Air Pollution*, H. Wolozin (Ed.), W.W. Norton, New York.

Dales, J. (1968) Land, Water and Ownership, *The Canadian Journal of Economics*, **1**(4), 791–804.

Day-Rubenstein, K. and Heisey, P. (2001) Agricultural Resources and Environmental Indicators: Crop Genetic Resources, in *ERS Agricultural Resources and Environmental Indicators*, agricultural handbook no. AH722, USDA-ERS.

Day-Rubenstein, K. and Heisey, P. (2003) Plant Genetic Resources: New Rules for International Exchange, *Amber Waves*, June.

Deans, B. (2007) The 400th Anniversary of Jamestown, *Time*, April 26.

Delgado, C. (2000) *The Coming Livestock Revolution,* background paper no. 6, submitted to the UN Department of Economic and Social Affairs, Commission on Sustainable Development, 8th session, April 24 – May 5, New York.

Dempsey, M.A. (1994) Fordlandia, *Michigan History,* 78(4), 24–33.

Department of Transport (2007) *Transport Statistics Great Britain 2007,* p. 156.

De Soto, H. (2000)*The Mystery of Capital – Why Capitalism Triumphs in the West and Fails Everywhere Else,* Black Swan.

DG Environment (2007) *Water Scarcity and Droughts,* second interim report, June.

Dial, J.B. (1996) speech at the FIA/SFE Asia-Pacific Futures Forum, Sydney, Australia, December 6.

Diamond, J. (1997) *Guns, Germs and Steel: The Fates of Human Societies,* W.W. Norton.

Domanski, D. and Health, A. (2007) Financial Investors and Commodity Markets, *BIS Quarterly Review,* March.

Dudley, K.M. (2000) *Debt and Dispossession: Farm Loss in America's Heartland,* University of Chicago Press, Chicago.

Dumett, R. (1985) Africa's Strategic Minerals During the Second World War, *The Journal of African History,* 26(4), 381–408.

Duvick, D. (2001) Biotechnology in the 1930s: The development of hybrid maize, *Nature Reviews Genetics,* 2, 69–74.

Eagleton, T. (1978) *World Trade and the Small Farmer: Can They Co-exist?* Speech at the World Agricultural Trade: The Potential for Growth symposium, Kansas, May 18–19.

Eckes, A.E. (1978) American History Textbooks and the New Issues of Trade, Payments, and Raw Materials, *The History Teacher,* 11(2), 237–246.

Ehrlich, P. (1968) *The Population Bomb,* Buccaneer Books, New York.

Electric Power Research Institute (2007) *The Power to Reduce CO_2 Emissions – The Full Portfolio Report,* discussion paper prepared for the EPRI 2007 Summer Seminar.

Elmore, R. and Abendroth, L. (2006) What is the Best Seeding Rate for Corn Based on Seed Prices and Yield Level? *Integrated Crop Management,* April 10.

Endlich, L. (2000) *Goldman Sachs, The Culture of Success,* Times Warner Books.

Energy Information Administration (no date) country analysis briefs – UK electricity, available at http://www.eia.doe.gov/emeu/cabs/United_Kingdom/Electricity.html

Energy Information Administration (1994) *Quarterly Coal Report January–April 1994*, pp. 1–8.

Energy Information Administration (2006) *Annual Energy Review 2006*, Appendix E: Estimated Energy Consumption in the United States, selected years 1635–1945.

Energy Information Administration (2007a) *International Energy Outlook 2007*, Chapter 6, Electricity.

Energy Information Administration (2007b) *Biofuels in the US Transportation Sector*, October 15.

European Copper Institute (2004) *Energy Efficient Motor Driven Systems...can save Europe 200 billion kWh of electricity consumption and 100 million tonnes of greenhouse gas emissions a year.*

European Copper Institute (2007) *The Essential Role and Benefits of Copper in Building a Sustainable World: Usage, Key Figures and New Applications*, March 13.

Faber, J. (2004) Heating oil futures began with high hopes, exceed wildest expectations, *Energy in the News*, 3, June 16.

Farm and Ranch Irrigation Survey (2003) **Volume 3**, Special Studies, Part 1 2002 Census of Agriculture, issued November 2004.

Fay, S. (1982) *The Great Silver Bubble*, Hodder and Stoughton.

Ferguson, N. (1998) *The House of Rothschild. The World's Banker 1849–1999*, Volume 2, Penguin.

Fernandez-Cornejo, J. (2004) *The Seed Industry in US Agriculture: An Exploration of Data and Information on Crop Seed Markets, Regulation, Industry Structure, and Research and Development*, USDA-ERS Agriculture Information Bulletin No. AIB786.

Fernandez-Cornejo, J. and Caswell, M. (2006)*The First Decade of Genetically Engineered Crops in the United States*, USDA-ERS Economic Information Bulletin 11.

Fernandez-Cornejo, J. and McBride, W. D. (2002) *Adoption of Bioengineered Crops*, USDA-ERS Agricultural Economic Report No. AER810.

Fetter, B. (1999) If I Had Known That 35 Years Ago: Contextualizing the Copper Mines of Central Africa, *History in Africa*, **26**, 449–452.

Finlay, M.R. (2004) Old Efforts at New Uses: A Brief History of Chemurgy and the American Search for Biobased Materials, *Journal of Industrial Ecology*, 7(3/4), 33–46.

Flannery, T. (2005) *The Weather Makers: Our Changing Climate and What it Means for Life on Earth*, Penguin.

Food and Agriculture Organization of the United Nations (2006) *Livestock's Long Shadow: Environmental Issues and Options*, The Livestock, Environment and Development (LEAD) Initiative.

Food and Agriculture Organization of the United Nations (2007) *Food Outlook, Global Market Analysis*.

Fowler, C. (1994) *Unnatural Selection: Technology, Politics and Plant Evolution*, Gordon and Breach.

Fraley, R. (2007) *Yield Can Fuel Ethanol Expansion*, the USDA Agricultural Outlook Forum, March 2.

Freese, B. (2003) *Coal: A Human History*, Perseus Publishing.

Frey, J.W. (1930) Economic Significance of the Mineral Wealth of China, *Annals of the American Academy of Political and Social Sciences*, **152**, 116–126.

Fullerton, T. (2001) *Watershed*, ABC Books.

Gardner, B.L. (2002) *American Agriculture in the 20th Century: How it Flourished and What it Cost*, Harvard University Press.

Garner, J. (2005) *The Rise of the Chinese Consumer: Theory and Evidence*, John Wiley & Sons, Ltd, Chichester.

Gibson-Jarvie, R. (1976) *The London Metal Exchange, a Commodity Market*, Woodhead-Faulkner.

Gomes, C. (2007) *Global Auto Report*, Global Economic Research, Scotia Bank Group, July 31.

Goodell, J. (2006) *Big Coal: The Dirty Secret Behind America's Energy Future*, Houghton Mifflin.

Gordon, R.B., Bertram, M. and Graedel, T.E. (2006) Metal Stocks and Sustainability, *Proceedings of the National Academy of Sciences of the US*, **103**, 1209–1214.

Gray, K.R., Frieder, L.A. and Clark, G.W. (2007) Financial Bubbles and Business Scandals in History, *International Journal of Public Administration*, **30**, 859–888.

Greenspan, A. (1997) *Government regulation and derivative contracts*, speech at the Financial Markets conference of the Federal Reserve Bank of Atlanta, Coral Gables, Florida, February 21.

Gurdak, J.J. (2006) *Human and Climate Stresses on Ground Water: Life and Water on the High Plains Aquifer, United States*, First International Symposium on Water and Better Human Life in the Future, Kyoto, Japan, November 6–8.

Hahn, R.W. and Hester, G.L. (1989) Where Did All the Markets Go? An Analysis of EPA's Emissions Trading Program, *Yale Journal of Regulation*, 6, 109–153.

Hahn, R.W. and Stavins, R.N. (1992) Economic Incentives for Environmental Protection: Integrating Theory and Practice, *The American Economic Review*, 82(2), 464–468.

Hall, P. (1998) *Cities in Civilization*, Weidenfeld & Nicolson.

Hansen, L. (2006) Wetlands: Status and Trends, in *Agricultural Resources and Environmental Indicators*, 2006 edition, Economic Research Service.

Harris, P. (2007) Water Scarcity Could Hit Chile's Miners: Thirsty Copper Industry Looking for Solutions, *Northern Miner*, May 7.

Harvey, F. and Allison, K. (2007) Clean Technology Investment Soars, *Financial Times*, November 16.

Heaney, A., Dwyer, G., Beare, S., Peterson, D. and Pechey, L. (2005) *Third-party Effects of Water Trading and Potential Policy Responses*, conference paper for the American Agricultural Economics Association conference, Rhode Island, July 25–27.

Heivilin, D.M. (1992) *National Defense Stockpile: Views on DOD's 1992 Report to the Congress and Proposed Legislation*, statement to the Subcommittee on Seapower and Strategic and Critical Materials, April 29.

Henson, R. (2006) *The Rough Guide to Climate Change*, Rough Guides Ltd.

Herfindahl, O. (1959) *Copper Costs and Prices: 1870–1957*, Johns Hopkins Press.

Herriges, J.A., Secchi, S. and Babcock, B.A. (2005) Living with Hogs in Iowa: The Impact of Livestock Facilities on Rural Residential Property Values, *Land Economics*, 81, 530–545.

Hofstrand, D. (2007) Energy Agriculture – Brazilian Ethanol, *Ag Decision Makers* Newsletter, June.

Hoppe, R.A. and Korb, P. (2006) *Understanding US Farming Exits*, USDA-ERS Economic Research Report No. ERR-21.

Howitt, R. and Hansen, K. (2005) The Evolving Western Water Markets, *Choices*, 1st quarter.

Hoyt, E.P. (1967) *The Guggenheims and the American Dream*, Funk and Wagnalls, New York.

HRH The Prince of Wales (2007) speech at the Business in the Community Awards Dinner, July 2.

Iacocca, L. (1998) Driving Force, *Time*, December 7.

Institute of the Environment (2006) *Environmental Report Card 2006*, University of California.

International Energy Agency (2004) *Energy Technology Analysis: Prospectus for CO_2 Capture and Storage*.

International Energy Agency (2005) *Act Locally, Trade Globally. Emissions Trading for Climate Policy*.

International Energy Agency (2006) *World Energy Outlook 2006*.

International Energy Agency (2007) *World Energy Outlook 2007*, China and India insights, p. 298.

International Monetary Fund (2007) *World Economic and Financial Surveys: Regional Economic Outlook, Middle East and Central Asia*, October.

Jaccard, M. (2006) *Sustainable Fossil Fuels: The Unusual Suspect in the Quest for Clean and Enduring Energy*, Cambridge University Press, Cambridge.

Jaffe, A.B., Peterson, S.R., Portney, P.R. and Stavins, R.N. (1995) Environmental Regulation and the Competitiveness of US Manufacturing: What Does the Evidence Tell Us? *Journal of Economic Literature*, 33, 132–163.

Johnson Matthey (2004) *Platinum 2004*.

Kagan Vitiello, J. (1997) *Trading through Time: The History of the New York Mercantile Exchange 1872–1997*, New York Mercantile Exchange.

Kanza, T.R. (1968) The Problems of the Congo, *African Affairs*, 67(266), 55–62.

KlimaFa Ltd (2007) *Vatican to Become World's First Carbon Neutral Sovereign State: Planktos/KlimaFa's New Vatican Climate Forest Initiative to Fully Green the Holy See*, press release, July 12.

Kynge, J. (2006) *China Shakes the World: The Rise of a Hungry Nation*, Weidenfeld & Nicolson.

Lambrecht, B. (2007) Political Road Gets Rockier for Ethanol after a Run of Victories in Congress: New Adversaries Put the Heat On, *St Louis Post-Dispatch*, July 22.

Landry, C.J. and Anderson, T.L. (1999) *The Rising Tide of Water Markets*.

Lazzari, S. (1994) *Alcohol Fuels Tax Incentives and the EPA Renewable Oxygenate Requirement*, CRS Report 94-785, October 7.

Leech, H. and Carroll, J.C. (1938) *Armour and His Times*, D. Appleton-Century Co, New York.

Levy, J.I. (2006) Contemplating Delivery: Futures Trading and the Problem of Commodity Exchange in the United States, 1875–1905, *The American Historical Review*, 111.2.

Lewis, L. and Smith, L. (2007) Water whets the Appetite of Commodity Traders with an Eye to the Next Fortune, *The Times*, October 19.

Lintner, J. (1983) *The Potential Role of Managed Futures Accounts in Port-folios of Stocks and Bonds*.

Lomborg, B. (1998) *The Skeptical Environmentalist: Measuring the Real State of the World*, Cambridge University Press, Cambridge.

Lovelock, J. (2006) *The Revenge of Gaia*, Penguin.

Lux, H. (2003) What Becomes a Legend? *Institutional Investor*, February 1.

Lynch, M. (2002) *Mining in World History*, Reaktion Books.

Mackintosh, J. and Morrison, K. (2005) Carmakers gear up for the next shortage – platinum, *Financial Times*, London, p. 22.

Malthus, T.R. (1798) *An Essay on the Principle of Population*.

Mayo, J. (2001) The Development of British Interests in Chile's Norte Chico in the Early Nineteenth Century, *The Americas*, 57(3), 363–394.

McLean, B. and Elkind, P. (2003) *The Smartest Guys in the Room: The amazing rise and scandalous fall of Enron*, Penguin.

Meadows, D.H., Meadows, D.I., Randers, J. and Behrens, W.W. (1972) *The Limits to Growth*, report to the Club of Rome.

Meekhof, R., Gill, M. and Tyner, W.E. (1980) *Gasohol, Prospects and Im-plications*, USDA Economics, Statistics and Cooperatives Service.

Millennium Ecosystem Assessment (2005) *Ecosystems and Human Well-being: Current State and Trends*, Summary, Volume 1.

Mills, E., Roth, R. and Lecomte, E. (2005) *Availability and Affordability of Insurance under Climate Change: A growing challenge for the US*.

Mingst, K.A. (1976) Cooperation or Illusion: An Examination of the In-tergovernmental Council of Copper Exporting Countries, *International Organization*, 30(2), 263–287.

Mitchell, D. (2004) *Sugar Policies: Opportunity for Change*, World Bank Policy Research Working Paper 3222.

Mitsch, W.J., Day, J.W., Gilliam, J.W., Groffman, P.M., Hey, D.L., Randall, G.W. and Wang, N. (1998) *Reducing Nutrient Loads, Especially Nitrate-Nitrogen to Surface Water, Ground Water, and the Gulf of Mexico: Topic 5 Report for the Integrated Assessment on Hypoxia in the Gulf of Mexico*, NOAA Coastal Ocean Program, p. 3.

Monteón, M. (2003) John T. North, the Nitrate King, and Chile's Lost Future, *Latin American Perspectives*, 30(6), 69–90.

Montgomery, D. (1972) Markets in Licenses and Efficient Pollution Control Programs, *Journal of Economic Theory*, 5, 395–418.

Morgan, D. (2000) *Merchants of Grain*, iUniverse.

Morrison, K. (2006) China Develops Capacity to Gain Top Spot: Increased Investment Could Help the Sector Exert More Muscle, *Financial Times*, May 10.

Mupimpila, C. and van der Grijp, N. (1998) *Global Product Chains: Northern Consumers, Southern Producers, and Sustainability. Copper From Zambia*, prepared for the United Nations Environment Programme.

Napolitano, S., Schreifels, J., Stevens, G., Witt, M., LaCount, M., Forte, R. and Smith, K. (2007) The US Acid Rain Program: Key Insights for the Design, Operation, and Assessment of a Cap-and-Trade Program, *The Electricity Journal*, 20(7).

National Energy Board (2007) *Canada's Energy Future: Reference Cases and Scenarios to 2030*.

National Energy Policy Development Group (2001) *Taking Stock: Energy Challenges Facing the United States*, US National Energy Plan, July.

National Oceanic and Atmospheric Administration (2007) *Warm summer in US ends with record heat in South, widespread drought continues in Southeast, West*, press release September 12.

National Petroleum Council (2007) *Facing the Hard Truths About Energy*.

National Renewable Energy Laboratory (1998) *A Look Back at the US Department of Energy's Aquatic Species Program: Biodiesel from Algae*, close-out report prepared for the US Department of Energy's Office of Fuels Development.

National Security Space Office (2007) *Space Based Solar Power as an Opportunity for Strategic Security*, report to the Director, released October 10.

NRDC (2004) *Energy Down the Drain: The Hidden Costs of California's Water Supply*.

O'Brien, T.F. (1979) Chilean Elites and Foreign Investors: Chilean Nitrate Policy 1880–82, *Journal of Latin American Studies*, 11(1), 101–121.

O'Brien, T.F. (1989) Rich Beyond the Dreams of Avarice: The Guggenheims in Chile, *The Business History Review*, 63(1), 122–159.

O'Connor, H. (1976) *The Guggenheims: The Making of an American Dynasty*, Arno, New York, reprinted from the 1937 original edition, p. 422.

OECD (1999) *The Price of Water: Trends in OECD Countries*.

Parker, D. (2007) *A New Zealand Emissions Trading Scheme*, speech by the Energy and Climate Minister of New Zealand, Banquet Hall, Parliament Buildings, September 20.

Payne, R.J. (1978) Mining the Deep Seabed: The Political, Economic and Legal Struggle, *The Journal of Politics*, 40(4), 933–955.

Pearce, F. (2007) Look, No Footprint, *New Scientist*, March 10.

Pointing, C. (2007) *A New Green History of the World: The Environment and the Collapse of Great Civilizations*, Vintage Books.

Poniachik, K. (2006) speech to Canning House, London on October 11.

Qin, W. X. and Ronalds, N. (2005) China: The Fall and Rise of Chinese Futures, *Futures Industry*, May/June.

Raghavjee, R. (2006) *Towards Commoditisation of the Uranium Market*, speech to the NEI Nuclear Fuels Seminar, Quebec, October.

Reilly, W.K. (2004) *The Worth of Water*, presentation given to the Fourth National Conference on Science, Policy and the Environment, Washington DC, January 29–30.

Reitler, I. (1931) The Metal Exchange, *The Annals of the American Academy of Political and Social Science*, 155, 127–132.

Reserve Bank of Australia (2007) The Recent Rise in Commodity Prices: A Long-run Perspective, *Reserve Bank Bulletin*, April.

Ribaudo, M. (2003) 'Dead-zone' in the Gulf: Addressing Agriculture's Contribution, *Amber Waves*, November.

Rippy, J.F. (1948) Economic Enterprises of the 'Nitrate King' and his Associates in Chile, *The Pacific Historical Review*, 17(4), 457–465.

Rippy, J.F. (1958) *Globe and Hemisphere: Latin America's Place in the Postwar Foreign Relations of the United States*, Henry Regnery Company, Chicago.

Ruttenberg, S.H. and Associates, Inc. (1973) *The American Oil Industry: A Failure of Anti-Trust Policy*, Marine Engineers' Beneficial Association.

Sandalow, D. (2006) Ethanol: Lessons from Brazil, in *A High Growth Strategy for Ethanol*, Aspen Institute, Washington, DC.

Sandor, R.L. (2004) *Market-Based Solutions to Climate Change: An Economist's Story*, address to the Graduate School of International Relations and Pacific Studies, University of California, San Diego, June 12.

Sansoucy, R. (1995) Livestock: A Driving Force for Food Security and Sustainable Development, *FAO World Animal Review*, 84/85, 5–17.

Sater, W.F. (1979) Chile and the World Depression of the 1870s, *Journal of Latin American Studies*, 11(1), 67–99.

Sawyer, J. (2007) Nitrogen Fertilization for Corn Following Corn, *Integrated Crop Management*, February 12.

Schlesinger, A. (2000) Who was Henry A. Wallace? The Story of a Perplexing and Indomitably Naïve Public Servant, *Los Angeles Times*, March 12.

Schmitz, C. (1986) The Rise of Big Business in the World Copper Industry 1870–1930, *The Economic History Review*, 39(3).

Schwager, J.D. (1993) *Market Wizards: Interviews with top traders*, Collins Business.

Schwieder, D. (1996) Iowa: The Middle Land, Iowa State Press.

Simmons, M. (2005) *Twilight in the Desert: The Coming Saudi Oil Shock and the World Economy*, John Wiley & Sons, Inc., Hoboken.

Simon, J.L. (1996) *The Ultimate Resource 2*, Princeton University Press.

Singer, J.W. (2006) Commentary on Crop Rotation, *Pioneer Growing Point*, January, p. 21.

Smith, A. (1776) *The Wealth of Nations*, Books I–III.

Smith, C.W., Betran, J. and Runge, E.C.A. (Eds) (2004) *Corn: Origin, History, Technology and Production*, John Wiley & Sons, Inc., Hoboken.

Smith, M. (2006) *DRC – Challenging Opportunities*, Mines & Money Conference, London, November 21.

Spilimbergo, A. (1999) *Copper and the Chilean Economy, 1960–1998*, International Monetary Fund, research department, April.

Stationery Office (2006) *Census 2006, Preliminary Report by Central Statistics Office*, Dublin, Ireland.

Stavins, R.N. (1998) *Market-Based Environmental Policies*, Discussion Papers dp-98-26, Resources for the Future.

Stern, N. (2006) *The Economics of Climate Change. The Stern Review*, Cambridge University Press, Cambridge.

Stone, I. (1968) British Long-Term Investment in Latin America, 1865–1913, *The Business History Review*, **42**(3), 311–339.

Swingland, I.R. (2003) *Capturing Carbon and Conserving Biodiversity: The Market Approach*, Kogan Page.

Tamarkin, B. (1985) *The New Gatsbys: Fortunes and Misfortunes of Commodity Traders*, Williams Morrow and Company Inc.

Tamminen, T. (2006) *Lives Per Gallon: The True Cost of Our Oil Addiction*, Island Press.

Taylor, J. (1993) CFTC Begins Attempt to Ban 7 Traders from Futures Pits, *The Wall Street Journal Europe*, July 21, p. 24.

Time (1940) Plastic Fords, *Time*, November 11.

Tyson Foods Inc. (2005–6) *Investor Fact Book*.

UNCTAD (2007) *Report of the UNCTAD study group on emerging commodity markets*, working paper, September 3.

US Bureau of Reclamation (2005) *Water 2025: Preventing Crisis and Conflict in the West*, status report.

US Congressional Budget Office (2005) *Policies that Distort World Agricultural Trade: Prevalence and Magnitude*, August.

US Department of Agriculture (2001–2) *Agriculture Factbook*, Chapter 2.

US Department of Agriculture (2007) *Historical Track Records*, April.

US Department of Agriculture Advisory Committee on Biotechnology and 21st Century Agriculture (2006) *Opportunities and Challenges in Agricultural Biotechnology – The Decade Ahead*, July 13.

US Department of Energy (2003) *Platinum Availability and Economics for PEMFC Commercialization*, December.

US Department of Energy (2006) *Key Challenges Remain for Developing and Deploying Advanced Energy Technologies to Meet Future Needs*.

US Environmental Protection Agency (1990) *Environmental Investments: The Cost of a Clean Environment*, report of the administrator to Congress.

US Environmental Protection Agency (2006) *Technical Summary – Global Mitigation of non-CO_2 Greenhouse Gases*.

US General Accounting Office (1988) *Financial Markets Preliminary Observations on the October 1987 Crash*, report to Congressional requesters.

US General Accounting Office (1997) *Information on the Condition of the National Plant Germplasm System*, report to Congressional Committees, October 16.

US Geological Survey (2001) *Policy – A Factor Shaping Minerals Supply and Demand*.

US Geological Survey (2007) *Mineral Commodities Summaries*.

US Government Accountability Office (2007a) *Biofuels: DOE Lacks a Strategic Approach to Coordinate Increasing Production with Infrastructure Development and Vehicle Needs*.

US Government Accountability Office (2007b) *Federal Farm Programs: USDA Needs to Strengthen Controls to Prevent Improper Payments to Estates and Deceased Individuals*.

US Office of Technology Assessment (1985) *Strategic Materials: Technologies to Reduce US Import Vulnerability*.

US Senate Permanent Subcommittee on Investigations (2006) *The Role of Market Speculation in Rising Oil and Gas Prices: A Need to Put the Cop Back on the Beat*, June.

US Senate Permanent Subcommittee on Investigations and Committee on Homeland Security and Governmental Affairs (2007) *Ranking Minority Members: Excessive Speculation in the Natural Gas Market*, staff report with additional minority staff views, June 25 and July 9.

Valdes, C. (2006) Brazil's Booming Agriculture Faces Obstacles, *Amber Waves*, **4**(5).

Valdes, C. (2007) Ethanol Demand Driving the Expansion of Brazil's Sugar Industry, *Sugar and Sweeteners Outlook*, June 4, p. 36.

Volk, S.S. (1993) Mine Owners, Moneylenders, and the State in Mid-Nineteenth-Century Chile: Transitions and Conflicts, *The Hispanic American Historical Review*, **73**(1), 67–98.

Walden, H. (1966) *Native Inheritance: The Story of Corn in America*, Harpers & Row.

Walters, A. (1944) The International Copper Cartel, *Southern Economic Journal*, **11**(2), 133–156.

Wara, M. (2006)*Measuring the Clean Development Mechanism's Performance and Potential*, Program on Energy and Sustainable Development, Center for Environmental Science and Policy, Stanford University, California.

Warburg, P.M. (1929) Commercial and Financial Chronicle, March 9, 1929, cited in Chancellor, E. (1999) *Devil Take the Hindmost: A History of Financial Speculation*, Farrar Straus Giroux, New York, p. 210.

Warman, A. (1988) *Corn and Capitalism: How a Botanical Bastard Grew to Global Dominance*, University of North Carolina Press.

Wauters, A. (1930) Belgian Policy in the Congo, *Journal of the Royal Institute of International Affairs*, **9**(1), 51–62.

Weiner, R.J. (2002) Sheep in Wolves' Clothing? Speculators and Price Volatility in Petroleum Futures, *Quarterly Review of Economics and Finance*, **42**(2), 391–400.

Whitbeck, R.H. (1929) The Chileans and their Geographic Environment, *Annals of the Association of American Geographers*, **19**(3), 149–156.

White, B. (2006) Goldman's Change of Guard, *Financial Times*, June 29.

Wilkins, M. (1974) *The Maturing of Multinational Enterprise: American Business Abroad from 1914 to 1970*, Harvard University Press.

Wilson, J. (2007) Farmland the New Hot Property: Demand for Corn Used in Ethanol Fuels Price Hikes Outpacing NY Lofts, *The Globe and Mail*, February 21.

World Bank (2005) *Shaping the Future of Water for Agriculture: A Sourcebook for Investment in Agricultural Water Management*.

World Bank (2007) *Commodity Markets, Prospects for the Global Economy*, world bank website, viewed May 29.

World Bank (2007) *At Loggerheads? Agricultural Expansion, Poverty Reduction, and Environment in the Tropical Forests*, policy research report.

World Nuclear Association (2007) *The Global Nuclear Fuel Market: Supply and Demand 2007–2030*.

Yergin, D. (1991) *The Prize: Epic Quest for Oil, Money and Power*, Simon and Schuster Ltd.

Young, O.E. (1983) Origins of the American Copper Industry, *Journal of the Early Republic*, **3**(2), 117–137.

Index

Index compiled by Annette Musker